Another Kind of Madness

Another Kind of Madness

A JOURNEY THROUGH THE STIGMA AND HOPE OF MENTAL ILLNESS

Stephen P. Hinshaw

St. Martin's Press   New York

www.stmartins.com

Design by Meryl Sussman Levavi

Cataloging-in-Publication Data is available from the Library of Congress.

ISBN 978-1-250-11336-8 (hardcover)

ISBN 978-1-250-11337-5 (ebook)

Our books may be purchased in bulk for promotional, educational, or business use. Please contact your local bookseller or the Macmillan Corporate and Premium Sales Department at 1-800-221-7945, extension 5442, or by e-mail at MacmillanSpecialMarkets@macmillan.com.

First Edition: June 2017

10 9 8 7 6 5 4 3 2

To the memory of my father and mother

*To my sister, Sally, who works every day to
improve the lives of people with physical and
mental disorders by increasing empathy and skill
on the part of practitioners*

Contents

Preface

This book has taken literally a lifetime to emerge. I tend to be a person of fast action, but some essential ventures don't come to fruition quickly—like understanding one's family, finding an authentic voice to recount difficult life experiences, and working to reduce the shame and stigma regarding such weighty topics as mental illness.

In college, I became increasingly invested in the field of psychology, spurred by my father's initial, revelatory talk with me during my first spring break back in the Midwest. Over time I began to believe that his story, and my own, might be of value not just to my family or those in my inner circle but to a wider audience as well. This work is my attempt to convey such remembrances and accounts to the best of my memory. I've tried to create dialogue and narrative that adhere as closely as possible to what transpired when I was a boy, a teen, a young man, and beyond.

The inspiration for the book's title comes from a quote from James Baldwin, in one of his masterpieces, *Giovanni's Room:* "People who remember court madness through pain, the pain of the perpetually recurring death of their innocence; people who forget court *another kind of madness,* the madness of the denial of pain and the hatred of innocence; and the world is mostly divided between madmen who remember and madmen who forget." [emphasis added]

I cannot, of course, claim to comprehend Baldwin's experiences, but his words are inspirational. Regarding the present narrative, as I try to make clear in the pages that follow, stigma itself is "another kind of madness," a form with consequences that are far worse than those linked to mental illness itself. More broadly, stigma fosters a denial of human potential. The silence and shame must be transformed into open dialogue. Unless we make progress toward this goal, we will never realize what we can become as a species.

I have altered the names of some individuals outside our family to protect their privacy, an unfortunate but still necessary action. Progress in the fight against stigma is a marathon, not a sprint.

In the end, I hope that the material herein provides solace, inspiration, and courage to all individuals affected by mental illness either in themselves or in those close to them—in other words, to everyone.

Another Kind of Madness

Introduction

In the late summer of 1936, scalding winds scoured the Southern California region. As the calendar reached September, the 16-year-old known as Junior couldn't shut off the voices now shouting inside his head. Preoccupied with the growing Nazi threat in Europe, day and night he roamed the sidewalks of Pasadena, the same ones that had carried him to grade school on his metal roller skates a decade before. Begging him to save the free world, the voices grew in intensity each day. Desperate to emerge with a plan to save the free world, Junior continued his relentless pacing.

Not long after midnight on Sunday, September 6, he paused. Silent houses surrounded him in the darkness. With his shirt soaked in sweat, he suddenly gasped as a new awareness took hold of his body and mind. With thrilling clarity, he now understood: *He* was the sole human destined to save the free world. His long days and nights of searching had not been in vain! The revelation filled him with wonder.

As his thoughts gathered speed another insight emerged. Alone among mankind, he had attained the power of flight. His arms, in fact, had become wings. Like Icarus, if he lifted them toward the sky, he'd be aloft. Once he soared toward the clouds, the free world's leaders would witness this magnificent signal and pledge to conquer the Fascists.

Alas, through his tortured logic, he reasoned that his flight would be seen around the globe only after sunrise. For now, he must await the dawn, using every ounce of his energy to shield his secret. Inhaling any stray cigarettes he could find before stubbing them out, he kept moving, inspired by his newfound mission.

For several years, international Prohibition leaders had attended periodic dinners at his family home, alongside his father, Virgil Hinshaw, Sr., an international leader in the movement. Inevitably, discussions turned to the world situation.

"The Fascists are taking over, Mussolini in Italy, Hitler in Germany," said one grim discussant. "They will dominate the world!" "You Americans are isolationists," called out another. "Who will preserve international freedom?"

Sitting with his five brothers at the table, Junior felt his alarm grow each time. But with so much to accomplish—homework, church, sports, and part-time jobs—the warnings gradually faded. After all, what could a family of Quakers, committed pacifists, really do to aid the world situation? Yet now, with his senior year of high school approaching and his parents out of town at a Prohibition meeting, a newfound surge of energy took possession of his being, his mind expanding as it never had before.

Amplified by radio accounts of the rise of the Fascists, the visitors' warnings called out to him: The Nazi threat is real! Black-and-white newsreels looped before his eyes: Brownshirts marching, Hitler's speeches before massive crowds. Repression grew but America did nothing to heed the signs. Possessed by his new mission, he understood that if he dared not step forward, who would?

But how? If not for him, the Fascists might prevail.

As the early-morning hours of September 6 inched toward dawn, the winds abated. Finally, a brilliant yellow-orange, the sun emerged to the east, spreading long shadows from roofs and palms. Enthralled by his energy and his remarkable insights, Junior reached his block on North Oakland Avenue, moving furtively past a few yards to find his own home, a dark-brown bungalow now directly in front of him. Breathing in, he crossed the lawn with muted footsteps. As the front door beckoned, he stared at it and then above. All was silent in the early daylight.

There was no turning back. The time was now.

But how to ascend? Thinking fast, he nimbly scrambled up the trellis, steadying himself as he found footholds. A final thrust and he was on the roof above the small front porch, the walkway 12 feet below. The sky loomed majestically before him, the air already torrid. The voices inside his mind reached a crescendo, pleading with him to perform his deed. *Save the free world!*

Glory would be his.

Approaching the edge, he shed his clothes and heaved them over, shoes, pants, and shirt floating to the ground beneath. Suddenly cooler, he held his breath. Calf muscles straining, arms outflung, he pushed off and propelled himself forward. For a second, there was only the feel of the air against his skin.

The ground rushed toward him before everything turned black.

I learned of this event without any preparation at all. In the middle of April 1971, I settled into the living room sofa, picking up a magazine. I needed to start some serious reading for my freshman-year term papers at Harvard but couldn't resist a short break. Back in Columbus, Ohio, where I'd spent my first seventeen years, I felt as though a heavy backpack weighed me down—each compartment filled with disbelief. Did I really belong here anymore?

From the couch, the multi-paned window revealed our white front-porch columns, framing the deep-green lawn and startlingly pink crabapple blossoms just beyond. As light filtered through intermittent, early-afternoon clouds, the mood shifted from dark to light and back again.

Was there some kind of stirring in the wind, a small signal of change in the air? If so, I paid no attention. Things would never change, I was sure, inside the stillness of our family home. In just a few days I'd be back in Cambridge and my new life back East.

All week, for my first spring break, I'd wandered the house in a half-daze. The colonial-soldier figures on my bedroom wallpaper, the half-deflated footballs and basketballs in our mud-hall closet, the sound-absorbing carpeting of the main floor: Everything appeared as though behind museum ropes.

After glancing through a magazine or two, I heard a soft shuffling sound. Peering up, I saw Dad approach awkwardly from his study. He must have returned from his morning classes on campus, where three mornings per week he lectured on the history of Western philosophy for masses of Ohio State University (OSU) undergraduates. My sister, Sally, was in eleventh grade at the huge high school a block behind our home. Mom was at OSU, teaching English.

Dad and I were alone in the house.

"Son," he began in a quiet voice, his eyes avoiding mine. He used the formal term when things were serious, a remnant of his Quaker upbringing. "Could we talk for a bit?"

Placing the magazine down, I turned to face him. His body was slightly hunched, his face tense. He no longer resembled the athletic, confident personage he'd once been, early in his career and early in my life. By now, a small paunch surrounded his stomach and a heavy gravity seemed to be pulling down the corners of his mouth.

"Sure," I replied, wondering vaguely if I'd done something wrong. A trickle of adrenaline coursed through my veins. He beckoned for me to follow him into his bookshelf-lined library, the room he'd planned when our house had been designed a decade before. The navy-blue, brown, and maroon hues of the book covers seemed to call out from the wooden shelves. Each time I entered, I felt overwhelmed by the world's knowledge of science, history, and math inside those pages.

Dad paused as I walked past and pulled the sliding door shut, the soft metallic whirr of its rollers filling the air until wood contacted wood with a small hollow pop. I sat down on a straight-backed chair he'd placed near his desk, close to the tangle of file folders, syllabi, and lecture notes crowding its surface. Underneath the window overlooking our front-yard pin-oak tree sat a small table holding his manual typewriter, the ancient one he'd used at Stanford and Princeton, a gift from his father. He typed 90 words a minute without error, the keys ablaze with rapid-fire clacking. His typing seemed faster than most people's thinking.

Dad's downward gaze and the quiver in his voice told me that our talk would not be about my freshman year or minor issues at home. As he cleared his throat, I clenched.

"Steve," he began, "there are sometimes experiences, situations in life that are, well, difficult to understand." To my surprise he was fumbling for words, far different from his usual orations on philosophy and science.

"What I mean is this: Perhaps it's time you heard about some events from my history." He paused. "There were times when I wasn't fully rational."

As he continued speaking time slowed. Worlds passed before my eyes as fast as I could process them. From his periodic talks with me when I was young, I knew of the Hinshaw family's tribulations and achievements. But something had always been missing, especially surrounding his strange disappearances, when he would vanish for weeks or months at a time. Nothing had ever been said.

From this first, revelatory talk in Dad's home library, from many more over the following 24 years, from discussions with his brothers that began during my twenties, and from long-preserved family letters, I pieced together the events as though witnessing them in person. It's as though I'd been transported back to Pasadena.

Moments later, stunned from the impact, bleeding from his head, his left wrist suspended at an awkward angle, Junior struggled to regain alertness. Startled by the early-morning commotion, his brothers rushed out to see him sprawled on the concrete. They'd been worried by his strange behavior over the past days but couldn't keep him contained inside the house.

"My God," cried Bob, 18, the first one out the door, "what's happened?"

"Be careful!" shouted Randall, three years older than Bob, rushing close behind. "Someone get Junior's clothes."

But couldn't they see what he'd accomplished? "It's hot—I'm cooling off," he whispered, as his brothers lifted him inside and phoned for the doctor. The emergency vehicle arrived and transported him to Los Angeles County Hospital, its huge white edifice crowning the hills east of downtown LA. His shattered arm was set in a cast but the bones didn't quite mesh. A nurse emptied a syringe into his arm and the world floated away.

Two weeks later he was transferred to a back ward at a public mental facility, Norwalk County Hospital, which housed patients with severe mental illness. His roommates included individuals with misshapen heads, victims of microcephaly and serious intellectual disability.

As I sat motionless before him in his study, taking in every word, Dad told me that perhaps he had at last found his true peers, as a deeply flawed individual. None of his academic accomplishments, none of his religious upbringing, none of his grand ideas could counter his newfound fate.

Each night at Norwalk screams echoed through the corridors, competing with the angelic choruses inside his mind singing of glory and salvation. His only treatment was being tied to his bed to prevent wandering. Some mornings he worked the garbage crew but there was no school at this adult facility, only interminable, empty hours each day. Alone except for his voices and invisible to the world, he had entered a different existence.

Over the next weeks he became convinced of a new idea, fueled by the relentless voices. The food at Norwalk was poisoned, part of an ongoing Nazi plot. To eat would signal his capitulation to the Fascist plans. As he refrained from ingesting anything but water, his body grew thinner and thinner.

In November, his father received an urgent telephone call from the hospital's superintendent, who stated that their patient, Virgil Jr., had lost 60 pounds, and was down to 120. "The situation is critical," he intoned grimly. "You must come with all speed." A pastor had been called to administer last rites.

Rushing inside after the frantic drive, Virgil Sr. gasped in horror at the sight of his emaciated son. Resigning himself to the inevitable, he wrote to his brother that night, convinced that he would re-encounter his fourth-born only in the next world. Yet over the following weeks the ideas and voices began to lose their force and Junior began eating once more. As his strength returned he pondered his surroundings, barren and forlorn. Wishing desperately to return home for Christmas, he was told by the doctors that he was too ill.

Weeks passed as the rainy Southern California winter finally yielded to signs of spring. By late February, staff noticed sudden, inexplicable improvement. Fully rational, he was released within a week. Following his return to Pasadena, shocked by his sudden re-emergence, no one—not his father, stepmother, or five brothers—dared to discuss the experiences of the past half-year. The shame was too great. Any talk might jinx his recovery.

He began twelfth grade six months late. By June, he had earned straight As for the spring semester and the previous fall as well. His life of inexplicable ascents and descents had begun.

To his family, his recovery signaled that a miracle had occurred. Like all miracles, it was enshrouded in mystery.

"It was during this stay that my diagnosis of schizophrenia was revealed," Dad told me on that blustery April afternoon. "There have been other times in my life with similar episodes. Perhaps we should discuss them during a subsequent talk."

Evidently, our session was ending. We stood up and awkwardly shook hands. I pushed back my chair, turned, and pulled open the sliding door. Walking slowly through the living room I stopped short. Were those actually the same blossoms and sky showing through the front window? Had thirty minutes passed, or half a lifetime?

While hearing Dad's words I'd fought panic but also experienced a deep stillness. At last I knew *something*. A current of air had entered the vast vacuum just a step behind me, which I'd tried to shut out my whole life. At last, a few sounds had emerged from the void. Only one thing was certain. From that moment forward my life would never be the same.

Sunday Dinner at
the Willard

Twenty years after my father's abortive flight to save the free world—and more than half a continent away—I was five, rushing home from morning kindergarten class. Yanking open the door to the basement, I raced down the steps.

I just *had* to find Dad. If he was home, he must be in his study, getting ready for his next lecture. But sometimes he vanished into thin air. Nothing was ever said; he simply disappeared. When it happened I had no idea that he'd been involuntarily hospitalized for bouts of inexplicable, wild behavior. All I knew was that one day Dad was present and the next day there was an empty space where he'd once been. Had some kind of silent abduction taken place in the middle of the night, under armed guard?

At the bottom of the staircase I felt the sudden coolness of the basement air. When it rained hard in the spring, water would collect in the middle of the slate-gray floor over by the washer and dryer. "Stevie, this is what's called a flood," Mom said. "The ground gets full of water and it collects beneath the ground level." Grunting lightly from the exertion, Dad would grab a mechanical pump from the garage and place it in the middle of the rising pool of water. I heard it grumble and growl while the pulsing liquid pushed through the rubber tubing, up the wall, and out a side window. As the water splashed onto the driveway, small streams slowly trickled down toward the street, the rivulets converging like the gradual clasping of long, wrinkled fingers.

I looked toward Dad's study. He had built it himself in a corner of the basement from cinder blocks and wood planks. Inside the open door the soft glow from his desk lamp illuminated the covers of his books, surrounding him on three sides.

This was our first house—colonial-style, brick and wood clapboard—on Wyandotte Road, named for a Native American tribe. We lived in the suburb of Upper Arlington, not quite two miles from the Olentangy River and, on the far bank, Ohio State. Inside the walls of the house, we were a model academic family in the Midwestern world of the fifties.

Weren't we?

I saw Dad sitting erect in a short-sleeved dress shirt, gazing intently at the open pages on his lap. The woodsy aroma of pipe smoke mingled with the musty scent of the dank basement walls. His elegant handwriting filled the lines of tall pads of yellow paper.

I hesitated. Maybe he didn't need an interruption while he was concentrating. But geography facts gripped me and my impatience was growing. Entering his workspace, I got up my courage. "Daddy, can I talk to you?"

Turning toward me and looking up, he revealed a small smile. His pipe lingered in his left hand while the arc of light from the lamp illuminated the rows of bookshelves. All those books!

"Certainly," he replied, putting down his pen. "What could it be?" The pleasure in his voice warmed my skin. On days like this, the sense of possibility sent a jolt of current through each nerve in my body. One day, perhaps, I would read books like this and make discoveries.

"Well," I replied, trying to get the words just right. "I heard that Russia is the biggest country on earth. Is that true?" Pondering, Dad looked into the distance. He seemed to understand the serious nature of my question.

"Yes, it is. It's now called the Soviet Union, which is even larger than Russia."

"But," I continued, not quite believing what I was about to ask. "I heard that China has more people than Russia. Is *that* true?"

"It is, indeed," Dad replied with growing interest. "China has more people than any nation on earth." I was shocked.

In reply, Dad emphasized his points with the kinds of verbal headlines he might make in a lecture on campus, saying that a smaller area could have more people in it, but in a larger region the population may be less dense. His words flew over my head but another question popped into my mind.

"How *many* more people live in China?" A number here might really help. Numbers have always given me comfort. I'm always mentally calculating sports scores, percentages, or statistics of some kind. Numbers are always the same, their order perfectly consistent. They don't vanish without warning.

"A great many more," Dad said, with a hint of lightness in his voice.

But the most daring question of all now formed in my mind. "Daddy, could there be . . . a *hundred* more people living in China than in Russia?" Even as the question left my mouth, the number seemed impossibly large. Yet in the calmest voice imaginable he replied, "I know this will be hard to believe, Steve, but there are actually *more* than a hundred more people living in China than Russia."

My eyes bulged, but his gentle look told me that what he'd said was the absolute truth. *More* than one hundred! Many things, I was learning, exist beyond everyday understanding. I lingered a moment before heading upstairs, hoping one day to understand such mysteries.

When Dad was home, I got answers. But what if, the next time he left, he never came back? The fear gripped me like the slow, inexorable tightening of a rope, squeezing the air from my lungs. The worst part was that no one ever talked about it.

A few weeks before, stripped down to a ribbed undershirt that revealed his still formidable muscles, Dad had taken the power mower from the garage on a Saturday morning for the first lawn-mowing of the spring. He poured gasoline from a bright-red can into the hole near the engine. Placing his foot down on top of the mower, he pulled the cord with a snap of his wrist. White smoke poured out as the engine started up with a roar. Pushing down on the handle, he dimmed the noise and began to walk the machine back and forth across the front yard. Lush grass flew out the side in moist clumps. The rows of grass heading up the street were a different shade of green than the rows heading the other way, the pattern symmetrical.

In a flash I rushed inside for my toy lawnmower. Hurrying back out, I fell in step behind him as we walked the rows together, single file. We were careful to avoid the bumpy roots of our large elm tree. When he lifted his hand to clear the profuse sweat that had formed on his brow, I did the same, even though my forehead was dry.

From the front steps Mom and Sally watched us. I desperately wanted to show them how hard I was working. That feeling, with all of us together in the yard: I wanted it to last forever. Even then, I knew that moments like this were precious. In the broad daylight of spring, no shadows could block our view of one another.

My favorite times occurred when Dad drove Sally and me to the Ohio State campus. On teaching days he always wore a jacket and tie, carrying himself with a subtle elegance. For him, being a professor was serious business. Some mornings, watching from my perch in the bathroom, I studied his crisp straight-razor strokes, whooshing through the white lather covering his face. Later, he switched to an electric razor, and I heard the buzzing noise whine up and down in pitch as he guided the round shaving heads over his chin. When finished, he blew sharply into the ridges of the blades, clearing out the heavy stubble before vigorously slapping his cheeks with aromatic lotions.

His actions were precise and intense. He had tasks to accomplish, readings to put together, historical and scientific perspectives to integrate. His preparations revealed the intensity of his mind.

With a new dress shirt, he struggled to button the top button against his still massive neck, a legacy of the shot-putter he'd been back in high school. He rifled through his bathroom cabinet for a straight razor, which he carefully extracted from its cardboard housing. With intense delicacy, he sliced through the cloth to add an extra eighth of an inch to the buttonhole. Finally, he buttoned the shirt to the top and tied his tie, in a perfect four-in-hand knot.

Dad's office in the philosophy department was inside University Hall, OSU's oldest building, a red-brick structure with gables, a slate roof, and a clock tower. It fronts the Oval, the massive lawn at the center of campus, criss-crossed by sidewalks for the masses of students walking to and from class. The sign in front of the building says 1870, the year it was built. On a small rock nearby another sign marks the fortieth degree of latitude north of the equator right at that spot. Back then I looked for a line in the grass but Dad told me that latitude lines were invisible, created by scientists to measure the earth and help people navigate, with each degree covering about 69 miles. On the globe, I could see that Madrid, over in Spain, and Denver, out West, were also right on the fortieth parallel. Looking at maps and globes I felt safe, knowing where I was in the world.

From University Hall we were close to the massive Ohio Stadium, the Horseshoe, home of the Buckeyes. Back then it held 88,888 people, which I always thought was a great number. When Dad and Mom took us to home games, we walked through campus amid excited groups of fans huddled together in the brisk autumn air. Each game was a scarlet and gray sea of humanity, filled with periodic eruptions of raw emotion from the crowd.

When Dad walked Sally and me inside his office, a small group of professors, teaching assistants, and secretaries would stop by to say hello to the young scholars in tow. Filled with questions and laughter, the air was rich, the thirst for learning unmistakable. One time Dad walked me over to the small radio station on campus, where he recorded his weekly program on philosophy and everyday life. At home or in the car, I heard Dad's voice on WOSU as he precisely explained how the search for knowledge could illuminate people's worlds. It was clear that I was visiting an exclusive club. Might I one day gain entry, if I worked as hard as I could? Having a purpose has always lifted me. My biggest fear was—and still is—that there might be nothing to strive for at all. Without warning, everything might come to a halt, my life frozen in an absolute zero of futility. Underneath my pride at being a favored son at Ohio State, a baited trap lay in wait in the grass, ready to reach up and snare me.

Half a year later, Dad was driving us to Grandmother's house on the other side of town, where Mom had grown up. I wanted to jump from the car, but we were moving too quickly through Columbus. Just early afternoon, the day had already turned into a nightmare.

In the days before freeways, the drive took us across the Olentangy River toward downtown, before heading out East Broad Street until the trees and manicured lawns of Bexley appeared. Usually a half hour full of anticipation, a chance for Sally and me to play in the back seat, the journey had become disastrous. Dad loomed above us, perched on some kind of invisible booster seat, his eyes fiery and movements abrupt. Was his expression a smile or a sneer? It looked like both at the same time. His usual patience and elegance had evaporated. Mom cowered in the front seat next to him.

"It's absurd," he half-yelled to no one in particular, "to think that any self-respecting philosopher would dream of making such a statement." He snorted derisively. "Completely absurd!" Although I didn't know quite what he meant, it was absolutely clear that he was right and everyone else was wrong. "I'll settle the academic scores forever!" he bellowed, but who was his audience?

Why was he shouting?

Our plan was to pick up Grandmother and head to the Willard restaurant down on Main Street, with its sumptuous fried chicken dinners. The Willard had been an institution since Mom was a girl. Every few weeks after church we made the trip. But Dad had been haughty and furious all morning. Why was the house not spotless? The OSU football team: *He* could have coached them better. Why had he failed to receive the acclaim he so richly deserved? Although usually close to perfect in his eyes, Sally and I had been too slow to get ready and didn't respond to his questions with sufficient haste. Mom was trying to speak calmly but he didn't appear to notice. Even back then, I sensed that he was *hoping* things would go wrong so that he could show off his wisdom and power.

Increasingly on alert, I prayed that he might snap out of his state. But what could I do to stop it? Instinctively, I knew that I had to be a good son, maybe a perfect son, to help hold the family together. But how could I keep up the act without anyone to tell me how?

Finally at Grandmother's, we pulled into the long, narrow driveway that took us to her back entrance. Mom rushed out to get her. But after Grandmother squeezed in the back seat with Sally and me, Dad scolded her, irritated that she hadn't been ready the instant we'd arrived. Mom tried to defend her but Dad talked right over Mom, which almost never happened. How all-knowing he was!

Who *was* this man?

As we slowed to turn into the parking area next to the Willard, my heart sank when I saw the enormous line, stretching to the back, inching forward glacially. Trapped in an itchy sweater, I felt the way I had in a shoe store the winter before when, exasperated by trying on so many pairs of dress shoes in my bulky winter coat, I kicked the salesman in the shin out of sheer frustration, to Mom's endless humiliation. I nearly always held things in. But when impatient, pushed too far, or overheated, I would sometimes burst in a split second of pure heat. Sometimes I still do.

As we clambered out of the car and stood at the back of the teeming line, I felt that I'd break out in a rash. "Come *on*," I called out to no one in particular, as beads of sweat trickled down my back. Sally took a step back, wondering who would erupt next.

"Stephen," Mom commanded—always the full name when there was trouble—"you must be patient. Think how good the dinner will taste." Maybe she could stem the tide through sheer force of will.

"Why can't Steve just stand still?" Grandmother was reaching her own melting point. After a few more minutes in the stuck line, I stalked off toward the parking lot. Exasperated, Mom clenched her fists. Finally, showing a triumphant gleam, Dad marched over, took me by the arm, and gently but firmly escorted me to the car. With a sweeping gesture of his right arm, he beckoned for everyone else to join. We silently climbed in as the crowd witnessed the strange retreat of our super-charged family.

The only sound was my own fast breathing. "Can we open the window?" I asked while Dad put the key in the ignition. But no one made a move. Nearly gloating with perverse joy at the afternoon's demise, he drove the few blocks back to Grandmother's, struggling to keep his speed down. Once inside the kitchen, Grandmother couldn't contain herself. "Well, I never!" she called out. "To think of how we looked to everyone!"

But Dad countered in a tone of voice I'd never heard. "Ruth," he roared, his face beet red, "if you didn't spoil him so badly when he and Sally spend the night out here, this would never have happened!" I had the strange feeling that he'd wanted to tell her off like this for a long time but never before had the nerve. Only far later did I understand that he'd been beleaguered by his conservative, controlling mother-in-law for years but simply put up with it. Even more, he was fast escalating into an episode of mania, one of the two poles of bipolar disorder.

At first lively, jovial, intensely social, and grand in their thinking, people emerging into a manic state—what's called hypomania—feel special and privileged. Only *their* ideas are worthwhile. Music is heavenly, colors brilliant, sensations magical. A strange, luminous energy infuses every moment. Why sleep? There's enough "juice" to go full-tilt all day and most of the night, too.

Soon enough, though, when hypomania uncoils into full mania, things get out of hand. The engine continues to rev at a super-charged speed and goals are pursued intently, but there's little comprehension that other people may not share in the individual's ravenous desire for new ventures, no matter how outlandish or outrageous. Life is a constant *now*, without patience for inevitable stalls and delays. Even more, when manic, people tend to go straight for the jugular, sensing any weakness in their compatriots as though by radar. Full-blown mania is a state where energy, superiority, and irritability—plus growing anger at the dawdling pace of others—combust in a potent mix.

In most people with bipolar disorder, manias alternate with periods of abject depression, on schedules that are unique to each individual. It's one of the core puzzles in all of mental health: how people experiencing the ultra-high of a manic episode can—a week, month, or year later—succumb to the despairing low of a major depression. Theories abound, many related to alternating levels of key brain chemicals. Indeed, bipolar disorder may be as much a disturbance of one's "clock" as it is a disturbance of one's mood.

A condition of fragmented, utterly dysregulated emotion, bipolar disorder is deadly serious. The suicide risk is enormous, especially when manic frenzy and depressive despair emerge at the same time in what's called a *mixed state* or *mixed episode*. These periods produce enough raw energy that the person may now be able to act on the paralyzing hopelessness of the underlying depression. The poor impulse control linked to mania makes it impossible to tolerate negative feelings for even a split second.

Untreated, up to half of people with bipolar disorder make attempts on their own lives, and a third of these attempters end up completing the act. Don't let anyone tell you that bipolar disorder is just a lifestyle choice or that manias are invariably pleasant. All too often, self-destruction results.

So why had Dad been diagnosed with schizophrenia since he was 16, following his initial episode of madness when he'd nearly killed himself? His massive energy, his grandiose plan to save the world from the Fascists, and his impulsive, pumped-up mind were clear signs of a fully developed manic episode. Yet as manias and depressions escalate in intensity, it's common for signs of psychosis to occur, including hallucinations (hearing voices or seeing imaginary objects), delusions (fixed, irrational beliefs), and highly illogical thinking. These are usually linked to the underlying mood state. Dad's voices and beliefs related to saving the world, for example, were highly consistent with his manic grandiosity.

But for much of the twentieth century, U.S. psychiatrists clung to the belief that the presence of any psychotic symptoms indicated schizophrenia, a thought disorder with persistent disturbances of logic and rationality. As a result, manic-depression, as it was then called, was almost never diagnosed. It took until the 1970s for the more accurate European perspective to take hold, which allows for a diagnosis of bipolar disorder even if psychotic symptoms are present. In fact, when diagnosed accurately, bipolar disorder—which afflicts up to 4 percent of the population when the full spectrum is considered—is around three times more common than schizophrenia.

In classic cases of bipolar illness, like Dad's, the periods of time between episodes witness a nearly complete return to normal functioning. No wonder I was so shocked when my calm, philosophical father suddenly became inhabited by a superior, rageful self—and then changed back again without warning. Yet during the scene at the Willard, what stayed with me was the look of utter defeat on Mom's face. How many times had she seen it coming and been powerless to stem the tide?

Back in Grandmother's kitchen, Dad was relishing his outburst. Mom finally pulled herself upright and rushed outside, covering her face with clenched fists. Dad angrily shooed Sally and me out the back door and opened the car. To stop Dad from yelling again, I kept quiet. Teeth bared, the hidden trauma hiding just beneath the surface of our family now stared us in the face. We drove back home in complete silence, as my ears filled with a hiss of white noise. Once there, Sally and I went to our rooms. I concentrated on blanking out the afternoon. It was the last time we ever went to the Willard.

Within a week Dad disappeared. It wasn't the first time. It wouldn't be the last. I waited blankly while the weeks dragged on. No questions were allowed, no answers offered. Concentrating on schoolwork and sports might keep my body and mind occupied—anything to stop questioning, anything to stop feeling. I had no idea that our parents were under doctor's orders never to even mention the subject of Dad's mental illness to Sally or me. Walking through the house each day was exhausting, as though I were a mountain climber scaling a Himalayan peak without an external oxygen supply. Every few steps, slowly asphyxiating, I stopped and gasped for air. How long would all this go on?

I usually have a strong memory, but around Dad's departures and returns, the computer inside my head simply shut down. Some kind of vacuum sucked out my recollections, just like the water pump in our basement, chugging away, spitting out the flood water onto the driveway. This one worked on my mind, emptying it of remembrance.

The following spring, preparations for the Saturday evening dinner party were in full swing. When Mom and Dad hosted such events, it felt like a portal opening onto a different world. For a few precious moments the brittle tension of the household evaporated. "Cocktails at six," the mailed announcement pronounced in italics.

Mom's worries were vast. Would Dad stay healthy long enough to host the event? The next time he departed, would he ever return? But if they somehow went forward as though nothing had ever gone wrong, perhaps relatives, neighbors, and the campus community would stifle any questions about Dad's mysteries. For Mom, who'd been raised in an era when appearance was everything, throwing such a party was transcendent. A top student her whole life, she'd met Dad in the late forties while earning her Master's degree in history from OSU. Now a proud wife and mother, she wore the hope for her family like a badge.

Making her preparations, she anticipated the house full of excited friends and colleagues.

Dad was in his element, too. A scholar of ultimate promise, he was a logical positivist who had also mastered classical philosophy. As Mom told me years later, during those years he was the apple of the Ohio State philosophy department's eye. At any gathering, he held court about the world's big ideas. In a few hours, the couple's charm and erudition would be on full display, the picture of grace and accomplishment.

High above the dining room table, the small chandelier illuminated plates of hors d'oeuvres—deviled eggs, asparagus spears, watercress sandwiches—while dinner warmed in the oven. In the living room, light-brown and pale-orange shafts of light from the lampshades provided a soft glow. A radio-delivered Eisenhower speech sounded while Mom bustled, straightening cushions and doling out ashtrays. Dad put his favorite records on the phonograph. The triumphal march from *Aida* filled the air, transporting the household to Egypt, before the resonant organ chords of E. Power Biggs, playing Bach, transformed our home into a cathedral.

Green, brown, and amber liquor bottles gleamed on the card table Dad had installed near the back porch, his bar station for the night. The shakers glistened, the metallic ice-cube trays so cold that your fingers would stick to the frosted silver surface if you dared touch them. The faintly medicinal smell of the liquor hinted at hidden pleasure.

As the hour neared Sally and I got into our pajamas, awaiting our sitter as we perched on the stairway. At last the doorbell sounded and guests began to pour in: professors, doctors, artists, neighbors. Filling the house with their excited voices, the men sported tweed jackets while the women glittered in jewel-adorned dresses. Stepping aside to remove their coats, the handsome couples beamed.

"Alene," one said, gazing at my mother; "you look splendid this evening! What a spread in front of us!"

"Where's Virgil?" said another, a grin covering his face. "Aha, just as I suspected, pouring cocktails behind the table! Get on over here and say hello, you philosopher king!"

A third bellowed, loud enough for everyone to hear: "I've searched for years for the perfect party, but here it is right in front of me, chez Hinshaw! Get me a drink, right away!"

When the guests spotted Sally and me, 1950s-style love flowed. "Let's see how tall you are, Steve! And Sally, you're nearly as big. How beautiful you are, just like your mother! Come here and give us a hug." Another guest entered. "Steve, will you become a scholar-athlete like your robust father?" A glowing faculty wife gushed: "Sally, are you taking ballet already?"

In the living room at his makeshift bar, exposing a wry grin, Dad carefully measured each shot before shaking the requested drink, then tossed in a bit more before serving it. His wit was on full display, his laugh infectious.

As the sitter arrived Sally and I groaned. Mom guided us upstairs but we could still hear bits of conversation. "Virgil, where is Bertrand Russell these days? What did you tell him at Princeton?" Dad had studied with the noted philosopher while in graduate school.

"Alene, how can you look as you do with two children in tow? But we must get you to campus; surely there's room in history or English for someone with your talents."

Among the men: "Can Woody bring home another national championship with the Buckeyes in the fall? On to the Rose Bowl!"

Bursts of excited laughter periodically reverberated up the stairway. At one point, an enthralled voice cried out, "It may be a Cold War outside, but the house is warm inside! Here's a toast to our charming hosts!" Glasses clinked. From upstairs I pictured the gleam of the stainless steel serving dishes, the blue-yellow flames underneath exuding a faint scent of burning fuel that made its way to our bedrooms.

I've surmised that, during a pause, Mom passed the living room's front window, suddenly shivering. I learned about this moment during a conversation I had with her twenty years later, a few years after Dad and I had held our first, fateful conversation during my initial spring break from college. At the window, she recalled the clear, cold afternoon a few months before the party when she and Dad had stood right at that spot, peering out at the homes of the neighbors. He had returned from Columbus State Hospital after a period of uncontrolled behavior, voices in his head, paranoia raging. The incident at the Willard had been a clear sign—in hindsight, he was climbing through mania at frightening speed.

At Columbus State Hospital, part of his regimen was electroconvulsive therapy, abbreviated as ECT, with electrodes placed on his temples to induce grand mal seizures in his brain. To cut his episode short, the doctors had also prescribed high-dose Thorazine, the original antipsychotic medication. Yet once Dad was home, something was amiss. Usually back to his normal self after a bout of madness, he seemed in a fog, his personality elsewhere. Had his condition lingered, Mom wondered, or was it the effects of his treatments? To shield Sally and me from Dad's confused state, she sent us to Grandmother's house for consecutive weekends.

Timidly, her husband had approached her one Saturday, his voice wan. "Dear, could you help me a bit?" he asked. Straining to find patience, she assented. Since his return, one overwhelming need seemed to follow another. "It appears that I've forgotten the names of our neighbors," he lamented. "What do I say when they approach me? Could you help?"

The names of the neighbors, the ones they'd known for years? What had happened to the brilliant scholar she'd married? With each episode, she understood with more clarity her unexpected role as mentor, guide, and caretaker. Yet she was immediately all business, pointing across the street. "Of course you recall the Caldwells, Pete and Angie? There, in the white house?" Dad followed her gaze, his expression blank. "We play badminton with them, remember? Pete's the life of the party, always with a joke or a story. Remember?"

Staring, he showed a glimmer of recognition. "Sure," he said softly, "I can picture them. What are their names again?" As though speaking to a child, she went through it once more. "And what about next door?" he asked. "The man seems to know me so well."

"Honey, you must remember the Barkers?" They laid their eyes on the beige home just across the driveway. "Bill, who always greets you when you're home from campus? A little shorter than you, crew-cut, bow tie? And three doors down," Mom continued, "the Drakes?" They craned their necks. "Tim is Steve's age. His older sister Mary is already well along in junior high school."

"What are the children's names again?" Taking in a sharp breath, she began afresh.

Back at the dinner party, Mom's brief reverie came to an end. She looked up to see her husband fill a glass and bring in a spare chair amid the scattered guests. He's as good as new, she thought, the convivial, eminent philosopher she'd married. He betrayed nothing of his inner mysteries, his chilling absences. It had taken a few weeks for his confused state to lift but his memory had finally returned, especially when the Thorazine dose was lowered. They exchanged a glance and nodded to each other, acknowledging the party's success. Yet when might the tell-tale signs return, the signs of incipient madness? She'd already made the crucial decision in her life: To survive, she would need to concentrate on the good times, like tonight. If she dwelled on the past—or thought too much of his next round of impossible behavior, along with the distance between them regarding his bouts of insanity—she wouldn't be able to face another day.

Back in command at the dinner party, she made sure each guest got seconds. As coffee was served, couples started to murmur about relieving their babysitters. By now Sally and I had been asleep for hours, weak starlight shining into our bedroom windows. Perhaps we dreamed of the party's continued excitement.

Conversations lagged as a few more revelers gathered their belongings. Dutifully, Mom saw them to the door with a brave smile. A few more guests made to depart.

Wait, she thought desperately. Don't leave! If only the party could continue just a while longer.

If only the magic could last.

Out in California

2

Did I live in two different worlds, depending on Dad's presence?

Was Dad two different people?

Was I?

His particular form of bipolar disorder—with episodes beginning during his late teen years, fast escalations into grandiose bouts of mania, miraculous recoveries after months of incomprehensible behavior, and remarkably normal functioning in between episodes—was striking. Some call this pattern "Cade's disease," named after the Australian psychiatrist who pioneered the use of lithium therapy for bipolar disorder during the late 1940s and whose accounts of the condition reflected this classic pattern of cycling. Not everyone with bipolar illness shows such distinct manias and depressions. In fact, a majority show lingering symptoms during the periods in between episodes. But until relatively late in his life, Dad showed the extreme, classic pattern. Not surprisingly, when he took on a separate personality, so different from his usual self, my world turned upside down. When he vanished, I was frozen in time, not even daring to wonder where he might be. Following his return after weeks or months of shut-down, he was rational, calm, and responsive, my go-to person when confused or upset.

As strong as Mom was—holding the family together through sheer force of will—she didn't want to see me sad or angry. It might remind her of another male in the house whose emotions could threaten destruction. I learned to keep things in.

Throughout, no one could let on that anything had changed. We were all engaged in serious play-acting, the costumes stiff and the scenes perplexing, without rehearsal. Over time, we ended up pretending that we weren't pretending—enacting the ultimate in fantasy role-play. Each performance was live, and we acted out our roles as though our lives depended on their success. Why were the most important things in our family's existence such an ongoing mystery? Whatever lay behind the silence must have been so devastating that it would have destroyed us if brought into the open.

For the past couple of decades, beyond my career-long research and teaching in child and adolescent mental health—which was inspired by what I began to learn from Dad all those years ago—I've been engaged with the concept of *stigma*. This term is defined as the shame and degradation meted out to members of social groups believed to be unworthy, dirty, or untouchable. From its Greek origins, stigma signifies a literal mark or brand. Coming to the agora, the public marketplace, a citizen in ancient Athens might have wondered who had fought for Sparta or who was a former slave. A burned mark into the skin publicly announced such status—a physical stigma, an observable mark of disgrace to define those not deserving of full citizenship, true outcasts.

In modern times, such actual marking still sometimes occurs. Concentration camp inmates in Nazi Germany were branded with numbers. During the early days of the epidemic, individuals with HIV in certain countries were also physically marked. Yet the vast majority of stigma today is psychological, referring to the subtler but still devastating mark of simply being part of an unfit group. Stigma pollutes any interactions between such individuals and members of mainstream society, containing the clear message that the outsiders are unworthy and despicable.

Throughout history and across cultures, many characteristics have been stigmatized, including physical deformity or disability, diseases like leprosy (now known as Hansen's disease), minority status with respect to race or religion, any sexual orientation other than heterosexual, being adopted, and having a mental illness. Some of these are overt and visible, such as race, physical disability, and many chronic diseases. "Lepers," as they were called—noxiously equating the person with the disease—could be distinguished by their scaly, dark-toned, disfiguring skin lesions. Yet other stigmatized traits, like sexual orientation, being adopted, or having a history of mental disorder, are potentially concealable. These kinds of hidden stigmas can be especially troublesome, because the individuals in question may constantly wonder whether their characteristics are "leaking," adding layers of tension and uncertainty to every social encounter.

Think of the questions and decisions people like my father faced—and, far too often, still do: *Can anyone tell? If my secret of being insane, a madman, comes out, I'll be shunned. Covering up completely is the only course.* Stigma breeds shame; stigma breeds silence.

As cultures evolve, a number of formerly stigmatized traits or attributes can become far more acceptable. Left-handedness was formerly disgraceful but hardly seems an issue today. Strikingly, rapid shifts in societal attitudes toward gay marriage have emerged over the past two decades, fueled largely by young people. Such positive trends are unmistakable, giving real hope for tolerance and acceptance. Yet mental illness and intellectual disability, a newer term for mental retardation, have both been extremely stigmatized throughout history and across nearly all cultures.

Three attributes, in fact, rank at the bottom of social acceptance in current attitude surveys: Homelessness, drug abuse, and mental illness. The general public does not wish for close contact with such individuals, revealing a strong desire for *social distance*. Even more, on the typical scales and questionnaires used in such research, respondents are likely to underplay their negative attitudes to avoid being perceived as bigots. Privately held attitudes may actually be far worse.

During the silent 1950s, when I was young, mental illness was stigmatized to the extreme, linked in the public's mind with utter incompetence as well as major potential for violence. Over half a million Americans were placed involuntarily in crowded, inhumane public mental hospitals, many of which resembled snake pits. The very term "mental illness" made one a complete outcast. Our family was caught in the crossfire.

As a boy I knew nothing of the term *stigma,* which became publicized after the 1963 publication of Erving Goffman's classic monograph on the topic. What I did know was that something unimaginable lay just beneath the calm exterior of our family—and whatever it was could never be mentioned. What I did feel, in the rare times I allowed myself emotions, was that I might plunge so far down a steep chasm I'd never claw my way up to the surface. To invoke an overused phrase, the shame and silence were deafening. There were no awards handed out to our family for acting ability but we deserved, at the very least, nominations in all the major categories.

While home, Dad would periodically take me aside to discuss his family out in California. In the beginning, he escorted me into the living room of our house on Wyandotte Road, with its soft carpet and long, flower-patterned drapes. Later, as I proceeded through grade school and began junior high, we would go to his library in our new home. Each time, he asked whether I might like to talk about his family. Not knowing when he might vanish again, I always nodded. He planned his presentations carefully, laying out an assortment of photos neatly on the table. The room was still, the eagerness in his voice impossible to mask.

"Take a look," he said. His brothers and all those other relatives out West seemed to be a mysterious tribe, as distant from Columbus as Siam or Brazil. Southern California was mystical, I was sure, with oranges growing on trees all year long and vast beaches fronting the Pacific. Dad's eyes lifted upward as he spoke. If I had questions, I stifled the urge to ask, taking in each syllable without interruption.

The family spent their early years in La Grange, Illinois, outside Chicago. Grandpa Hinshaw was chairman of the Prohibition National Party from 1912 through 1924. The Eighteenth Amendment, enacting Prohibition, was ratified during his leadership, in 1920. I hoped that someday I might make history, too. Yet the wait seemed interminable. If I wondered, over the years, how the son of a Prohibition leader delighted in making cocktails at dinner parties, I kept that thought to myself.

Virgil Sr.'s interest in Prohibition arose from his Quaker background, including the firm belief that alcohol was the root of many social problems, like crime or the abuse of children. At 12, he joined the "Band of Hope," the children's branch of the Women's Christian Temperance Union. Dad showed me old newsletters he'd saved, which reported that while in his twenties, his father toured 203 college campuses to speak about the evils of alcohol before obtaining his law degree. I was inspired but stunned. Where did that kind of energy and devotion come from? What kind of family *was* this?

Photos revealed the four boys: First was Harold, known as Bud, born in 1912. Strong and athletic, he began to have troubles as a teenager. Showing the ultimate in defiance, he took up drinking. He worked sporadically as an adult, including a long stint as a golf caddy. Though I didn't yet know the meaning of the word "irony," I had a sense of the utter shame related to becoming an alcoholic in a Prohibition home.

Next, Randall was born in 1915. Slighter in build than the other boys, he contracted rheumatic fever as a pre-teen and was confined to bedrest for a year. To make up for his lost schooling he decided to read the Encyclopedia Britannica from cover to cover, starting with volume "A" and proceeding in order. There was no masking the high levels of scholarship in the Hinshaw family.

Early in 1918, Robert emerged. Dad said that he and Bob were close. As an adult Bob became both a psychologist and psychiatrist. Years later he told me that when he witnessed the aftermath of his younger brother's fateful flight from the porch roof in 1936, he decided then and there to become a professional in the mental health field and work toward both an M.D. and Ph.D.

The fourth of four, Junior came into the world in November of 1919, a year and a half after Bob.

Dad sometimes spoke of other relatives. One was a second cousin who had become one of the first woman physicians in the West. Another relative, my great-uncle Corwin Hinshaw, was a research physician on the team performing the first trials of antibiotics to treat tuberculosis in the 1940s. It was reported that he had just missed receiving the Nobel Prize. There was no mistaking the message: Big causes and high accomplishment were part of the Hinshaw family.

But other relatives, I learned as I got older, had experienced serious problems. Beyond Uncle Bud with his drinking issues, a cousin of Dad's died in her late twenties. She had problems with eating the right foods and keeping up her weight; she might have even killed herself. Dad's voice trailed off; it was clear that this was not an easy topic to discuss. Others had spent time in asylums, the old name for mental hospitals. The more I learned, the clearer the divide became: In Dad's family people either did great things or collapsed. I told myself that I'd need to push hard to stay on the right side of the divide.

Dad spoke of his mother, a missionary to Latin America who later became committed to the Prohibition cause. Tenderly, he showed me close-up photos of her broad, kind face. But then he glanced down. "A tragedy occurred early in my life," he said when I was further along in grade school. I didn't know the meaning of the term, so he explained grimly. "If Mommy were to die, that would be an utter tragedy." In early 1923, his mother became ill and had complications during surgery. Shortly after his third birthday, she died at a hospital in Chicago.

Dad's first memory was of standing in his living room. A large box was in the middle of the floor—a coffin, though he didn't know the word. Holding Junior above it, his father told him sternly, "This is your mother. You'll never see her again in this lifetime."

Among Dad's folders I saw an international Prohibition newsletter entitled *World Dry*. The spring 1923 issue featured a long article on the life of the recently departed Eva Piltz Hinshaw, describing her early missionary work outside the United States and praising her dedication to the Prohibition cause. It included a striking photograph of her four sons, aged 3 to 11, in and around a wagon on the sidewalk, captioned "The Motherless Hinshaw Boys." Bud stood to the right; Randall, Bob, and Junior sat inside.

In this photo, as I study it today, Dad's three older brothers show half-smiles for the camera. But from his seat in the wagon, Junior—three years old, dressed in a kind of androgynous gown—displays a facial expression those who study attachment might term *frozen*. He's neither sad nor happy nor shocked. Instead, his facial muscles appear paralyzed by a distant fright, which he may be trying to ward off.

Accumulated research reveals that the loss of a parent between the ages of three and five places a child at particular risk for a mood disorder later in life. There's something about grief during those tender years that may be hard to comprehend and resolve, given the child's lack of full development of language, memory, and attachment bonds to others. Yet the quality of the child's remaining relationships, inside and outside the home, is an even stronger predictor of life outcomes. Early loss, in other words, does not inevitably lead to lifelong emotion dysregulation. It would take many years, though, before I learned about the impact of those remaining relationships on Dad.

In a large cardboard box, Dad had kept copies of many of his father's letters. In one from the spring of 1923, written to a relative, Virgil Sr. stated that Junior cried inconsolably for his mother at bedtime while the older boys tried to soothe him. There was nothing anyone could do to calm him down.

Dad discussed his family's subsequent move to Southern California. He cleared his throat as he began speaking, as though beginning a small seminar. Needing a fresh start after losing his wife, Virgil Sr. moved his brood of four boys out West. Two years later he remarried, to another missionary who'd worked in Latin America, just like his first wife.

Dad beamed as he talked about his new home in Southern California. He attended a public school dedicated to John Dewey's progressive ideals. The San Gabriel Mountains lay close behind, with the Mt. Wilson Observatory at the summit. It was there, Dad recounted, that the first evidence for the Big Bang was detected. Through the huge telescope, the astronomer Hubble saw that the colors of faraway stars were shifting toward red and realized instantly that the universe was expanding. When a train passes a station, Dad explained, you know it's heading away because the clanging bell gets lower in pitch, the wavelengths longer. Red light, with long waves, is like a lower sound, so the stars must be rushing away from one another as space expands. The deduction was clear: There was a beginning to the universe eons ago, everything initially merged but soon flying apart, perhaps for eternity.

All that knowledge, I thought, right behind Pasadena. Mysterious patterns could be discovered if you knew where to look and had a prepared mind.

Dad's father resigned as head of the Prohibition National Party in 1924 to become president of the International Reform Federation—a worldwide extension of the Prohibition movement—expanding his horizons to the global scene. Two more boys joined the family, Dad's younger half-brothers Harvey and Paul. With my grandfather away so much for Prohibition work, Dad was involved with their upbringing, later helping them with their homework.

In 1929 the stock market crashed. All the older boys, including Junior, pitched in to support the family. Virgil Sr. lost most of his legal and real-estate work but kept up his international reform efforts. Dad's first real job, assisting a gardener in Pasadena, paid 17½ cents an hour. Later, he hauled huge blocks of ice to homes and businesses, to restock their iceboxes. One evening, Dad recounted, Grandpa Hinshaw pulled the family together to see who had money for dinner. Only Junior had a dime in his pocket, funding the meal of apples. Listening, I couldn't remember having ever been really hungry. I silently vowed that one day I would leave my complacent life and try to do something important.

In eighth grade Dad was P.E. squad captain for a group that included Jackie Robinson, the multi-sport athlete who became the first African American to play major league baseball. "I taught him everything he knew about sports," Dad said, with a wicked grin. As a teen he put on muscle. He played football and was a shot-putter. Years later, his half-brothers Harvey and Paul told me that they never forgot the sound of Junior's grunts during practice sessions at home, including the thud of the shot as it landed in the gravel driveway. At the same time, he was a regional debate champion. Academics and sports: The model was right there in front of me.

Dad showed me a letter his father had written to a relative at the height of the Great Depression. One sentence stood out: "I never saw a day that I did not want to live a thousand years." Where, I wondered, did that energy and dedication come from? With hindsight, I can only imagine that Virgil Sr. possessed a kind of chronic form of manic energy, though he never appeared to experience major depression.

As I heard of Dad's past, two concepts lingered in my mind: achievement and mystery. It was completely clear that the stakes were high for learning in the Hinshaw family, but why were some relatives ultra-successful while others crashed? Something frightening, something unexplained lay just out of reach of my understanding. The weight of the unknown sometimes stopped me in my tracks.

Dad's departures hung like lingering smoke after a long expired fire, ashes smoldering. I half-wondered whether something I'd done—or maybe something I wasn't doing enough—made him leave. The terror hovered below the surface of my controlled life.

Elementary school was my salve. The structure of each lesson, the homework I performed with almost religious devotion, the regular hours of the school day: My focus and effort constituted a futile attempt to keep any wandering thoughts at bay. All through school, when tests were returned in class and I saw another near-perfect score, I exulted. Like mainlining a narcotic, the bliss was overwhelming but fleeting, the surge of joy quickly evaporating as I faced another walled-off day.

As I got older, victories in football, basketball, baseball, and track yielded moments of triumph but each loss stung, filling my bloodstream with venom I couldn't seem to extract. How was I supposed to solve our family puzzles completely on my own?

Ever so slightly, things could leak. Sometimes, entering a room where Mom and Dad were talking, I could sense it: a furtive glance between them, a hidden signal to keep things in check, a message transmitted up in that adult zone, above my line of sight. What is it, I kept wondering, I'm not allowed to know?

Looking up at Dad's makeshift home library one cloudy afternoon, I asked, on a whim, if he were writing any books of his own. He turned quiet for a moment before replying. "I'm pulling together my ideas," he said softly. "But this takes real time." He told me several years later that he had never been able to organize his thoughts and ideas into a book, only single articles. As he spoke, frustration covered his face. As an adult I came to understand that his episodes and hospital stays had robbed him of his prime academic years. Back then, though, what I saw for the first time was his vulnerability, some kind of hole inside him.

Sitting in his library I asked him where ideas come from. He replied that this was a fascinating question, explaining that philosophers debated whether ideas existed inside people when they were born or whether people learned ideas from looking out on the world. I wasn't quite ready for discussions of nativism versus empiricism, but this was the kind of issue he pondered all the time. "How few new ideas there really are," he continued. Even though a person might believe he had an original thought, it usually turned out that someone else had already thought of it, maybe even centuries ago.

Right then and there I felt it: Dad feared that he had no original ideas of his own. To my surprise, he was expressing regret over his life. Something was blocking him; something that had cast a pall over his life—but what? Another side of Dad existed, somewhere I couldn't see.

Once our own set of conversations began when I was a grad student in clinical psychology, Mom told me that, when Sally and I were quite young, she drove out to the old Port Columbus airport to pick up Dad from an academic conference. She'd dropped us off at Grandmother's in order to have an evening with her husband after his half-week trip.

In that era anyone could go right to the gate to greet returning passengers. With real anticipation, Mom got there early to watch him walk down the small stairway leading from the plane's front entrance. As he made his way across the tarmac and opened the door to the terminal, she caught a glimpse of his eyes. Without warning her knees buckled. She nearly collapsed.

There it was, unmistakable: the glint in his gaze, the inevitable sign of an episode ready to emerge. It was a particular sparkle, giddy yet menacing, which only she understood. She struggled to stay upright. From past experience she knew all too clearly what would soon take place: exuberance, wild energy, suspicion, sexual fervor, quick bouts of rage. She knew, too, that there was nothing to stop the runaway train once it had left the station.

The worst thing, she told me, was her utter powerlessness to do anything about it. The terror was hers and hers alone. Would he end up in the hospital again, after her secretive calls to the philosophy department chairman or to Dad's doctors, telling them just how outrageous his behavior had become this time? Would someone need to contact the police?

Mom rarely showed anger. But as she recounted the story her eyes narrowed. The ultimate in frustration, she said, were those times she tried to tell Dad's doctors of her intuition about his quick changes of mood, when it was completely apparent to her that his brain chemistry was undergoing a radical shift. Yet each time the doctors let her know that the perspectives of a mere spouse were preposterous. Unless he were in grave danger and required imminent hospitalization, confidentiality must be upheld, so they typically refused to speak with her at all. And even if they engaged her, what could a Midwestern housewife—even a brilliant one with a Master's degree in history—know about the unconscious mind, the standard of the day for understanding mental disorder? Her ideas about biological changes related to the onset of mental illness were obvious folly. Only those trained in psychological theories could comprehend deep personality dynamics and initiate lasting change through years of interpretive therapy.

Given the accumulated knowledge of the ensuing decades, it turns out that Mom's intuition was entirely correct—alterations of key neurotransmitters are undoubtedly linked to bipolar episodes, and the psychiatrists of the time were betraying their ignorance and arrogance. Part of the reason for the continuing stigma of the entire field, I've come to believe, is its longstanding resistance to bringing serious science into the enterprise. How could the doctors of the 1950s believe they knew it all? People who experience mania are notoriously poor historians, so it's essential to include significant others in the process of diagnosis, in order to get the right information. And how could professionals relegate underlying biology to the stuff of myth? The treatises of the time betray elitism, arrogance, and the ultimate in narrow-minded thinking.

As I listened, my rage smoldered. Going further back in Dad's history, why did the superintendent at Norwalk fail to call Virgil Sr. until the eleventh hour in 1936, when his son was about to receive last rites? Do people with mental illness, and their families, deserve such callous neglect? Only recently did I learn of the 1975 film *Hurry Tomorrow*, a searing documentary from the 1970s about Norwalk (later renamed Metropolitan State

Hospital), with torturous images of forced medication and utter dehumanization. The history of "care" for people with serious mental illness reveals how stigma predicts an unspeakable lack of concern for basic human rights, too often leading to brutality.

Back in the airport, Mom gathered herself and hugged her husband as if everything were fine. They walked slowly toward baggage claim as she attempted to conceal her panic. She knew enough not to set him off once he'd begun to escalate. Over the following days, completely helpless, she watched and waited until he once again emerged into complete madness.

Who supported her? She couldn't tell her mother, a Daughter of the American Revolution, that her husband sometimes went insane. Or even her closest friends, whom she'd known since kindergarten. Some had seen Virgil as he'd bulled his way through a social event, but how could she speak of the voices he heard, Columbus State Hospital, or electroshock therapy? The shame was so great that she always covered: He's visiting family; he's at a conference; he has a physical ailment. Even when his brother Bob had to fly in from California to find treatment for Virgil, no one else knew. The stigma was supreme.

The aftereffects of the silence and suppressed terror stayed locked inside her as she held the family together year after year. It took every ounce of her fortitude to maintain the family. Until one day, 20 years later—after Sally and I were grown—the cumulative effect would unleash its force and erode every cell and tissue in her body. For the last four decades of her life, she battled severe rheumatoid arthritis, which was clearly triggered by the stress from the mortal battles she'd fought, alone and without support, throughout her marriage.

Dad's talk of grown-up relatives got me excited about the idea of becoming an adult. In first grade, my teacher announced an assignment that caught my interest. Older than the other teachers, with her stiff black hair molded into a severe flip, Mrs. Deacon always spoke calmly.

The first-grade classroom was in a brand-new, low-slung building down the block from the main school building. The grassy fields behind had dirt areas, perfect for making trails for the marbles I brought in from home. Scents of paint, crayons, and construction paper permeated the colorful, airy room, but the sticky, sour scent of white paste was the strongest. Some kids said that the paste was made from horses' hooves.

"Today, class, we have a special project," said Mrs. Deacon with enthusiasm. We were to draw a picture of the job we wanted to have when we grew up. To prepare us, she asked us to think about what we'd want to be. Some kids raised their hands right away: *teacher, fireman, doctor, policeman, dancer, nurse.* But my idea was still forming.

As the others started drawing I called her over, telling her that I wanted to have two different jobs. She thought for a moment before asking whether there was one that I'd like more than the other. I replied that I couldn't decide on just one. "I want to be an astronomer, to learn about the stars and planets. But if I practice a lot, I want to be a pro basketball player, too."

She pondered before slowly raising her head. "Yes, Steve, I believe that you really could try to be both." Excited, I asked whether I could divide my drawing into two parts. She nodded.

I finished the next day. On the left side, the astronomer peered through a telescope, a few stars showing through the opening in the observatory's ceiling with the roof retracted. On the right, a tall basketball player took a shot on a wooden court, as the crowd—little circles in the stands—cheered.

Several years later, Mom and I sat in the kitchen of our new house as I pondered my future. Thinking back on that drawing, I asked if I could be both a pro basketball player and a scientist. Starting off brightly, Mom replied, "Now Steve, playing sports is wonderful. Keep it up as long as you can." Yet her tone quickly changed as she stated, with authority, that they'd never be the main thing I'd do in my life.

"It will be fine to keep playing sports," she went on, "but remember: Your contribution to the world will be with your mind. Not through sports, but with your mind."

I started to protest but stopped in my tracks. I knew Mom was right before I could emit a word. The legacy in our family was to contribute through learning and knowledge. Yet as she made her pronouncement I had the strange sense that I'd need to stay alert at all times and keep my mind sharp. Without real effort, things might happen to a person's mind. I couldn't say precisely what, but something about Dad's relatives who hadn't fared well—and something unspoken about his disappearances—gave me a chill I couldn't quite comprehend.

First grade was coming to a close. On a bright Saturday afternoon our back yard felt wondrous. Each blade of grass invited my bare feet. As dusk approached the sky turned luminescent, faint yellow streaks off to the west. Smoky shadows from the neighbor's trees crept up our lawn. I could sense myself growing up, the possibilities endless. I walked over to Mom's chair, hoping she'd agree that becoming an adult was as exciting as I thought.

"Can I be older?" I called out. "Big people know so much and get to do so many things. It's unfair to be small!" I paused. "Can't I grow up sooner?"

She gazed at me with a smile and then looked out toward the middle of the yard. Light on my feet, I wanted to run somewhere just to feel my body moving. Yet before she answered, her mouth drew in at the corners.

"Stevie, you shouldn't be in such a rush to grow up." Though devastated, I tried not to show it. I can still picture her silhouette and the sky behind her, while she spoke with a blend of tenderness and conviction I'd never before heard.

"You don't know this yet, Steve, but there are many worries when people get older, many important things to take care of." I stood there, staring. "Once you're grown up, you'll wish you could be a boy again."

What did she mean? What was she protecting me from?

Grown-ups have big responsibilities, she went on, telling me to be glad that I was still young. With a wistful look, she summed up. "There's no rush to grow up."

I couldn't think of anything else to say. We lingered outside for another few moments but it was by now getting seriously dark. I tried to hold on to the rapturous feeling I'd had all afternoon but it was fading faster than the daylight. Deflated, I trudged inside. For a long time I couldn't shake the glimmer of doubt in Mom's face as she talked about all those responsibilities grown-ups have.

On a warm evening not long after, Dad was barbequing outside on the grill. He started up the fire by dousing the briquettes with gasoline from the red can he used to fill up the lawnmower and then waited a few·moments before throwing in a match or two. I knew it would take a while for the fire to get going, so I tried to be patient. Yet once the fire was raging, he reached in toward the fire, squirted extra gas right on top, and quickly leapt back. Roaring ever louder, the flames shot up straight toward the sky, the *whoosh* tremendous, everything wavy in the air above the yellow-orange flash.

As Dad looked back toward me, his eyes gleamed with supreme enthusiasm. With a sly grin he did it again, once more revealing his thrill.

I was excited but scared. I half-knew you shouldn't pour gas right on the flames, but the feeling was tremendous all the same. The updraft and surge: What power! Yet I was terrified over what might happen if things got out of control. Dad craved this kind of thing, but I couldn't help thinking of the consequences. Something pulled me back from too much excitement.

Toward the end of the school year we examined my first-grade school photos, the group shot of the whole class and the individual, wallet-sized ones of me. I was wearing my favorite shirt, silvery-gray with thin black and red stripes, the opalescent buttons fastened all the way to the top. "School Days 1958–9," said the small writing at the bottom.

"Do you see it?" Dad said to Mom, gazing at the photo. "Steve has a Mona Lisa smile!" Mom nodded.

I didn't know what they meant, so they got out an art book and showed me da Vinci's *Mona Lisa*. "It's a small smile but a profound one," Dad said. "It's the smallest part of a circle, an arc. From some angles it hardly looks like a smile, but from others you can see it. Look from here, then here."

I looked at the page, tilting my head for different angles. I *did* see it: mysterious, slightly thrilling.

When people came over to the house, Dad opened his wallet and showed off the photo. Could everyone see Steve's Mona Lisa smile? he asked eagerly. Each time, heads nodded. At those moments I was weightless, floating through the day, larger than life. The surge in my body was overwhelming, just like the flames shooting above the glowing coals.

But I knew I couldn't stay there for long. Strange things might happen in that zone above my line of sight, where adults conversed and flames flared. When I came back down from such heights, where might I land?

The Midnight Drive

Sitting handsomely on its tree-lined street, Grandmother's three-story house exudes a quiet majesty. It's still there on the other side of Columbus, out in Bexley. The new owners have modernized it, removing some of its charm although undoubtedly adding to its value. But if you half-close your eyes, it's possible to imagine what it looked like all those years ago: the side porch with its wicker rocker; the lift of the wood- and stone-framed floors heading toward the roof; the detached garage at the end of the driveway, abutting the back yard and alley. The garage held the wooden scooters that Mom and her brother Buddy used years before, preserved for Sally and me when we visited.

When we got tired from scootering, Sally and I explored the rooms of the house. Each one featured dark wooden floors made from the lumber of our grandfather's mill in West Virginia. Student boarders at the college a half-mile away rented rooms up on the third floor, heading out the front door to class with a curt nod. Even into her nineties, Grandmother changed their sheets and did their laundry on a regular basis.

Sally and I gazed into a second-story bedroom with its polished floor and heavy woolen bedspreads. We tiptoed in to the room, taking in the smell of varnish on the floorboards and the view through half-drawn shades across Fair Avenue to the Tudor homes on the other side of the street. Mom's older sister, Virginia—Ginny Ann—had been born with mental and physical problems of some kind; no one knew what to call them back then. She limped with leg braces and called out some barely intelligible words. But her life nearly ended at age nine when she crashed headlong while trying to navigate the steep steps to the stone-floored basement far below, a fall to near-oblivion. Bleeding from her head, immobile, she survived but never spoke or walked again. Once out of the hospital, she lived in that bedroom for the next 25 years.

When friends came over to play back in the 1930s, at the time Mom was in grade school, she heard them warn one another to be quiet. "Alene's sister is very sick," they'd whisper, looking down. "Don't disturb her; she needs rest in her room upstairs." *I didn't know my sister was sick,* Alene thought. It's just the way life was.

She and Buddy would sometimes go in and sit with Ginny Ann. No one talked about any kind of tragic fate; life just continued. That kind of fortitude, laden with silent denial, provided the model for the responses Mom exhibited throughout her marriage.

By the early 1950s Grandmother had finally needed to send Ginny Ann—a vacant stare in her eyes, wheelchair bound, mute forever—to Columbus State Institute, the massive building on the west side of town for those with feeblemindedness, as it was called, right across West Broad Street from Columbus State Hospital, where insane patients were sent. Miraculously, though, by the early 1970s the institute suddenly downsized and Ginny Ann entered a beautiful community residence. She lived there until the age of 89, having never walked since she was 9. The loving attention of the staff showed that, at least in some domains, respect and dignity have turned stigma on its ear.

On the first floor of the house was a sitting room with a low sofa and reclining chairs that looked directly out to the back yard and the grape arbors in the garden. Grandmother made grape jelly each year. We watched as she poured the deep-purple boiling fluid into glass jars with bronze screw-tops and vacuum-sealed wax. When we spent the night, Sally and I played board games in the sitting room after dinner. On the huge Zenith in the corner, Grandmother watched her favorite shows, *Lawrence Welk* and *Rawhide*.

But back in the late 1930s, when Mom was 12, her father spent a year there in a reclining chair after his first stroke. There was no way to transport him upstairs to the bedroom. Drooling, he could no longer speak intelligibly. Mom and Buddy spent time with him but everyone knew he'd never be the same. A year later, he died from a second stroke. Grandmother soon took over the family business. Once again, quiet forbearance was the order of the day. No one moped or complained; life proceeded.

After hearing these stories, I wondered how any problems of mine could even begin to compare to theirs. And if I did wonder where Dad went, or why everyone kept silent about the issue, wasn't it clear that the only way forward was just to not think about it?

A small breakfast area abutted Grandmother's kitchen, leading the way into the formal dining room. A large painted mural filled an entire wall of the small nook: a sailing boat on the blue-gray ocean, with billowing white clouds above a rocky coast. Eating at the wooden table, I secretly sailed to faraway lands, the cliffs and mountains beckoning, far from the house's memories, far from the quiet terror of our own home.

Mom finished high school in 1942 and then continued to live at home while taking the streetcar all the way down Main Street and then up High Street to Ohio State. For her last years, she lived in a sorority on campus. Dark haired and beautiful, she was an honors student as World War II raged overseas. Despite the losses she'd experienced, she persisted. A few years later, as a grad student, she would meet a new philosophy professor, changing the course of her life forever.

Sally, with her light-brown hair cut just above her shoulders. Sally, with the small gap showing between her front teeth, once her baby teeth were gone. When I was two and Sally one, she would bite my arm if I bothered her too much. The wet sting of her teeth and the tiny tooth marks indenting my skin lingered for hours. But while growing up, we were mostly inseparable.

One day back on Wyandotte Road, I heard Sally's screams from upstairs. Running through the bathroom, she'd slipped, and her forehead had crashed straight down on the rock-hard porcelain rim of the toilet. Mom and Dad rushed in. I hurried behind, my eyes huge when I saw the pale towel coated with fresh red blood. Suppressing the frightened look in his eye, Dad stayed with her as Mom ran to call the doctor, arranging for the stitches Sally soon got. The horizontal half-moon of the scar marked her forehead for years afterward.

Many days, Sally and I played together, petted our hefty black-and-white cat Slim, and huddled together when it was cold or stormy outside. As we got older I showed her how to throw a spiral and helped her with homework. But when Dad was gone, we never talked about him, not once. Maybe it would threaten his ever coming back if we spoke. We were co-passengers on the same plane, flying to unknown destinations, strapped into our seats and staring straight ahead, neither of us able to steer.

The difference was that when Dad returned from his mystifying absences, he spent private time with me, discussing his family out in California—but not with Sally. It's as though he didn't quite know what to do with a daughter. Far more than I, Sally was left to fend for herself.

In her bedroom Sally built a make-believe world of small plastic animals on the bottom layer of her nightstand, with tiny trees, a beach area, and a blue-colored mat serving as the ocean. We played with the animals in their land, where they spoke their own special language, which we called Hossareeneum. It sounded like English but with different words: "lea" meant "please"; "dip, tonk" meant "yes, thanks." Some days, Sally and I spoke to each other in this dialect. Perhaps we needed a special language amid the silence surrounding us.

Sometimes I could see it in her eyes: a hint of fear, a need to stay close at home, to protect Mom. Maybe I'd be the one, when the time came, to explore the world further.

First grade had ended. I noticed that Dad wasn't home. The air outside was warm, the pavement baking in the noonday sun. I asked once or twice but Mom said that he'd return from his trip pretty soon, maybe a few more weeks. *What trip?* I inquired as softly as I could, but she said nothing more.

One afternoon in the early summer, crossing the living room toward the back porch, I stopped short. Something seemed to be hovering nearby though I couldn't figure out what. My skin grew cool. Soon, my eyes were pulled upward as though by a magnet. With a start I saw them, near the ceiling: a string of balloons.

Incredulous, blinking, I looked outside through the porch, where another strand hovered over the back yard. All those different colors!

Had there been a parade nearby, or maybe some kind of celebration? Limp and deathly still, their tight skins glistening, they floated there without a sound. As I continued staring it dawned on me that the balloons were filled with poison gas. Hidden by the stretched plastic skins, the molecules inside were pressing for release. The danger was huge. Thoroughly frightened by now, I scurried upstairs to my bedroom.

Was this a vision of some sort? To this day I'm not certain.

But I told myself back then that if I kept my eyes focused right in front of me, my gaze pointed straight ahead, I might never see them again.

I rode my bike more than ever that summer. Tearing down the streets and sidewalks, I felt the wheels under me vibrate as the asphalt whizzed by, the rush of wind on my face. At least I felt *something*. For a few moments I could forget about Dad and where he might be. One day in the vacant lot half a block from our house, I met up with a boy I didn't know very well, Howard, who lived on a side street. As we rode down the sidewalk, the air was stifling, streets and trees bleached in the white sunlight. We stopped in the parking lot behind the stone church a couple of blocks away, where we got off our bikes and walked down a shaded stairwell, where it was cooler. Eventually we hopped back on and pedaled, single file, up the gentle incline toward Wyandotte Road.

Behind me I heard a muted crash. I stopped and turned. Howard was lying still on the sidewalk, his bike half on top of him. He must have hit a bump; he couldn't move. I stared at his face, partially covered by the bike but numb with pain. He didn't cry out. He didn't say anything.

Time slowed. My legs turned to lead. The street was empty, no cars or pedestrians anywhere to be seen. Any breeze had stopped as the searing sun beat down. I looked at the houses behind the lawns, the air wavy in the heat, curtains drawn. Maybe I'd get blamed for all this, even though it wasn't my fault. Was it?

Ever hotter in the stillness of the afternoon, I staggered to the door of the closest house and knocked, but no one was there. With all my energy now drained, I couldn't imagine trying anymore. Strangely inert, I felt paralyzed.

I then did something I've never understood. Back on the sidewalk, I looked down at Howard again—immobile, silent—jumped up on my bike, and rode home. I went inside and found something to play with. For the rest of the afternoon, I tried to clear my mind of all thoughts. All I could remember was that feeling, outside in the oppressive heat, of being unable to move, my ears filling with a strange static.

The next day, Mom asked if I'd been riding bikes with another boy the day before. Looking down, I meekly assented. She'd heard something from a neighbor. Apparently Howard had been injured pretty badly.

"And what did you do, Steve?"

How could I tell her that I'd just left him there? Like venom, the shame spread to each cell of my body. "I didn't know what to do," I replied, a flush rising to my face. Looking confused, Mom stared back at me. Neither of us said another word.

I heard a few days later that Howard had ended up all right, even though he'd hit his head after falling from the bike. But I couldn't escape that I'd left him there. During the school year I saw him occasionally but never played with him again. The humiliation was overpowering.

I still feel it today, the shame like dry ice, frozen fire.

I'd learned, by instinct, to place anything frightening into an airtight, vacuum-packed bag. I had no language for discharging negative feelings. Any failings pulled me down into a region of self-hatred so deep that I wasn't sure I could ever climb back out. Turning my back on Howard was part of the pattern, created by the shame and silence, of how I approached anything outside my usual rigid routines. Walling myself off may have seemed the ticket to survival, but—though it's hard to admit—I'd turned my back on someone who was clearly suffering.

Throughout my adult career, I've fought a dual battle: trying to understand, dispassionately, the causes of and treatments for mental illness, while nourishing my humanity at the same time. The struggle continues to this day.

One day a couple of months later Dad was back. No announcement from Mom, no discussion with Sally or me. "Can we throw the football?" I asked timidly as I saw him walk through the house. "Certainly," he replied. After trudging out to the back yard, he patiently showed me how to hold the ball correctly and coached my weak passes into longer throws. But should I ask about where he'd been? No one else was making any kind of fuss about it, so maybe I shouldn't either.

We renewed our play-acting. I co-wrote the script and performed the lines every day.

Resuming our talks, Dad said he missed much of his twelfth-grade year because he was ill and needed to make up the work later. It wasn't until the bombshell discussion in his study during my first spring break from college that I understood the reason why. When younger, what I often sensed were gaps.

From our periodic conversations I pieced together his continuing trajectory. After graduating as valedictorian, Dad spoke at the Rose Bowl in front of thousands. Admitted to both UC Berkeley and Stanford, he chose Stanford, deciding to double-major in philosophy and psychology. His voice swelling with memory, Dad said that his father wished for him to return to Southern California after he graduated to help with Quaker causes, such as international famine relief related to the tragedy of World War II. But his own passion was philosophy, and at Iowa he earned a Master's degree with Gustav Bergmann, a member of the Vienna Circle who had escaped the Nazis. A conscientious objector because of his pacifist and Quaker background, Dad received a fellowship to attend Princeton's doctoral program. He overlapped for a time with his older brothers Randall, a grad student in economics, and Bob, in psychology, who'd already started there. Dad also had a 4-F deferment, given his half-year as a mental patient, though that issue never came up in those early discussions when I was young.

During Dad's initial year as a grad student, the chairman of the philosophy department informed him of a weekly, one-on-one tutorial arranged at the home of a visiting professor from Great Britain. Asking about his host, Dad learned that he was to have those sessions with Bertrand Russell. Wait! I thought. Weren't those Russell's books right there in Dad's library, small ones like *Why Men Fight* and the huge one, *Principia Mathematica*? Dad said that Russell gave him many insights about philosophy.

Three years later, while finishing his Ph.D., he was introduced to Albert Einstein, at the Institute for Advanced Study. Pulling a book from his library shelf, Dad showed me the final chapter of an edited book on physics, about Einstein's social and moral philosophy. The author was Virgil Hinshaw, Jr. I was in awe.

It would be well over a decade before I knew that soon after completing his dissertation, he ended up in a mental hospital outside Philadelphia, called Byberry—named for the district north of the city in which it had been built. As a grad student, Dad had followed the Allied war effort, sometimes leaving campus to pack boxes of supplies in support of the fight against Fascism. Yet he became convinced that he'd gained the power of telepathy to predict the war's end. Early in 1945, with his degree in hand, he became acutely paranoid, believing that others might discover his powers. Agitated and raging over a failed relationship, he took the train to New York to seek out his ex-girlfriend. After he banged on her apartment door and windows in the bitter cold and yelled up to her room, neighbors called the police. Dad was booked and ended up being transported to Philadelphia on an involuntary psychiatric hold. He would spend five months in the huge, overcrowded institution, where inhumanity, beatings, and early death were daily occurrences.

Why was Byberry located in the countryside, far from downtown Philadelphia? Even Norwalk, when it had been built in the early twentieth century, was well outside the downtown Los Angeles area. Indeed, large public mental facilities were typically built a day's carriage ride from major cities, supposedly to provide refuge from daily stress but actually to protect the populace from insane patients—and, too often, from the barbaric practices that occurred within their walls. Clearly, stigma was part of the formula. By the 1950s, nearly 600,000 Americans were held involuntarily in such large state-run facilities.

I wouldn't know of the details of Byberry for some time. But when released in the summer of 1945, Dad took the train, along with his older brother Randall, back to Southern California. Unsure as to his future after his second bout of madness, he found whatever work he could. With a doctorate in philosophy—and his half-year at Byberry intentionally omitted from his résumé—he applied for teaching positions around the country. Ohio State's philosophy department was growing. He had published several articles from his graduate work in prestigious journals and received an offer. With a starting salary of $2,000, he could move from instructor to assistant professor and eventually receive tenure. He moved to Columbus, beginning his new life in the Midwest.

By my late twenties, Mom had learned that Dad and I had been speaking about his life for nearly a decade. It hurt her, she told me, that I knew far more about many aspects of his history than she did. But she didn't exude bitterness. Long before, she'd learned that there were major parts of his life that would remain walled off from her. Stigma and its consequences can impede the closest of relationships, eroding chances for mutual support.

By that time Mom and I had started our own private conversations. During one, she talked about an episode of Dad's when Sally and I were young. As her alarm peaked back then, she once again sent us to Grandmother's for the weekend.

"Dad was having a terrible time," she said. "He was irate over something, I don't know what." She said that, one afternoon, he stormed out of the house and into the garage, where he kept his golf clubs. Dad liked golf back then, often playing at the

OSU course. Afraid of what he might do next, she peered out from the kitchen window.

"Steve, he hauled his golf bag onto the yard and was pulling out the clubs one by one. You should have seen the look on his face." He took each club, she continued, and snapped it over his knee like a matchstick, ranting the whole time. He grabbed the broken pieces and flung them into the neighbor's yard, screaming at some unseen threat to his well-being. Concluding, Mom added that he never really played much golf much after that.

What else had I missed, all those years ago? From what else had I been shielded?

During our discussions, her most vivid story concerned an early-fall evening in the 1950s, which I've reconstructed from her words and from my adult understanding of how bipolar disorder appears when it's unchecked. Remarkably, I knew nothing of the event until 25 years after it occurred.

The scent of burning leaves infused the air while living room and bedroom lights illuminated the neighborhood on Wyandotte Road. Inside our house, I was four and a half and Sally three, fast asleep in our bedrooms upstairs. After the dishes had been dried and stacked, Mom stole a few minutes with her husband in the living room to watch a popular variety show on the giant black-and-white television set. Such a break was a real treat, but the way he'd been acting recently had placed her on full alert. On the 10:00 p.m. program, live from Cincinnati—a hundred miles away—an attractive entertainer sang a show tune, swaying her hips to the rhythmic beat of the studio orchestra. Dad had seen her before but tonight he glowered at the screen. He suddenly sprang from the couch and fixated on her sequined dress. "Come here," he commanded his wife, kneeling directly in front of the screen. "Listen—can you hear it?"

Wishing desperately to support him but terrified of what was coming, Mom dared not answer. "She's sending messages to me," he whispered with reverence. But the only thing Mom could hear was the song and its bouncy melody.

For several days he'd been awakening at dawn, rushing to his basement study to scrawl incomprehensible notes on his legal pads. He saw coded signs everywhere, in looks from people on campus, in the supposed patterns of cars parked at the curb. Essential messages were being transmitted, but only to him. Such occurrences are initial signs of paranoia, called *ideas of reference,* when special meanings are ascribed to everyday events—a stepping stone on the path to delusions.

Where was the scholar who courted her before their wedding in Columbus seven years before, the handsome, intellectual figure with whom she fell in love so deeply? Had anyone else seen this different, peculiar Virgil? Far too loud, Mom recalled, Dad played religious music on the phonograph and burst into Spanish, the adopted language of his mother and his stepmother from their missionary days. Its sensual sounds transported him back to California, as he launched into its rapid rhythms: "Yo soy yo y mi circunstancia," from the philosopher Jose Ortega y Gasset ("I am myself and my circumstance"); "el mundo tiene una belleza rara!" ("the world has a rare beauty").

In the living room that night, more excited by the second, Dad became entranced by the singer's words and dance moves. It was a personal semaphore, with hidden meanings encoded in the lyrics. "We must go to the station!" he cried. "Right now, before she leaves!"

Frantically, Mom calculated. If she let him drive off alone, what would he do at the station, if he even got that far? And she couldn't just plop Sally and me in the back seat: We would wake up terrified and we certainly couldn't see our father in this condition. What's poorly understood—even now—is that when full-blown mania hits, irritability and anger are part of the picture just as much as euphoria and expansiveness. Impulse control vanishes, judgment disappears, and irrationality takes over. No one dare stand in the way of the plans and snap judgments getting made.

Heart pounding, she decided to go along and try to contain him, praying that we would remain asleep upstairs until they returned. If not, she might never see her husband again. What kinds of choices were these, which she now had to make?

She longed for someone to call. But who would understand her impossible story? How could she keep her conversation private from her agitated husband? Alas, there was no time; he was grabbing the car keys and heading for the door. Dashing up the stairs to check on Sally and me, she heard our soft breathing. "Please, God, keep them asleep," she half-whispered before pulling herself away.

They rushed outside to their 1956 Ford Victoria with its V8 engine. Clearly, he must drive; she would never go fast enough to make it to the station on time. He forced the key in the ignition and, as the engine turned over, punched it into reverse before jamming the lever into first. They screeched down the street.

Once outside the city limits he managed to stop for signs and lights on the two- and four-lane highways but it was torture. "We must get there!" he shouted, though Mom was right next to him. "Can't this car go any faster?" But he mainly remained silent, determined to receive his messages from the singer, who intended them only for him. The speedometer's thin, blood-red dial glided past 60, 70, and 80 on the open road. He muttered each time they reached the next town.

Once back in the countryside, the car hurtled through the darkness. Mom felt that she had entered a different existence. With every ounce of effort she could muster, she tried to stay in control and urge him back home when the opportunity arose.

Unimaginably, an hour and a half later they arrived in the outskirts of Cincinnati, the station's huge broadcasting tower providing a beacon. It was nearly midnight. They swerved into the parking lot, gravel shooting out from the spinning tires as he slammed on the brakes. "Stay in the car; I'll find her," he ordered, leaping from his seat and rushing to the fence. Mom feared an ugly confrontation with the station personnel.

But wait! The gate was locked and the lights were off in the station's brick building. Even with the windows rolled up, she could hear the clanging as he shook the fence, hard. Would he climb it and jump over? Emerging calmly from the car, she left the door open, a soft dome of light in the dark lot. Approaching him, she saw his chest muscles heaving, his shirt soaked despite the cool night air.

"Honey, the station's closed," she said in a quiet voice. Hands clinging to the chain links, he peered ahead, panting. Careful, she thought, careful. "Remember, Virg, Stevie and Sally are still in their bedrooms. Maybe we should head back. The singer is sure to be on the air again in another few nights."

Wiping his face with a handkerchief, he was clearly torn. He shot another glance toward the station. "Yes," he said, abruptly changing course, "we must go." Doors opened and slammed shut. They flew back onto the highway and retraced their path.

Somehow, no one seemed to be following. In the silent world of the car's interior, the roadway, fields, and trees approached at blinding speed before disappearing off to the sides, headlight beams glued to the onrushing pavement. What would have happened, Mom asked rhetorically as she recounted the endless night, if a highway patrolman had pulled them over and he resisted? Would Dad have tried to prove his strength? If things got ugly, who would have come to the house to get Sally and me? Where would we have been sent?

But the only sound was the rush of the tires spinning madly over the highway. Foggy with adrenaline and exhaustion, she silently prayed. *Please, no accident; please, no police.*

They slowed as the car miraculously reached Columbus

sometime around 3:00 a.m. and stopped with a jolt in the driveway. The block was eerily silent, the houses dark and remote. Departing the car, she heard their footsteps echo faintly off the stone walk, the only sound for miles. She finally grabbed the keys from his hand and raced up the stairs to our rooms. There we were, fast asleep, our mouths slightly agape, oblivious to the night's events. Within moments she nearly collapsed on the bed she and Dad had shared since their wedding, the bed she'd be sharing with a stranger tonight.

Stilling her breath, she began to drift. The last thought in her mind following the terrifying midnight drive to Cincinnati was that the evening's events, and others like them, must stay locked inside her for the rest of her life. For the sake of the family, and because of doctors' strict orders, the pact of silence must remain in place.

Forever.

Some nights after dinner Dad would sit me on his lap at the kitchen table on Wyandotte Road, the air still warm from the oven. My knees and elbows would be covered with Band-Aids from falling off my bike as I continued to race around the neighborhood. At the table I might wear a construction paper crown, a single Indian feather sticking up, as Dad told me of Nickershoe, the Indian boy, and his adventures in a canoe or on the plains.

"Indian boys and girls didn't go to school the way you and other modern children do," Dad said. "But they learned all the time. The tribe's elders taught him how to carve from wood, how to fish. As he got a bit older and approached manhood, Nickershoe learned to hunt, using only his bow and arrow. He practiced and became extremely skilled. This is how Indians existed; the tribe lived off the land."

"Please, Daddy," I begged, "the great hunt in the fall!"

With a small grin, sitting erect at the table, Dad continued. "It was time for the great autumn hunt. The young braves had been preparing all summer. On glorious days, Nickershoe went with the other boys, plus an older guide, to gather food before the snows arrived. The journey took them into the forests to find bear and deer." Each detail became imprinted in my mind. Dad went on to say that Nickershoe had to prove his courage with his bow and arrow. In an early snowfall, he might find shelter in a cave and wait out the storm. He would then ride like the wind on his Appaloosa for the final hunt.

"Finally, the braves returned, with their kill draped over the horses in back. Everyone gathered to welcome them. As the braves headed into the camp, the elders were proud. The new group had done a fine job; Nickershoe might one day be their leader. What a feast they had, to celebrate the end of the great hunt."

Dad told me that he'd learned about Nickershoe when *he* was a boy, while camping in the mountains of Southern California. I wasn't sure that I could ever be as brave as Nickershoe, but if someday put to the test, I might try. I felt sure that a test *would* come one day, when I would need to be braver than I'd ever been. But what the test might be, and when it would happen, remained a mystery.

All these events took place in the silent 1950s, an era that seems lifetimes ago. Haven't we traveled a vast distance since then, especially regarding attitudes about mental illness? Isn't the stigmatization of people with mental disorders receding at a fast clip, just like fast-improving attitudes toward gay marriage?

If only such were the case. On the one hand, the general public knows far more about mental illness than previous generations. After all, psychology courses are routinely taught in high schools, and mental illness isn't the secret it once was. Many more people in the United States can correctly identify symptoms of mood and anxiety disorders, psychotic conditions, and childhood forms of mental illness than ever before.

Yet at the same time, several large-scale investigations reveal that public attitudes toward mental illness, dismal during the 1950s, have stayed essentially flat since then—meaning that the desire to keep one's distance remains high. And three times as many people believe that mental illness is inevitably linked to violence today than people did 60 years ago. In key respects things are actually going backward.

A major factor is the intensive media focus on horrific acts of gun violence. Photos of deranged-looking killers have become the public face of mental disorder, conveying the image that mental illness automatically produces aggression. In reality, individuals with mental illness are far more likely to be *victimized* by violence than others—but with rare exceptions, no more likely to commit aggression. Yet this point is almost never publicized.

Cycles abound in the history of mental illness and its treatment. Back in the late 1700s and early 1800s, a movement occurred in Europe, soon spreading to the United States. The goal was to release those with chronic mental disorders—often believed to be possessed by evil spirits—from chains and shackles within inhumane "madhouses" to retreat-like, rural settings, staffed by sensitive, well-trained caregivers. This practice was termed *moral treatment,* a clear attempt to humanize people who had lost their way, through calm, therapeutic settings far from everyday stresses.

As so often happens with even the best-intentioned reforms, these retreats became ever larger and more medicalized. As the nineteenth century progressed, with the full onset of the Industrial Revolution, state legislatures aimed for cost savings and protection of the general public by re-creating huge institutions, usually far from urban centers, under the supposed edict of moral treatment. In the aftermath of the Civil War, such massive public facilities came to dominate treatment for severe mental illness. Dad experienced the full horror of the "care" they offered. Although he'd been raised in a middle-class, Prohibition home and attained the status of professor, involuntary mental hospitalization knew no class distinctions. Brutality was widespread.

By the 1970s, deinstitutionalization had finally led to the closing of nearly all public mental facilities, to promote community care and humanization. Who could argue with such a trend? Yet these community-based alternatives were never funded adequately. Indeed, many contend that deinstitutionalization was actually reinstitutionalization, as huge numbers of people with mental illness began to flounder in jails and prisons or in poorly staffed, isolated, urban "community" centers. In addition, too many of today's homeless population have chronic forms of mental disorder, fueling fears of contagion—as though a serious mental disorder can be transmitted by close personal contact—and promoting the view that everyone with mental illness is incompetent and potentially exploitable.

What about deeper currents regarding attitudes toward mental illness? One view is that when people encounter individuals who struggle to maintain psychological balance, their own stability is threatened. When reminded of the fragility of life, or of their own imperfect self-control, many observers try to keep the source at arm's length. Even more, illnesses enshrouded in mystery, like cancer several generations ago or leprosy before its bacterial origins were uncovered, become highly feared and stigmatized. Today, breast cancer is a "cause," the subject of huge fundraising campaigns. Leper colonies are a thing of the past, as people with Hansen's disease receive state-of-the-art antibiotics. Yet mental illnesses—still viewed as the result of irrationality, weak personal will, unpredictability, or maladaptive parenting—receive contempt and outrage rather than compassion. As noted by Princeton social neuroscientist Susan Fiske, those with mental disorders are typically viewed as the "lowest of the low," perceived to be deficient in both warmth and competence.

Little wonder that teaching factual information about mental illness may actually *increase* social distance. "Facts" promote stereotypes, while the information that needs to be conveyed is the great potential for coping and recovery if treatment is made available. Emphasizing the fundamental humanity of those affected must be the main objective of any outreach. With greater openness and discussion, mental illness can take its rightful place on the national agenda. With access to effective treatment, people within the entire range of mental disorders can thrive. Still, the road ahead is long and steep.

By the end of the fifties, Mom had reached a crossroads. When Dad would return from an episode, she'd know nothing of the details. What if he didn't come back next time? Where would the family go, whatever was left of it? Once she and I began speaking in earnest, Mom told me that Dad had divulged very little about his past during their courtship, saying only that he'd had "some trouble" back in high school and at Princeton. This phrase was the sum total of what she knew. "Steve, no one ever talked about mental illness back then," she said. The stigma was supreme.

After they were married, the truth became clear, especially when Mom became pregnant with me and then with Sally. Each time, before her eyes, he escalated into full-blown mania. It's well known that women with histories of mood disorder show high risk for postpartum depression. In fact, this diagnosis is now recognized as a key public health problem. Far less understood, however, is that men with genetic risk for bipolar disorder often become symptomatic when their partners become pregnant. Obviously, a direct hormonal link does not exist here, the way it does for postpartum depression in women. Is the lack of sleep a trigger—or perhaps an existential fear related to bringing a child into the world after experiencing years of cyclic madness?

By my after-the-fact count, Mom experienced at least six of Dad's episodes during the first ten years of their marriage. Each time, her fear grew. At the end of the decade she took stock of the situation and scheduled a meeting with a lawyer. Although keeping it private, she wished to explore the possibility of divorce, in case Dad never returned or became too debilitated. She was also making plans to return to graduate school and find a job, in case her income would become the sole support for the family.

"This was a high-priced attorney," she told me. Yet when she got to the well-appointed office near downtown Columbus, she froze. She'd planned out just what to say, but once her hour began she could hardly speak. She knew that the talk was confidential because of attorney-client privilege but still couldn't describe the actual problem: her husband's periodic plunges into serious mental illness. Instead she spoke in vague, general terms about the potential for separation.

"The attorney must have wondered what was wrong with me, fumbling around as I did," she said. "I'd wasted the appointment." She summed up by telling me that back then, mental illness was off limits. Her bitterness permeated each word. It's hard to think of a clearer example of stigma.

Over the ensuing months, as the fifties wound down, Dad stabilized once again. Mom and he contracted with an architect to design a new house, and Mom gradually let go of her silent idea of the need to separate. The new home was a vote, made from blind faith, for the family's continuation.

When I was in second grade we sometimes drove to the building site. Nearby, like a giant spaceship, its spindly legs holding a vast mother ship to earth, a huge cylindrical water tower loomed over the farmland. Pretending to be explorers, Sally and I walked on top of the house's foundation, crossing through the wood-framed doorways and skeletal walls.

Heading back to Wyandotte Road in the car, we saw strings

of colored lights next to the vast parking area for the new shopping center near the water tower. "Can we see, Daddy?" we cried out in unison. As he turned the car around, we made out silhouettes of carnival rides and begged to go. The makeshift fair smelled of dust, metal, sweat, and the gasoline that powered the rides. Like pink and purple glue, cotton candy stuck to our hands as the rides twirled and spun.

In mid-summer, the enormous van arrived, men packing up everything. Our new house on Kirkley Road was a split level, fresh white paint against the jet-black driveway. Inside was Dad's new study, which he'd asked the architect to design, with golden-hued shelves built right into the walls. Our new high school was to be constructed on the large city block right behind our own.

But just before school started, I noticed that Dad was missing once more. I calculated that he'd be back in a couple of months, like last time. But I had no real idea, only hope. Third grade began at my new school, and I came home each day vaguely wondering about him. Yet no phone call ever arrived, no letter. Dad had entered a void.

Ever so slowly, my world began to cave in. It was a fight to keep up my morale.

Maybe I'd done something to make Dad disappear yet again, but what? As the weeks wore on, I needed some answers. I had to figure out how to ask Mom.

Looking for the right moment, I braced myself.

The View from Right Field

4

After Mom said good night, I tried to lie still on the top bunk in my new bedroom. Shutting my eyes as tight as I could, I hoped in vain that sleep would overtake me. Dad stayed missing that entire school year, and all my thinking made it impossible to relax.

Somewhere in the hazy territory between wakefulness and drowsiness, I saw something in the distance, as if projected on the bedroom's far wall. I couldn't make it out at first but it soon came into focus: a large silver machine hovering in the air, whirring softly. From an opening at its front, white ribbon slowly spilled out. Folding over on itself, the ribbon floated through the air. As it wafted downward, its folds and loops revealed shadows underneath. Always at the same steady pace, the ribbon continued to emerge, filling in the space in front of me. It was the ribbon of time, eternal time.

It never stopped.

Dad had told me about infinity, which is more, he said, than googol, more than googolplex. "It's not even a number," he told me; "it's a concept beyond numbers." Was the universe infinite? Or infinitely finite? My mind reeled as he raised the questions.

But eternity was far more frightening. I thought about time constantly: How little there was to get everything done, how slowly it passed when I thought of my questions that never got answered. Yet if time never stopped, what did anything mean? Fractions no longer made any sense. What did it mean to travel a third of the way somewhere, a tenth, even a hundredth? If time is eternal, you can never get closer to the end. However far you might go, exactly that much more ribbon keeps pouring out, so you're just where you started. With eternity, there's no progress, only another day's futile attempt to get somewhere. Nothing had any meaning against the eternity of time.

Finally I began to drift off. At school, I'd once thrilled whenever my teacher returned another test or assignment. But now, as each day wore on, it felt as though a gauze bandage was wrapping itself around me, insulating me from the world.

Some nights, my head filled with thoughts I couldn't stop, especially swear words like *God damn* and *hell*. A little song repeated itself: *darn damn God, darn damn God*. No matter how hard I tried, the words kept coming. What would happen if God heard these awful words?

Lying there, trying to calm myself down, I started to wonder whether I'd peed enough. If I tried one more time, squeezing out those last drops, maybe I could finally relax and fall asleep. I hauled myself up from my bunk bed, climbed down the ladder, and walked across the hallway to our bathroom, with its double sinks and aquamarine tile floor. Straining, I made a trickle into the toilet and marched back to bed. But within a few minutes I started wondering whether there might still be a little left, starting the whole process once more. What I didn't know is that giving in to ruminative thoughts by performing compulsions—peeing to stop the fear that I'd not cleared my system—provides only fleeting relief. In an endless cycle, the obsessive thoughts roar back, ever stronger.

I couldn't tell Mom how upset I was because she'd get that look on her face letting me know that she couldn't bear to see me unhappy. I'd never been lonelier in my life. I sometimes felt like smashing things. Didn't anyone know how hard I was trying? All the pretending was getting harder every day. I finally made up my mind that I just had to find out something about Dad.

During the fall, Mom sat at the kitchen table on a bright afternoon. The sliding glass door overlooked the back yard, revealing our skeletal new trees and the squares of sod that were gradually turning yellow-brown. The house was deathly still. Hesitating, I forced myself to walk toward her.

"Yes, Stevie," she said, looking at me, "what is it?"

It was now or never. I took a large swallow of air. "Mom, I have a question. Where's Dad?"

Her smile quickly faded. She didn't seem angry but her look was plenty serious all the same. Moments ticked by. In her clearest voice she finally spoke up. "Your father is resting in California. We don't know when he'll be back." She held my gaze. "It's best," she concluded, "if you ask no more questions."

I replayed her words in my mind and managed a choked reply. "He's resting?"

She nodded. That was it. Head down, I walked slowly back upstairs.

I pictured Dad taking lots of naps, keeping his mind fresh for all the books he read and all the ideas he had. I tried to be happy that he was resting, but where in California was he, exactly? Why didn't we ever hear from him? That evening in bed, the ribbon of time once more unfurled from the machine, softly folding on itself, its flow never ending.

Our third-grade teacher, Miss Searler, told us at the beginning of the school year that this was her first year of teaching.

Young, with wide eyes, she had a round face and an eager look that made me want to answer all her questions. After the final bell one afternoon, the kids whooping as they departed, Miss Searler asked me to stay. The empty desks formed straight rows, workbooks lining the shelves. High up was the American flag and beneath it those forest-green vinyl strips featuring print and cursive letters of the alphabet written neatly on them. Handwriting was my worst subject. I bore down hard, really hard, almost snapping the pencil lead as I wrote or drew. Even now, I can still see the ultra-dark letters and words I formed on the lined paper, graphite thick on the page. I can still feel it today, the stab of pain inside my right shoulder blade from all that bearing down, the muscles and tendons permanently knotted.

The afternoon sun shone obliquely through the high window as Miss Searler looked toward me, all the hope in the world on her face. "Steve, I have a question for you."

"OK," I replied, hoping this wouldn't take long so I could get outside.

"Where's your dad? We haven't seen him around."

For a few seconds I stopped breathing. Did she know something? Or was she just curious? Those big eyes of hers: She really wanted an answer. I suddenly remembered that back-to-school night had been the week before, so maybe she was just wondering why he hadn't been there. Nearly all my classmates had two parents attending.

I swallowed. "Miss Searler, my dad's in California," I said, trying to sound assured. "He's resting there."

As she pondered what I'd just said, she still smiled but the look in her eyes shifted. Squinting, she tilted her head slightly to the right, her bottom lip starting to push up against her top lip. "Really?" she asked, trying to keep her voice bright, but it was hard with her mouth at this new angle.

"Yeah, that's what my mom says."

"All right," she replied. "But does anyone know when he'll be back?"

I thought but no answer appeared. "I don't know," I said softly.

After an awkward silence, Miss Searler asked about something else, maybe an assignment. I answered woodenly, said good-bye, and walked down the stairs to the playground. For a long while afterward I thought of her expression. That shift in her eyes, the slight tilting of her mouth when her face went from hopeful to doubtful.

I finally told Mom about needing to go to the bathroom each night, as she'd been wondering why I was going back and forth across the hall so much. With a worried look she called our pediatrician and made an appointment with a specialist.

A week later we drove to the offices near downtown. The nurse asked me to put on a pale-green gown. Inside the changing room I took off most of my clothes and put my arms through the thin straps. "No, little boy," she said when I came out. "It goes the other way. What seems like the back is actually the front. I can help you tie it when you're ready." Trying not to feel stupid, I finally got it right but felt really skinny in the gown.

I swallowed some chalky liquid from a paper cup and lay down on a table, with a huge, pale-green x-ray machine looming above. I got moved around after every few pictures, for shots from different angles. I held my breath to make sure the pictures didn't blur. Finally finished, I got dressed again.

From the car's back seat during the drive home, I couldn't think of anything to say to Mom. I looked out at North High Street and the low-slung brick buildings under the slate-gray sky before we turned left, driving past the OSU football stadium toward our house. Next to me I could almost feel those poison balloons hovering, the lethal gas inside pressing for release.

A few days later Mom said that the new doctor had called

to say that the x-rays hadn't shown anything. She looked puzzled, but I wasn't surprised at all. I'd known that the problem
was more in my mind than anywhere else in my body.

Every few weeks Sally and I spent the night at Grandmother's house. It had long been our haven during those times
when, far beyond our knowledge, things were unmanageable at
home. Grandmother took us to movies—the Elvis movies she
loved or, when she wanted to show us religion, *The Ten Com-
mandments,* which I thought would never end. Religion was on
Grandmother's mind. In the small anteroom near her bedroom,
she lectured to us after Bible readings. One afternoon she delivered her sternest lesson.

"The Bible tells us that there are many things you can do and
be forgiven," she said. "But certain words are the worst. If you
take the Lord's name in vain, you will be eternally damned."
Suddenly frightened, Sally and I asked what that meant. "You
will go to hell forever," she replied with force. "The flames are
hotter than anything on earth; the burning would hurt more
than you can ever imagine. You can do many things and be
forgiven, but you can never take the Lord's name in vain."

Stunned, I couldn't believe it. With those chants and songs
I said to myself in bed each night, each one damning God, I was
going to end up in hell for eternity. Although I tried not to let
my horror show, I was in supreme agony.

The next time Sally and I went to Grandmother's house, I
put my plan into action. Making sure they were busy in the
kitchen, I tiptoed upstairs to the anteroom, which looked out
over the back yard and the alley beyond. I might lie up there
near the radiator if I'd had too much to eat for Thanksgiving or
Christmas Eve dinners, but there was no time to rest today. Getting up my courage, I walked straight into Grandmother's bedroom, finding her Bible with its pebbled, soft-black cover and
onionskin pages, lying on the stand near her bed. Sitting at her
desk, which smelled of hairbrush and perfume, I looked for the

part in the Old Testament about taking the Lord's name in vain. To my amazement I found the passage within a few minutes. My world reeled. Right there, the Bible stated exactly what Grandmother had said, that taking the Lord's name was unforgivable. I stared blankly. My only hope was to try even harder in school and at home, which might count for something in the final reckoning. But what good would that do? My fate was sealed.

During January, after a forlorn Christmas with Dad nowhere to be found, Mom surprised me with a 45 r.p.m. record of a song I liked from the radio, "Big Bad John," by Jimmy Dean. She'd gone out of her way to buy it. I rushed to put it on the turntable in the family room, as the snow lay thick on the ground outside the windows. I put the vinyl disc on top of the cylinder as the small arm clicked over and pushed the record down onto the rubber circle, the big arm swinging around and dropping down on the lined black grooves. After a mild hiss, the song started for a second or two. Yet suddenly the music stopped, static over static. I tried again but the arm skipped once more.

"Oh, God," I said with an exasperated sigh. Couldn't anything go right? But when I looked back I realized that Mom had quietly walked downstairs in the interim, witnessing the scene, her face frozen with disappointment. And here I was taking the Lord's name in vain, not just lying in bed when I couldn't help it but on my own, out loud.

Might it be noticed, in the end, how hard I was bearing down at school and at home? Yet in light of my sins, I was certain that none of that mattered.

Years later Mom told Sally and me about her childhood during the Depression, especially the time when she wanted more than anything to get the new board game Monopoly. Grandmother had made it clear, though, that there'd be no presents until Christmas, half a year away, without exception. After pleading to no avail, Mom thought hard and made a plan. Gathering tracing paper, tiny small household items for the pieces, construction paper for the Chance and Community Chest cards, colored paper for the money, and cardboard for the property deeds, she constructed her own version by hand, an exact replica. For a model she used the real version at a friend's house.

She'd kept it all those years. The handmade game lay right in our closet inside the new family room. As Mom pulled it out to show us, Sally and I couldn't believe how real it looked. But I was also ashamed. Compared to the kind of patience Mom had displayed, I had to be the most indulged kid imaginable. How could I ever complain? I was forgetting, though—if I even knew it then—that pain is hard to compare. What I needed back then was even the slightest dose of reality. Instead, I lived in a make-believe world where, if a family simply closed its eyes hard enough, everything would be all right. We lived in the shadow world of stigma.

In the dismal cold of February, Mom and Grandmother planned to take Sally and me to a children's concert of the Columbus Symphony on a Saturday morning. Excited for once, I fell asleep earlier than usual the night before. When I awakened, pale light glowed behind my curtain, a deep snowfall covering the driveway and yard. The sky was a soft gray above the snow cover. Everything outside had a primordial look. After a quick breakfast, I put on my boots, gloves, and coat and raced to the garage to get a snow shovel. I could clear the way for Grandmother's car!

The snow was powdery and easy to lift off the driveway, the white landscape majestic all around. I made up the game on the spot, running in my boots and pushing the shovel in front of my face like a racing plow, as the snow mounted in front and splayed off to either side. With one row done, I pivoted back to start another. Bitterly cold at first, I soon warmed up, my legs churning. Like boats gliding in turgid water, a few cars floated by on our street, their tires humming over the hardened snow cover.

I turned and started a new row, regaining speed. But an instant later I heard a cracking sound as something smacked me in the mouth. With my lips stinging, I stopped short and the shovel flew out of my hands to make a muted clang on the half-cleared driveway. Stunned, I realized that the blade must have hit a patch of ice beneath the snow, flinging the metal handle back into my face. Using my tongue, I felt something funny in my mouth.

Mom and Sally heard the commotion as I rushed inside to the bathroom, my lip bleeding. Maybe, I prayed silently, it was just a cut. "Oh, no, Steve," Mom cried, gasping while she looked inside my mouth. "Your front tooth—it's chipped!" I looked in the mirror and couldn't believe it: A corner of my front tooth was missing.

"It's not that big a deal!" I pleaded, trying to stop the panic. But Mom was frantic. "Your beautiful permanent tooth—it's ruined forever!" she half-sobbed. How had things changed so quickly from that glowing feeling outside to the scene in here?

Grandmother arrived a moment later. Once she heard the story and studied my tooth, she shook her head in a kind of horror. While changing clothes inside my bedroom, I heard Grandmother's voice across the hall. "Well, Alene, the dentist can fix this. But this is a man's job, to shovel the snow! If Virgil were here, this would never have happened." She continued. "Where *is* he, anyway? Why isn't he at home?"

I felt hot all over. I wanted to charge out of my room and tell them to stop worrying about the tooth. And no more arguing about Dad: He's just resting in California! But I didn't move.

How could I have known at the time that Mom was constantly covering for Dad's disappearances into mental hospitals? What was true? What was a half-truth? Everyone felt the strain of the shame and cover-up.

Finally calmer, they called me in for one more look, deciding that the dentist could polish off the tooth's corner. "Let's hurry and get on our warm coats and head out," Grandmother said.

After the drive downtown, we walked through the slushy parking lot and joined excited families crowding the hallway of the huge auditorium. But I was overheated and utterly deflated. Slumping in the cushioned chair, I couldn't wait for school on Monday. It was now certain that if I got too excited, disaster loomed. Life went far better if I tried not to feel at all.

By early spring, I had made a new friend, Brian, who always had something kind to say. His back yard bordered a corn field, part of the university's agricultural school, with greenhouses off to the side. Baseball season was approaching, so we pitched to each other. Each of us half-worried that if we hit a long one, it might break the glass of those low-slung greenhouses just beyond his family's yard.

On a warm morning in April, I watched the ball all the way in from his hand. Taking a big swing, remembering how Dad had taught me to wait and then extend my arms, I made solid contact. A moment later we heard the crash.

"It's OK," his mom said after we rushed in to tell her, "things like this happen." There was no way to get the ball back but there was a spare. I sighed in relief.

Whenever I was at his house, only his mom and sister were present. After more baseball a week later, Brian and I sat in the shade drinking lemonade. He looked toward the horizon and said that his dad had died two years ago. "My daddy is in heaven," he said. "My mom says that we'll all join him one day." His face tilted upward as he spoke, as though gazing where his dad now resided.

I swallowed hard. Although terribly sad for him, I couldn't think of anything to say. I still had a dad, didn't I? Yet what could I say about *him*? That he was resting out in California? I had no words to console Brian, or myself.

Brian had been orphaned by his father, but had I? As far as I knew, Dad was neither alive nor dead. At least Brian understood where his dad was.

After that spring, he and I found other friends. Once again, I was frozen in silence.

All the boys were joining Cub Scout baseball, so I begged Mom to sign me up. I'm sure she felt that doing so would help me endure Dad's long absence. All the teams were named for Indian tribes. We were the Osage, with bright-yellow T-shirts sporting dark-blue numbers. The other boys always seemed to have their fathers with them at practices and games but I rode my bike to and from the fields alone.

The league was for third, fourth, and fifth graders, so third-grade boys like me were usually the smallest kids and worst players. With my December birthday, I was the youngest third grader of all. But the rules said that everyone had to play at least two innings. The coaches hoped that no balls would come to us during our limited time in the field, and prayed that we didn't head up to bat with anyone on base.

On a warm, hazy-orange May evening, it was the fourth inning and we were ahead by a run. Peering down the bench, our coach spotted me and, with a sigh, put me into the lineup in right field, where almost no balls were hit. I trotted out, noting the smudged sun low in the sky and the red-brown bricks of our school looming in the background. I smelled the newly cut grass, white clovers mixed in with the green blades. I heard the chant of our infielders, "Hey, batter; hey, batter, batter—swing!" Maybe the inning would pass quickly.

A couple of their players got hits or walks. There was one out, two runners on base. Please, I begged the ball, don't come my way. But a left-handed batter came to the plate. I cringed, knowing that lefties are likely to pull the ball to right field. Looking strong, he took a couple of hard practice swings. As our pitcher threw the ball in, I saw it first: a flash of white coming off the bat. An instant later the sound arrived, CRRRACK, the ball streaking over the second baseman's head, bouncing in front of me. Their crowd began to cheer.

I ran to my right to retrieve the ball. Running was no problem, as I was even sort of fast. But when I reached the ball and plucked it out of my glove, a strange thing happened: I froze. My right arm was cocked above my head but the ball stayed glued to my fingers.

I saw the pale sky above me as their runners circled the bases, legs churning. The opposing fans were now screaming: The Hopi were about to take the lead!

"Throw it in," my coaches yelled from a distant corner of the universe. The infielders waved at me frantically to do something, anything. But I just stood there, the ball flash-frozen in my hand above my head. By now, both the baserunners had scored. The batter rounded third base and crossed home plate with his arms upraised. Their fans erupted.

As though waking from a trance, I brought my arm down and jogged in, tossing the ball underhand to an infielder, who snatched it with a disgusted flick of his wrist. Our shortstop threw his glove into the infield dirt. Numb with shame, I trotted back out to right field. Maybe I'd just melt into the grass out there. Somehow, the next couple of batters popped up or struck out and the inning was over. Shielding my face, I jogged back to our dugout, took off my glove, and stared straight ahead. No one looked at me; no one said a word.

During the next inning one of the assistant coaches came over to me on the bench and said, with kindness: "Well, you didn't really know what to do out there, did you?" But all I'd needed to do was throw the ball in. I knew *that*. Most of all

I remember that frozen feeling, watching the runners circle the bases as I stood there with the ball planted in my hand. I thought the humiliation would never leave.

After we lost, our team went out on the diamond to face our competitors: "Two, four, six, eight, who do we appreciate? Hopi! Hopi! Hopi!" They did the same for us, but their smiles were those of victors. I hopped on my red bike and headed back home. A few minutes later I placed it down quietly in the mud hall and walked upstairs.

"How was the game, Steve?" Mom asked, in the kitchen.

"We lost," I replied softly. If I'd told her or Sally what just happened, they'd have felt awful and tried to cheer me up, which would have made me feel even worse.

Before drifting off to sleep, I wondered what Dad might say about my spiritual and physical failure, if only he were back. The darkness surrounding me seemed eternal.

On a bright morning in June, I went downstairs for breakfast. After sitting at my spot at the table, I noticed Dad not far behind me, cooking at the stove. As usual, he was busy and slightly rushed, reaching with a slight grunt to dish out scrambled eggs onto my plate and Sally's, then hurrying to get bread out of the toaster. It was warm and close in the kitchen. He was wearing his ribbed undershirt, already perspiring. He always sweated when he exerted himself, a robust intensity lurking underneath the quiet philosopher.

But what was he doing there? I couldn't remember any kind of hello or even what day he'd arrived. There must have been a celebration, even a small one, right? He'd been gone the whole school year. I'd pretty much given up hope.

"Is the food all right?" he called out, looking over the counter at Sally and me as he juggled the pans and utensils. "Yes, it is," we said, as yellow sunlight suffused the kitchen.

Compared to Mom's more deliberate style, Dad's hurried

gestures were jarring but their familiarity was reassuring all the same. I wanted to ask him if he got enough rest out in California, but he didn't bring it up and neither did I. If we went off script, what might happen? Instead, I asked whether he'd be going to campus and he said that he would. We'd meet up in the afternoon back at home, just like before.

If I had any plan, it was to keep trying as hard as I could with my schoolwork and in sports, despite my huge failings in the latter. Trying as hard as I could might prevent Dad from leaving again and hold off the eternal punishment awaiting me. My staying busy might also allow him to get some more rest. The burden of effort sometimes seemed enormous, like standing at the bottom of a towering mountain with no trail in sight. All I could do was trudge forward blindly.

Even today I sometimes plunge. Each time the feeling is the same. Rejection of some sort is usually the trigger—a missed connection with someone close; the first sign of failure at one of my ventures. Before I know it, I make the leap that everything I've attempted is futile. Back in the familiar, breathless terrain of my childhood, I'm desperate for answers that will never come.

The poison, a toxic dose of frustration and despair, spreads to each cell in my body. It feels as though the chunk of rock under my feet has severed from the mainland. Rushing out to sea in a cold, swift current, I can see everyone I know as they recede before my eyes, but I'm powerless to stop their retreat.

Too thin, my arms can't hold up the world any longer. I'm as paralyzed as I was back in right field.

For a few hours—sometimes as long as a day or two—my expression is frozen. Anyone I encounter wonders what's wrong, my usual energy having totally evaporated. I'm embroiled in a torrent of nothingness, lacking the power to get back in contact with myself or anyone else. It's like those "gestalt" figures, such as the black vase against the white background that suddenly turns into two white faces staring at each other. One moment I perceive my world as full of life and spirit, but when the bottom drops out, all hope vanishes. I've entered my personal circle of hell.

It's as close as I come to madness. I may have dodged the bullet of developing a psychotic-level mood disorder but there's no stopping my fall.

I now understand that the abyss has always been right there next to me, created by the early silence and the role-playing, never quite vanquished by my desperate efforts to shut it out.

What brings me back? A fragment of music, a warm memory, or perhaps a signal from my wife, Kelly, that we're still connected, that things will be OK. Oxygen fills my mask and the venom gradually flushes from my system. But the next descent lurks.

You'd think I'd have figured it out by now. Still, I'm overpowered each time, sliding headlong into a place of no return, finally certain that all motion will stop. Somewhere deep inside me, fundamental pieces are still missing.

Maybe, I sometimes think, all this should have changed once Dad and I started our regular conversations about his life, following our initial talk during my first spring break. Yet our pact—our unspoken contract—was that he spoke about his episodes, diagnoses, and hospitalizations while I sat there listening, making an occasional comment. It was far from a two-way street.

Even so, I've come to think of that initial talk as my second birth: my psychological birth, as my therapist once put it. That 30-minute session in his study, and those that followed for the next quarter century, propelled my life mission to study psychology, understand mental illness, and reduce the huge burden of stigma blanketing the entire enterprise.

Even so, I carried the solo burden of figuring out the way forward. Dad's seismic upheavals had dominated our family while I worked to stay in control, trying to place my own nagging fears under wraps. I couldn't quite admit how affected I was, a common theme for kids in families overshadowed by a parent's mental disorder. Without a true back-and-forth experience, I held my breath each time, wondering what else I might learn about my tortured family.

Breaking through to a more open way of living would take decades. It was the hardest project of my life: to overcome my own personal shame and stigma.

I'm still in the middle of the process.

5

Miracles of
Modern Medicine

Why had Dad chosen that first spring break, in April of 1971, to start the process of filling me in on his past? Couldn't he and Mom have opened up earlier, averting all those years of shutdown? I got the answer during one of my talks with Dad when I was in college. With a wistful look in his eye, he said that when Sally and I were quite young, he'd been extremely worried about what to tell us about his bouts of psychosis and hospitalizations. Shouldn't we at least know *something*, he wondered to his doctors, especially as we got older?

Yet Dr. Southwick, his main psychiatrist, responded to Dad's plaintive question without hesitation. "*Never* discuss mental illness with your children," he told Dad; "any such knowledge will permanently destroy them." Unconditionally and professionally ordered, the entire topic was off limits. Mom was part of the pact as well.

Talk about stigma! During the 1950s the psychiatric profession forbade family members from knowing about the very forms of illness under its care. Would an oncologist direct a patient never to divulge his or her cancer to family members, including children—or a cardiologist, heart disease? It's unthinkable.

But mental illness was so shameful that banning all discussion was believed to be therapeutic. Our family's role-playing was off and running, professionally sanctioned—even ordered.

This stance is mind boggling and, quite literally, mind numbing. Stigma is another kind of madness, the worst kind of all, far beyond mental illness itself. Enforced silence—motivated by shame and advocated until recently by the mental health profession—produces disastrous consequences for all involved. Of course, disclosure to one's family, friends, or colleagues is always a matter of timing, judgment, and prudence, but the fight must take place against the default assumption that opening up is disastrous and must never occur

Once I turned 18, perhaps Dad reasoned that I was no longer a child, so that any disclosure at that point wouldn't go against the medical advice he'd received. Or maybe he was finding it impossible to pretend any longer. Given the one-way nature of our conversations, I never asked. But if I could reconfigure history, what might our family have said all those years ago about Dad's condition? I can't really imagine, because of the magic act we tried to pull off every day. But saying almost anything might have taken away the sharp edge of blame, anger, and terror that were my barely acknowledged companions.

My colleague at Harvard Medical School, the noted child psychiatrist William Beardslee, has developed a form of family therapy for situations in which one or both parents has a major mood disorder, like depression or bipolar illness. Beyond the individual treatment needed by such parents, usually including medication and psychological intervention, this therapy targets the huge tendency to hide what's happening inside the family. In other words, it directly addresses silence and stigma.

During the 16-week program, the therapist encourages the parents—initially without the children present—to work to find clear language to capture the family's experience. Understandably enough, most parents initially resist such disclosure: *They're too young to understand; wouldn't it just hurt them? Why would we open up about such a shameful topic?* Yet through prompting and coaching from the family therapist, the parents develop a narrative their children can comprehend. Eventually the whole family convenes and the therapist guides the parents to talk about Mom's absences, Dad's anger, family drinking patterns, time off work, or whatever the particulars may be.

The overall goal is to prevent what typically happens, which is that the children blame themselves. In fact, when families experience problems but nothing is said, kids usually take on the blame by *internalizing* the conflict. This stance may appear puzzling, but at least the child maintains some control over the situation—and this perspective is probably better than believing the world to be a cruel, random place. Yet such responsibility obviously increases the child's self-blame and guilt, enhancing later risk for depressed mood. If open discussion of the family's realities can occur, this process of internalization may be headed off at the pass.

Children in families receiving this form of family therapy function better immediately afterward than children in more traditional family interventions, with improved social and academic performance and better overall adjustment. Even more—and intriguingly—their risk for developing mood disorders is substantially reduced up to four years later. The implications are remarkable: Although part of the risk for mental illness is transmitted via genes, and strongly so for bipolar disorder, another part of intergenerational transmission is related to communication. Even in our biochemical age, breaking the silence is essential.

When I was a sophomore in college, back home for another family visit, Dad discussed his second major episode, which led to his hospitalization at Byberry, just after he'd received his doctorate from Princeton. A particular incident stood out. One Sunday, the only church service that Byberry offered was a Catholic mass. He must have been feeling pretty good about himself, Dad reflected, because he made a loud joke from the benches serving as pews about the priest, his chalice, and what he was doing to the assembled staff and patients: "He's jerking us off!" Dad shouted to the fellow worshippers.

When manic, people see humor and irony in non-traditional, often sexualized ways and typically lack any inhibitions about sharing their perspectives. But the audience was outraged rather than amused. That same night, Dad continued, his peers captured him, with one of the attendants standing guard, and took him to an occupational therapy room. Securing the door, they placed him against a pommel horse and beat him. It became a weekly ritual. In the aftermath, his wounds were covered only by his ragged uniform.

Stunned, I listened in silence. But I also wondered privately whether this was the truth or part of a delusion, with Dad's schizophrenia—the illness with which he'd been diagnosed for 35 years—doing the talking. I wanted to believe everything he told me, but maybe his recollections were tainted by his madness.

It was at Byberry, Dad continued, where he first received barbiturates to calm him down from agitated behavior, along with insulin coma therapy. This primitive treatment involves giving the patient enough insulin to induce a temporary coma or even seizures, under the now-discredited theory that people with epilepsy are immune to contracting schizophrenia. It became popular in the United States during the 1940s, largely because patients with schizophrenia seemed unresponsive to traditional talk therapy and because ECT—the direct induction of seizures through shocks to the skull—was not yet in wide use. ECT had its own set of side effects, especially regarding memory, as Dad (and Mom) would learn during his episodes and hospitalizations in the 1950s. ECT can be an extremely effective treatment for serious depression, if done in the right ways, but back then it was often used barbarically. In the end, insulin coma treatment failed to provide any real evidence of benefit, incurred risk for potentially severe side effects, and terrified patients once they awoke. All in all, Dad's accounts of Byberry were horrific.

While a grad student in Southern California during my late twenties, I attended a family reunion at the home of Randall, Dad's older brother by nearly five years. Randall was the one who'd scoured the Encyclopedia Britannica while bedridden as a pre-teen. He was a quick, jittery, and sometimes anxious man with a vibrant mind, keenly interested in his chosen field of international economics. Knowing of my interest in psychology and acutely aware of his younger brother's psychiatric history, he pulled me aside and launched into a protracted story. Throughout his talk, his face revealed the intensity of his remembrance.

In the winter of 1945 he'd been working in Washington before becoming a consultant to the Federal Reserve Board— and later, a distinguished professor. As the winter progressed, he recounted, the Allies were pressing eastward through Europe following the brutal Battle of the Bulge. On the Eastern front, the Russian army was ever closer to Berlin. Each day, news of imminent victory arrived. In March, however, he received an urgent telephone call from the longtime graduate dean at Princeton, where, a couple of years earlier, Randall had received his doctorate. To his complete surprise, the dean was in tears. Knowing that his younger brother Junior had just completed his own Ph.D. there, Randall was on full alert.

"Your brother Virgil is being held at Philadelphia State Hospital, called Byberry," the dean reported grimly. "Reports are that his behavior became quite serious shortly after he received his degree." Moved by the dean's emotion, Randall recalled

September of 1936, when he saw his younger brother splayed on the pavement below the porch roof in Pasadena. Had it happened again? Could Junior actually be in another mental hospital?

Shaken, Randall approached his superior, a female general, asking for permission to purchase a series of highly prized gasoline ration cards. His objective was to spend his single day off each week, every Sunday, driving to Philadelphia to visit his brother. Contact back at Norwalk eight years earlier had been sporadic at best. This time, Randall told me with emphasis, it would be different. Each Sunday he awakened early and made the long drive to the huge facility located in the countryside. His plan was to keep Junior company and observe his behavior. By communicating his notes of weekly progress to the staff, perhaps he might facilitate an early release.

The first visits were tense, as his brother was clearly disturbed. Randall despaired of a long bout. Yet by late April he detected a glimmer of hope, as Junior's preoccupation with sin, religion, telekinesis, and Fascism appeared to be fading. From Washington, Randall sent a telegram to the ward chief and asked that his brother receive a day pass so that the two of them could have lunch together outside the facility. Randall's observations might continue to build momentum for discharge.

Full of optimism when the request was granted, he arrived before noon. Walking through the imposing entrance corridor and finding a spot in the waiting area, he searched the faces. But when Junior came into view his eyes were strangely veiled. Randall kept his thoughts positive—after all, Junior had not left the facility in over six weeks—and they departed for the parking lot, mostly empty except for staff cars. Not so many visitors to an imposing state mental hospital.

As he continued his narrative Randall looked puzzled, recalling the growing apprehension he experienced on that Sunday afternoon more than three decades before. Something was amiss. His brother remained tense and guarded as they got into the car. Once out on the narrow highway, Junior quickly spotted a road sign and then a billboard, calling out the words in German, his voice shrill.

"What's going on?" Randall inquired with a start.

"There is danger," his brother replied back in English, his voice reflecting mortal threat. "What danger?" Randall countered, trying to conceal his exasperation. "We're on a day pass, driving to get lunch. We've just left Byberry. Remember?"

But Junior's glare was ominous. "Stop your lies. We've departed a concentration camp in Germany. How can you think of assisting my escape?"

Randall struggled to remain calm. "Junior, this is absurd. We're outside of Philadelphia, in Pennsylvania. Come to your senses," he begged.

"Silence," Junior cautioned, his voice commanding, before issuing more German pronouncements and then, back in English, warning that if he were found missing, a search party would be sent. The idyllic drive was fast becoming a nightmare but Randall pushed for reason.

"We're near Byberry, Junior. There is no concentration camp nearby."

"We must return," Junior shouted. "We'll both be shot if I'm outside the camp!"

Desperate, Randall made one more plea, yet his brother was having none of it. Throwing up his hands, Randall found a cross street, reversed direction, and drove slowly back toward the hospital. So much for this week's progress notes, he thought bitterly.

Once the car was parked in the lot, Junior bolted for the entrance. Back in the corridors, he avoided eye contact with staff. Randall hurried to follow but the visit was clearly over. In Junior's mind, any further communication with a collaborator would only increase the danger. Despondent, Randall called out that he'd return in a week but wasn't sure that his brother even heard.

Randall and I had been in a side room, away from the rest of the reunion, for some time. It was time to rejoin the group. Summing up, he said that on the road from Byberry, the drive back to Washington was endless.

I was now in fourth grade and Dad had been back for a few months. My frame of mind was better than the year before during his seemingly endless absence. On a cool fall afternoon he pulled me into the driveway as soon as he arrived from campus. "Hold out your hands in front of you," he said, pausing while I lifted my arms. "That's it, make a ball of air." He was starting some kind of science lesson, maybe a deeper lesson, too. With him it was hard to tell.

"How many molecules of air, how many atoms of oxygen or nitrogen composing these molecules, do you suppose are inside your hands? Can you make a guess?"

I knew that atoms were small. "Umm, maybe millions?"

Dad shook his head. "Many more," he replied, a look of wonder filling his eyes. "The answer is probably closer to quadrillions, even quintillions. Imagine! More than the grains of sand on a vast beach, on scores of beaches." He went on to say that most of an atom is empty space, the nucleus and electrons tiny compared to the vast area in between, like planets orbiting a sun. "As Einstein said, the nucleus is like the fly inside a cathedral," Dad continued, my everyday world long vanished. "The world around us is full of miracles," he concluded, "beyond our powers of observation."

Making small talk at family gatherings with a strained expression, Dad might answer politely about the weather or what might be served for dinner. Yet when speaking about science or different eras in history, his voice filled with quiet exultation. One version of him was slightly lost at sea, struggling to maintain a presence in the world everyone else inhabited, but the other—impassioned and persuasive—sought the essence of existence. When I thought about his two styles a chill shot up my spine, though I couldn't quite say why. I didn't yet understand that his first, awkward self was tainted by a fundamental belief that he was different from the rest of humanity, flawed to the core, a deviant mental patient.

Mom was now far busier, as she'd returned to Ohio State to earn a second Master's degree and a teaching credential, with the goal of instructing English and history to junior high school students. I had no idea of her deeper reason or of her futile visit to the attorney downtown a couple of years before. In fact, her decision seemed progressive, now that the sixties had begun: a step toward women's rights. Out on the picnic table in the backyard during warm weather, I saw Dad sitting next to her as they craned their necks over the text on transformational grammar from her linguistics course. Patiently, he explained the intricacies of Chomsky's analysis, the diagrams appearing like spider webs. Their heads and torsos tilted toward each other as they shared their deep concentration.

Back then, I zeroed in on a landing strip of planning, school, and athletics, aiming right for the middle. Like a medieval map of the flat earth, the world ceased to exist beyond the controlled borders of those three activities. Everywhere else the unspeakable lurked. Something lay in waiting just beyond my controlled life but I couldn't imagine what.

Night times were still hard. The swear words didn't come into my mind like the year before, when Dad was absent, but I worried that if I couldn't sleep I'd become desperately ill. The fear clung to me like a chronic fever. Just like Dad, I reasoned, maybe I needed rest. One evening in the late fall I fell asleep quickly but in the middle of the night sat bolt upright, with my heart pounding. Stricken, in the confused state of the wee hours, I was convinced that I'd not slept at all, overwhelmed with the belief that if I lay there any longer my heart might stop. I jumped down from the top bunk, rushed across the carpet, and banged hard on my parents' bedroom door. I should have kept quiet for Sally, sleeping in her nearby room, but I couldn't help it.

"Mom! Dad!" I shouted, sobbing. "I'm getting sick. Help!" No answer; I pounded once more. "Please, help me. I might die."

After a moment, I heard a soft padding sound. Opening the door slowly, Dad peered out. Wearing pajamas, his eyes ringed with sleep, he whispered: "What is it?"

"I've been up all night. I can't sleep. I don't think I can live."

He paused, turned, and spoke softly back in the direction of Mom. Then, gesturing for me to lead the way, he followed me back to my bedroom. After I climbed the ladder up to my bunk, he rubbed my forehead.

"Tell me again what's troubling you," he asked quietly. Half choking, I blurted it out. "I've been up all night; I can't sleep. I could die by morning." I began sobbing again.

He pondered for a moment. "There's no need to worry," he said calmly but with assurance. "Simply resting helps your body; it's perhaps 70 percent as good as sleep." Picking up force, he continued.

"You may not know it, Steve, but you live in an age of miracles. Even if you were to become sick, doctors can now treat many diseases with new medicines." When he was a boy, he continued, antibiotics and other current medicines didn't exist. Many people died, some tragically young. He reminded me that my great-uncle Corwin was on the research team discovering the mechanisms of antibiotics for treating tuberculosis. "Imagine the time before such medicines," he continued, "the rates of death were tragic."

He summed up: "Why, with the progress being made today—with these miracles of modern medicine—if you take good care of yourself, you'll probably live to be 100 years of age!"

In a flash the ceiling retracted, like the one above the astronomer in my first-grade drawing, starlight pouring in from the observatory's opening. A hundred years!

Dad began to talk about additional discoveries but I'd already started to drift. He soon said good night and walked back across the carpet. Nearly asleep, I held the number in my mind. Not eternity, perhaps, but 100 years seemed a vast span.

As an adult I began to consider my father's interest in the miracles of modern medicine he'd described. Undoubtedly, he was wondering why no such miracles had ever been available for him. Why were his mysterious episodes so unexpected, so shameful—and so far removed from any satisfactory medical care? He felt, as he told me in his later years, that no one understood his plight and that he was not even deserving of help.

When individuals belong to groups that receive strong stigma and inevitably hear society's messages about their group, there's a good chance they'll absorb the underlying content. In other words, social stigma transforms into *self-stigma*, completing a vicious cycle. Such internalized stigma—the view that one is fundamentally flawed and unworthy—carries devastating consequences. It's bad enough to be part of a group outside the mainstream. But when individuals are convinced that their own weaknesses and moral failings lie at the root of the problem, things hit bottom. Not surprisingly, in the case of mental illness, high levels of self-stigma predict a failure to seek treatment, or early drop-out if treatment has actually begun.

Not all members of stigmatized groups show self-stigma. Despite the persistence of racial prejudice and bias, many members of racial minority groups in the United States have healthy levels of self-esteem. A protective factor is solidarity and positive identification with other group members. Think of Black Power, gay pride, or the women's movement, which can thwart negative identification while promoting advocacy and positive self-regard.

But until quite recently, who would have ever wanted to identify with a group that, by definition, was crazy, insane, or psycho? The isolation and shame associated with mental illness perpetuates internalized stigma, which in turn propels even more despair. Self-help groups and movements did not exist in Dad's time, but today they're a major part of the mental health landscape. Although they cannot, by themselves, eradicate either public stigma or self-stigma, they're part of the solution.

The following spring Dad came to most of my games during baseball season. I rode my bike, getting there early for warm-ups, while he drove over for the contest. I actually got some hits and was now tall enough to be playing first base.

I could never stand losing. Back then, Sally knew whether our team had won or lost on the basis of pure sound. Some nights, she heard my bicycle come slowly down the driveway and the jaunty footfall as I walked upstairs. "We won tonight! Is there anything to eat?" Other evenings, though, I flung open the mud hall door and the crash of the bike, which I'd thrown down hard on the linoleum floor, reverberated through the house. After storming upstairs I slammed the bedroom door.

"Not too hard to tell whether your team won," she teased. But she saved her teasing until later, avoiding the crossfire of my sudden rage.

Sally and I remained close. In the years to come, I might hear her plaintive voice in the evening: "Steve, can you help me with my math problems?" With her doe eyes and pixie haircut, now growing out, Sally looked sheepish, her tone imploring. "I'm stuck."

"Hold on, Sal. Let me finish up my stuff. I'll take a look in a couple of minutes."

When Sally was struggling with math she sometimes went to Dad, but his answers were cerebral and abstract. He couldn't simplify the material. I carefully went over the problems with her, trying to make her see that if she just followed the steps she could get it on her own. But her response was always the same. "I can't see it the way you do, Steve. My brain doesn't work the same way." I began to sense that I might cast a pretty long shadow.

A Campfire Girl, she was always into activities and full of energy. Her friends crowded our house. Though always on the lookout for others, she had trouble bringing such care back to herself. Ultra-sensitive to her classmates, Mom, our cats, or anyone in pain, she often let her own needs take second place.

As a boy, I was freer to look to the outside world to escape the clogged silence inside our home. Dad's intuitive support for me when I needed it most didn't extend to Sally. Raised with five brothers in a competitive, male-dominated household—and with his mother gone forever by the time he was three—he never received real communication from the opposite sex. He had lived most of his life in all-boy enclaves, later competing in the male-dominated world of philosophy. Although he could reach out to his wife to ask the names of neighbors following mystifying episodes of madness, he never filled her in on where his mind had gone—or what the hospitals were truly like. That realm of his existence was too private and shameful. He chose to open up to me during my freshman year of college but not to his daughter or even his wife. Self-stigma held him back; perhaps, he thought, a female wouldn't really comprehend.

As close as we were, Sally and I lived in different worlds. There were other reasons why Dad felt uneasy about getting too close to females, but these remained a mystery until I was much older.

For spring break of my fifth-grade year we planned a trip to Southern California. I'd finally be able to see where Dad and his brothers grew up. While loading up the car in the driveway, Dad was moving fast, sweating and grunting as he rearranged the suitcases, periodically checking his wristwatch to make sure we'd depart for the airport on time. From inside the house where I was packing my own bag, I heard a sharp cry of pain. Rushing outside, I saw Dad bent over, grimacing, his left hand covered with a handkerchief soaked in blood. Mom and Sally hurried out too.

"I was trying fit in another suitcase," he muttered through clenched teeth. "In my haste, I slammed the tailgate door on my left hand. I don't think the finger is broken."

"Virg, perhaps we should cancel the reservation," Mom said tentatively.

"By all means no," he replied. "We must make this trip. If you get some ice, maybe I can wrap it up and we can still make the plane." Underneath the handkerchief, his finger was distended and purple. He reminded us that he'd broken this hand and wrist in high school; it wasn't set right and had been weak ever since. No one knew, of course, that it had been shattered at the end of his brief flight off the porch roof.

Dad vigorously chewed a couple of aspirin without water. Mom got into the driver's seat and we were off. Once in the plane, on the runway, Sally asked whether the take-off would be scary. Dad replied that once you're up in the air you don't even know that you're flying. "Think of the physics involved. How do all these tons of metal get airborne? Consider the wing shape, creating less pressure above to give lift." Even in pain, Dad couldn't resist teaching.

In Pasadena, we met my step-grandmother, Nettella, at the house where Dad grew up, 935 North Oakland Avenue. The house seemed small, set back a little from the street, dark wood downstairs and bedrooms upstairs, with a small, flat roof above the front door. Sally couldn't believe it: Kumquat trees grew right in the yard.

"What a festive occasion," Grandma Hinshaw repeated as the family arrived for a reunion the next day, her white hair pulled up with pins. Food covered the dining room table. I'd packed the autobiography I'd written for a school assignment, entitled "My Life, By Me." On the first page, I'd stated how fortunate I'd been throughout my life, with all the advantages I'd experienced. After dinner, I overheard Uncle Randall and Uncle Bob remark to Dad that I was philosophical, just as he was.

A day later we drove to a department store in Arcadia called Hinshaw's, located in the San Gabriel Valley below Uncle Bob's modern, low-slung house in the foothills. I marveled to see our family name in such huge letters on the store's sign. Uncle Paul, the younger of Dad's two half-brothers, worked at the other Hinshaw's, in Whittier, when he wasn't singing as a soloist for the Roger Wagner Chorale with his magnificent baritone voice. At the offices in back, I got introduced to my great-uncle Ezra, the store's founder, who drooled as he sat in his wheelchair, his white hair ragged. I tried not to stare.

"Ezra has a disease called Parkinson's," Dad remarked as we drove back. "His mind works but the brain area that controls his muscles can't function." He said that no one knew how it happened. It was a medical mystery scientists were trying to figure out.

One of the great shocks of my youth occurred when we traveled again to Southern California as I began high school. Once there, we again headed to Hinshaw's, where in the back offices I saw an older man with white hair, walking, smiling, and saying hello to many staff. A moment later, my uncles re-introduced me to my great-uncle Ezra. "You met him a few years ago, Steve, remember?"

I started to argue about their obvious mistake, as Ezra had been the incoherent man in a wheelchair. Yet I did see the resemblance. Once more, I tried not to stare.

Dad spoke up again that evening. "Ezra has been taking a medication for Parkinson's called L-DOPA. It works on the affected brain area. In many cases it can bring back the functions an individual has lost." Finally, here was proof: Miracles of modern medicine actually did exist. I longed to be part of a team one day making such discoveries. There was much to do to relieve human suffering, I was sure, and it would take both science and the right frame of mind to make it happen.

For a school performance in the spring of my last year of elementary school, we sixth graders put on a festival for which I was the host and narrator. Dad wasn't around but I was so busy I hardly noticed. On the evening of the event, families poured into the auditorium. Afterward, Mom found me in the hallway. "Why didn't you tell me you had such a big role?" she gushed. "My goodness!"

To work off energy and avoid the reception, some guys and I played a chase game, racing in and out of the school building. Inside the foyer, I gained on a guy outside, who pushed hard on the door so I couldn't tag him. As I gave it my strongest shove, it opened an inch and I grabbed the door jamb for leverage. But when he slammed it back everything stopped, a scalding ring of pain filling the air. Crimson blood gushed from my finger.

Mom was near the long tables of food nearby. "What have you done?" she cried, eyes wide, surveying the damage. I got stitches and a shot for the pain, and a splint secured my broken finger for a month. Almost as a ritual by now, I reminded myself what happened when I got too excited. Despite my ignorance of Dad's condition, I had a sixth sense about what happens when someone loses control. My fear was stronger than any urge to explore.

A few weeks later, Dad was back. As usual, nothing was said. The routine had been set for years. For summer vacation we drove to the 1964 World's Fair in New York, taking Grandmother with us. After the long subway ride to Queens we saw the huge stainless steel globe and the exhibits. Dad and Grandmother were getting along well. Heading out to dinner one night, Grandmother asked where. A sly smile on his face, Dad replied: "How about the Willard?" They all laughed hard, even Mom. But I was stunned. How could they even think of joking about that place?

Back at the hotel, there was a call for Dad from California. "This may be important, everyone; I'll take it in the bedroom," he told us. "I hope everything's OK," Sally said.

A few minutes later he emerged, his face grim. "My step-mother died today," he said somberly. "She'd been ill, but this is still unexpected. My brothers think I should attend the service in Pasadena, and so do I." Mom looked sad and hugged him.

"Wait!" I called out, frustration rising. "Our vacation is ruined!"

"Well," Mom said, "this is a terrible loss for your father, and you should tell him how sorry you are. But maybe Grandmother and I can continue on the car trip up to Boston and Cape Cod, as we'd planned." Gaining confidence, she asked what Dad thought.

"Of course," he replied, "if you're up to it."

The next morning, Dad headed off to the airport in a cab. We drove through New York's maze of yellow taxis, pressing on to Cape Cod, Boston, and Niagara Falls. A week later, we arrived back in Columbus, where Dad had recently returned from the other coast.

We asked one another about our respective trips. "The service was sad but dignified," he said. "All my brothers were there. What a chance to be together."

As he spoke I caught a wistful look on his face. Something seemed to be on the tip of his tongue. Might he tell us something more about his family and his past? Would doors be thrown open, hidden worlds revealed? Were there memories of his stepmother and childhood that I'd never heard? I held my breath.

But when I looked back the expression on his face had vanished. Secretly crushed, I gave it one more chance, glancing over a final time. But the moment was gone. Deflated, I knew that things would return to the way they always were, my eyes focused straight ahead, mysteries sealed over.

6

The CBS
Evening News

To this day I remain baffled by how our parents shielded Sally and me from the worst of Dad's frantic episodes, including the midnight drive to Cincinnati and his sudden departures from our home. Had it not been for Mom's superhuman efforts, we might have perished.

When Dad was climbing through a manic episode, his judgment was horrendous and his behavior outrageous. He needed to save Western philosophy and made late-night calls to unsuspecting colleagues around the country with his wild plans. At the same time, he might become convinced that others were stealing his ideas. When in a frenzy about such supposed theft, he disrupted OSU faculty meetings. The looks he got from strangers, or the alignment of dates on manuscripts he was reading, signaled cataclysmic events that could shape world history, leading him to rush home and type up incomprehensible notes. Despite the usual, careful organization of his lectures, he might skip from idea to idea like a flitting hummingbird.

It's hard to imagine that he had the self-control to lie low in front of his children at those times, especially when the police came to get him to a hospital or his brother Bob appeared from California to intervene. Yet somehow, Mom—and he—kept the utter insanity hidden.

But if the truth be told, they didn't do it completely on their own. I was a collaborator. I didn't *want* to know what was happening. Whatever lay out there beneath the measured tone of our household, I never pressed to find out. During his year-long absence when I was in third grade, I gave up after my single, futile inquiry to Mom. If amnesia powder had been placed on our breakfast cereal, I sprinkled it there. If a memory pump was at work, I must have been the one dragging it from the garage and placing it atop my skull. To this day I fight the long-held belief that I must suppress anything troubling, which is part of my learned pattern, too often keeping me stuck even now. It's one of the key battles of my lifetime.

"Steve, look here." Mom handed me a blue book from the huge stack on the kitchen table as I paused from my algebra homework in seventh grade. Now an instructor at OSU, she was teaching freshman composition. The head of the English department, where she'd taken coursework for her new Master's, convinced her to forgo secondary education and teach on campus. As an advanced instructor, each quarter she taught composition courses for international grad students as well as several sections of the required freshman English class.

Every few nights a batch of essays was strewn across the kitchen table, ready for grading. Back then there was only one admissions requirement for entering Ohio State, a high school diploma. First-year English was the make-or-break class. One of the topics for the current assignment—any issue to give some practice in writing—was the recent homecoming weekend. I peered down at the page. In a scrawl, the student had written his final lines: *It rained and rained and rained. It was very muddey. I was so sad.*

My eyes bulged. *This* was college English? I'd been practically raised on paragraph structure and spelling. If I didn't attain near-perfection, my world came crashing down. I felt bad for that freshman. Mom did too, as hard as she tried to teach grammar and writing style. We were a privileged family, steeped in education, while many Ohio high school graduates had little preparation at all.

Our amusement—and horror—provided a touch of relief. It was similar with Dad when we watched the Three Stooges or Laurel and Hardy down in the family room. He loved those old films, his face convulsing with laughter. He was a boy once more in a Pasadena theater, the weight of the universe lifting. For a precious moment, the house's unspoken tension evaporated.

Yet every so often the dam burst in a different way. Stuck outside in a thunderstorm after a swim at the town pool, chilled to the bone, I banged hard on the locked storm door, frustrated that no one could hear. I punched so hard that I slammed my fist right through the glass, avoiding a severed artery by sheer luck. Another time, when I thought Sally was teasing me too much, I slammed the door to my bedroom with such force that the full-length mirror—hinged to the back—crashed straight down to the floor, the sound of the five-foot-high rectangle of glass reverberating through the house. Somehow, it didn't shatter.

What was it that lay a quarter-inch beneath the surface of my skin, ready to explode at a moment's notice? My efforts to uphold the silence took their toll, leading to an occasional boiling point. Even more, I clearly carry a partial dose of Dad's genes for bipolar illness. Although they yield a pale shadow of his own unchecked emotion during the worst of his episodes, I share similar tendencies of dysregulated affect. All too often, mental disorder is a family affair.

When I was in junior high school, Dad joined the choir at the large church he and Mom attended, a progressive Protestant congregation. The choir was ultra-high quality, sometimes accompanied by musicians from the Columbus Symphony. Every Thursday, after an early dinner, he attended rehearsals. During the week he practiced vocal scales and lyrics in his study, his voice penetrating the sliding wood door. On Sunday mornings, I saw him standing in his robe behind the pulpit of the large church sanctuary, his gaze alternating between the music in his hands and the heavens above. Where did he travel at those moments? Forward in time to the eternal life awaiting him if he kept his faith? Or back to his early religious training in Pasadena?

He told me how he combined his worlds. "I remain convinced that a supreme being created all that we see. Philosophers and scientists might attempt to comprehend a portion of the mystery." My worries about eternal damnation were losing their grip but I still demanded perfection from myself. Suspended above a deep chasm, I clutched the narrow rope bridge, my arms and shoulders ready to give way from the strain.

At OSU Mom taught American novels, like *The Great Gatsby*, plus nineteenth- and twentieth-century poetry. She showed Sally and me one of her favorite poems, Edward Arlington Robinson's "Richard Cory." The first and last verses stayed in my mind:

> *Whenever Richard Cory went down town,*
> *We people on the pavement looked at him:*
> *He was a gentleman from sole to crown,*
> *Clean favored, and imperially slim . . .*
> *. . . So on we worked, and waited for the light,*
> *And went without the meat, and cursed the bread;*
> *And Richard Cory, one calm summer night,*
> *Went home and put a bullet through his head.*

Mom said that she was trying to get her students to understand the poem's main theme: the difference between the

surface—what everyone saw as a perfect life—and the mysteries beneath, the despair no one knew. This poem, in fact, was
the closest Sally and I got to any real truth about our family's
situation. Mom was committed to the sworn pact never to reveal Dad's situation to us. It was only through discussion of
literature that we received even a hint.

The famed Berkeley sociologist Erving Goffman coined the
term *courtesy stigma* to signify society's strong tendency to de-
grade anyone associated with a stigmatized individual or group.
Sardonically, Goffman contended that if society rebukes and
stigmatizes a certain class of people, it's only common courtesy
to denigrate those individuals affiliated with that group. Think
of the relative of a leper—or someone, in the eighteenth or early
nineteenth century, who aided a slave in the South. Such people
were total outcasts in the mainstream societies of their day. Cur-
rently, family members of those with serious mental disorder
bear the huge brunt of courtesy stigma: How much closer can you
get than being related to someone carrying that kind of taint?

Even more, throughout much of the twentieth century the
professions of psychology and psychiatry directly blamed family
members, especially parents, for causing mental illness in their
offspring. Autism was linked to "refrigerator" parents who provided no emotional bonding; schizophrenia resulted from
"schizophrenegenic mothers," whose hostile and dependency-
promoting styles drove their children to madness. Spouses,
siblings, and offspring were part of the ongoing curse. Any
consideration of biological vulnerability—including the clear
findings that genetic risk is formidable for conditions like schizophrenia, bipolar illness, attention deficit hyperactivity disorder
(ADHD), and autism—was discounted.

Regarding courtesy stigma, families encounter considerable
objective burden linked to their relative's mental illness, including time taken off work and expenses for obtaining help, which
all too often promote economic deprivation and major stress. Yet

families also describe, quite vividly, what's called *subjective burden*, linked to the shame and humiliation about the entire issue, including heroic efforts to keep things secret. As costly as objective burden can be, most families report that subjective burden—the discomfort and anxiety over admitting the very presence of family mental illness—takes a far larger toll.

As the wife of a man who periodically went mad back in the silent 1950s, Mom lived each day in the deep chasm of courtesy stigma. The psychiatric profession didn't listen to her or value her insights in the least, and family support was completely off the radar of available mental health interventions. Rightfully, Mom felt that if anyone came to know the truth, our family would be shunned for carrying a "moral flaw," the ultimate in unfitness. Any social standing we had would have evaporated.

Courtesy stigma isn't just for relatives. Think of the entire mental health profession, including psychologists, psychiatrists, and social workers—those individuals entrusted with the care of people with mental disorders—along with scientists who investigate causes and treatments. Bluntly, the unspoken view is that all such individuals spend their lives dealing with crazy people. In fact, people working in mental health fields encounter low status and even ridicule. Clinical psychologists are at the bottom of the totem pole of status among other psychologists; psychiatry is widely known to be an undesirable residency following medical school. Funding levels for mental health remain lower than those for physical disorders—that is, "real" illnesses. Stigma, self-stigma, and courtesy stigma fuel a crippling vicious cycle of defeat and despair, with shattering consequences for everyone touched by mental illness.

In a sudden burst, I grew several inches in seventh grade. First base was an increasingly good position in baseball, as I could reach off-target throws from the infielders. During the late spring we had a doubleheader on a bright Saturday morning.

Sally was at a friend's; Mom and Dad brought lawn chairs to watch. By noon, the heat was rising up in waves from the dusty infield. Even with my cap pulled tight around my head, I had to squint. Jogging in between innings, I stopped, blinked, and saw it in front of my eyes: A pinpoint of light, turning into a zigzag and then a lightning bolt blocking the right half of the sky. Fast-orbiting lights, bright as a thousand flashbulbs, pulsed outside my eyeballs. I reached up to cover my eyes.

"Steve, what's the matter?" Mom said, rushing over.

"I can't see anything," I said back, fighting panic. "How can I make it stop?"

Dad told my coach I was sick and went for the car. Half of my vision was now covered by a yellow-gold blizzard. During the drive home the lights mysteriously faded, but the pain soon started on the other side of my head, deep in the temple, like the tip of a sword piercing my skull. If I moved a millimeter, the throbbing got worse.

Mystified and half paralyzed, I limped to bed. When Mom came in, her whisper sounded like a cannon shot. The trickles of light at the edges of my nightshade looked as bright as stadium lights. A few hours later, I rose up despite the crushing pain, feeling as though I'd swallowed a gallon of bilge. I barely made it to the bathroom. Retching over the toilet, I threw up explosively—juice, water, bile, who knows what. Panting, I sat on the floor tiles. Getting up to a wobbly standing position, I flushed the toilet, lightly brushed my teeth, and noted that the pain in my left temple had let up slightly. I slowly hoisted myself back into bed.

Sometime during the night I woke up from a deep sleep, parched. Walking gingerly to the bathroom, hardly believing I felt almost normal again, I dared drink only a few sips of water before going back to bed. The next thing I knew it was morning, the air radiant. Famished, I went downstairs, the poison inside me somehow purged. Food hadn't tasted that good in months. It was as though I lived in two universes, one full of inexplicable pain and the other an exalted reprieve. Dad said I'd undoubtedly had my first migraine, just like he used to get as a teen. Just like Virgil Sr. and all the boys in the Hinshaw family. Just like Sally, about to begin hers. I was now linked to my relatives by pain.

After dinner, the whole family sometimes talked about Mom's and Dad's past lives. "How did you meet?" Sally and I asked them when we were pre-teens.

"On a blind date," Mom answered. We didn't yet know the term. Did you pretend to be blind? "It's when two people who don't know each other meet for the first time," Mom replied patiently. "Friends of mine at OSU knew Dad, who was teaching in philosophy, and wanted the two of us to get together. We ended up falling in love."

We peered at the wedding photo album, dated June 12, 1950. It was hard to believe that Mom looked so formal in her white gown. Dad seemed impossibly young in his tuxedo. Mom explained that they drove out West for their honeymoon, ending up in Pasadena. It was her first auto trip across the nation. Years later, in a private conversation when I was grown, she elaborated on meeting the five brothers and their families. "It was incredible," she said. "As soon as they'd sat down for a meal, they talked over one another at the dining room table, vying for position, trying to one-up the rest. Virgil Sr. and Nettella glowed over their brood. Who knew the most about world events, politics, history, science? We wives could hardly get a word in edgewise." Such a competitive male bastion—bonded by religion and academics—fueled Dad's intellectual fires.

During the family discussion, Mom added: "We made another trip in 1952 when I was first pregnant with you, Steve, seeing all the California relatives again."

"But there was a tragedy," Dad continued. The first night of their drive up the coast to San Francisco, a message awaited them at the front desk of their hotel. Dad's father had been in a car accident outside Bakersfield. Given his age of 76, he'd employed a driver. Yet a drunk driver had come across the road and hit the back of the car, killing my grandfather instantly. Sally and I were silent.

"We got in the car and drove through the mountains," Dad continued. "I had to identify the body." I pictured Dad at the coroner's office, exhausted and grim. Familiar with irony by now, I couldn't believe how my Prohibitionist grandfather had died.

That fall, following their honeymoon—and following the loss of his father—Dad escalated into mania, the first time Mom encountered an episode. He wasn't hospitalized when I was born, Mom told me later, but it was a close call.

Sally and I asked what it was like when we were little. "You were *so* adorable," Mom said. "All those bottles, boiling in the kitchen back on Wyandotte Road. But it was worth every minute." Looking at photos, I saw one of me, a baby in the arms of my strong, shirtless Dad, squinting in the bright sunlight. Little did I know that Dad was floridly psychotic a few months later, as Mom's pregnancy with Sally was coming to a close, requiring hospitalization out in California during a severe bout when she was born in February of 1954.

Mom gave birth to both Sally and me essentially alone.

"Here's something you used to do when you were small," Dad said. "You liked to pull my books off the shelves. Your favorite was my leather-bound dictionary, with embossed pages, a gift from my father. You would grab a page and just rip it out, a huge smile on your face. You loved the feel of those thin onionskin pages."

I remembered that dictionary. When closed, the edges of its pages displayed a light gold tint between the covers. But had I really been that destructive as a toddler? Dad said he'd been tempted to punish me but realized that this was my way of exploring books. Because any punishment might thwart my desire to read, he took the book from my hands and placed it out of reach.

"Never," he repeated, "did I wish to diminish your love of books."

What if Dad had been manic or seriously depressed during such times? Would he have been outraged and screamed at me? Instead, while in his normal state—the "euthymic" period in between manias and depressions, as it's formally called—he favored me with his patience and forbearance. What predicts when a person with bipolar disorder flies into mania or sinks into depression? Despite decades of research, it's extremely hard to gauge. There's a major genetic vulnerability to bipolar illness, but life stresses can trigger particular episodes. Patterns are specific to each individual. That Dad was in his right mind much of the time undoubtedly saved the family. But the stark contrast between his moods silently colored every interaction in our home.

Girls were on my mind like never before. Back in fourth grade, I stared at blond-haired Mary Ann, feeling strange sensations all through my body. Now in junior high school I felt that way just about every day. Would I ever feel connected with a girl and tell her about my feelings, if I could only figure them out myself? The mixture of longing and fear was overpowering.

On Saturday afternoons in the winter, I wandered through the shopping mall amid the freezing air, cars searching for spaces amidst piles of slush, the sky darkening by late afternoon. I was searching for a ring that I might give to some girl, if only I might get up the nerve. Inside a store, displays held jade-like rings that caught my eye. But when the saleslady asked if I wanted to see one, I looked away, my face scarlet. My longing stayed locked inside. What would I say to any girl about who I really was?

In fact, I was saying as little as possible to myself. Staying busy, striving for success in school and sports, and keeping my focus removed the temptation to actually feel. It was far better, I calculated, to keep things in.

When I was in eighth grade, one evening Dad and I sat down in the kitchen to watch *The CBS Evening News* with Walter Cronkite. Dad often had a bourbon and Coke or some other drink during pre-dinner hours. "It's the common man's religious experience," he would say of his cocktail, though I'd never seen him drink more than two. What insights did the alcohol provide him?

Watching the news was a highlight of Dad's day. He loved Cronkite. One of the lead stories that night was about a recent increase in gasoline prices throughout the country, a couple of cents per gallon. But Dad glared at the set like a cobra ready to pounce, a strange gleam in his eyes.

"It's outrageous!" he snarled at the screen.

"What is?" I asked, hoping he'd bring it down a notch.

"Those prices are criminal," he retorted. "Riots have broken out over far less than this. Class warfare won't be far behind!" He was incensed, his moral outrage palpable. "History will prove me right," he continued, holding a menacing edge in his voice.

Come on, I told him, but only in my mind: We aren't heading toward a class war over an issue as trivial as this. For a moment, I felt older and more mature than my own dad. I was actually embarrassed by him. At least no friends of mine were over, I thought with relief. What would they make of a father so silly, immature, and overemotional?

Should I say something? But the edge in his look, as he stared down the television monitor, warned me to hold my tongue. I murmured something about how the price increase wasn't all that much but he was utterly dismissive. His tone of assured superiority gripped me like an alien force.

During a rare glimpse, like this one, into my father's early signs of mania, the biggest shock was the contrast with his usual demeanor and tone. I flashed on the scene at the Willard seven years before but quickly shut it out. During the next commercial, I made an excuse to leave. At school, I started bearing down even harder. Some days the pencil lead nearly snapped underneath my fingertips.

The fog of forgetting has blotted out my recall of how far he escalated after that scene. By that time, it's conceivable that his doctors had increased the dosage of Mellaril—a newer cousin of Thorazine, an antipsychotic medication that can reduce delusional thinking and paranoia—and kept him home. Remember, I was a collaborator: I actively sought to block out key memories.

A year later, all of us were in the living room, reading magazines or various parts of the Sunday paper. The phone rang and Mom got up to answer in the kitchen. As she talked her voice rose and fell but I couldn't make out any specific words. She hurried back in and told Dad, with a concerned look, that his brother Bob was on the line from California. Dad walked quickly into his study, closed the sliding door, and didn't emerge for half an hour. Finally, he padded slowly back. With a slumped posture, he started to speak, then paused. Finally, he cleared his throat.

"Well, that was quite a long conversation with my dear brother Bob. There is troubling news. As you know, his work is as a psychiatrist, sitting all day and talking with patients. With this sedentary life, one of his legs began hurting. Gangrene soon set in." Dad concluded by saying that Bob needed to have his leg amputated to save his life.

Mom's eyes were wide, Sally's too. Amputated? A vague suspicion descended over my shoulders. An amputation caused by too much sitting? As hyper-rational as Dad sounded about his talk with Uncle Bob, I couldn't quite believe what I'd heard.

Or perhaps I could. I'd learned to accept what was placed in front of me. Questioning things, inviting in the unknown, seemed far too risky. A few weeks later Dad said that Bob had received his artificial leg, which seemed to be working fine. I was relieved. But that initial morning, I witnessed the erection of barricades, a wall against the truth. What else was hidden?

When I was still in junior high, Dad started talking with me about history. It was sure to be another lesson. "Do you ever think," he asked me, "that full understanding of a person's life history would reveal the underlying reasons for his behavior?" He continued. "Take Hitler. If we knew his full past, would we understand his actions?" Finishing his thought, he wondered specifically: "Is to know all to forgive all?"

I nodded halfheartedly, but my gut reaction was that this was way too soft. How could pure evil be forgiven if we simply knew the person's past? But the bigger question was why Dad was so possessed by good and bad. His obsession with Hitler was complete. He recounted that a million people at once, completely captivated, would stand in the plazas of German cities, listening to Hitler's speeches. Watching TV documentaries together, Dad and I stared at the Führer's animated gestures as he harangued the throngs. A nation idolized him, but repression, purges, war, and unfathomable extermination were close behind. Dad couldn't seem to get these images out of his mind. At that point in my life, I had no idea how far his obsession had taken him when he was 16.

On a frigid night before Christmas, Dad and I drove to deliver gifts to a family who'd done housework for us years earlier, an African American family on the other side of Columbus. Shivering, we rang their doorbell. After inviting us in to their overheated apartment, they seemed incredibly grateful that we'd come by. The interchange was warm and upbeat. But I felt sick with shame over how much I took for granted every day.

Driving home, as the heater blasted in the front seat while

streetlights provided an amber tint to the ice-covered streets, Dad began speaking.

"Steve, we must discuss civil rights and the history of oppression in this country. Black people have been denied fundamental rights for far too long." He brought up Gandhi, Martin Luther King, and separate drinking fountains and lunch counters in the South. As the bitter wind blew outside the frosted windows, I lamented how little I ever really thought about oppression. Yet if Dad was so attuned to these issues, why didn't he seem to do much about them? Much of his life took place while sitting in his study, everything filtered through his mind. There was no mistaking his passion, but where was his action?

And where was mine? What was it that held me down and locked me in? Pure and simple, it was fear. But at that point, I didn't know what I was afraid of.

I first heard the sound through our screen doors on a mid-August morning, three weeks before I was to start high school as a tenth grader. In a rhythmic chant, a hundred voices in the distance barked out hoarsely: "One-two-three-four; one-two-three-four." At first puzzled, I quickly placed it: The football team had started their initial morning of two-a-day practices, counting off for calisthenics. I walked outside to gaze through a crack in the wooden fence bordering our back yard. Across the street the entire squad was arrayed on the fields, wearing white practice uniforms with gold helmets.

All morning I heard the distant smack of shoulder pad on shoulder pad, sharp whistle blasts ending a play, the rhythmic hand-clap of a coach. If I gazed from a bedroom window on the second floor, peering over the fence to an angled view of the field, I saw passes whizzing through the air, running backs breaking through the line and sprinting 20 extra yards before jogging back to the huddle and flipping the ball to an assistant. I marveled at the huge linemen perfecting their blocking techniques. Getting ready for my cross-country workout that afternoon, I witnessed a repeat performance as the sun began its slow westward slant. With each sharp whistle from the field the realization hit me like a blast furnace. I'd blown it, my opportunity lost. The despair clung to me like a shroud—*I should have joined the football team.*

It's always been this way for me. After weeks or months of planning, something might topple the structure I've assembled. With a single setback, the balloon punctures. There's no middle ground between moving forward and hopelessness.

I'd gone out for tackle football the year before, in my last year of junior high. In Ohio football was king. I'd become a decent baseball and basketball player and was pretty fast in middle distances for track, but I'd always wondered whether I could handle the contact of football.

I'd brought up the debate with Mom and Dad. Not realizing I was upstairs, they quietly argued from behind their closed bedroom door. "Football is too dangerous," Mom said, with emphasis. "There can be major injuries." Dad countered with his own quiet determination, trying to keep his voice low but not quite succeeding. "When I played there were just leather helmets. The equipment is superior now. I say we let him."

Dad prevailed, and it was time to prove myself. At the first practice I put the shoulder pads, rib protector, and hip pads on my 135-pound frame, wondering how I'd be able to run in all that equipment. At twice-daily workouts in the sweltering humidity, I hit the blocking sled, firing out from my three-point stance, shoulder square into the huge pad, digging my legs in at the same instant, as grass and dirt flew out from my cleats. I tried to make tackles during defensive drills when a fast, strong kid tried to run right through me, the dust and heat overpowering. But after a rare good play, pride poured over me like a soothing bath. I made the team and played in every game. I'd passed the test.

Before I knew it the issue loomed again the following spring. The reminders poured in each day as I saw the mammoth new high school structure and endless playing fields a block behind our house. Our high school team was ranked among the elite in the state. I'd be lucky to make junior varsity as a tenth grader, and earning a spot on the varsity was no guarantee after that.

I started to think about joining the cross-country team, instead. I reasoned that cross-country might be a safer option, physically and mentally. Maybe I could get a varsity letter, even as a sophomore, during my initial year of high school.

By mid-summer I headed to the river with the cross-country team, lacing up my shoes after some stretches. The running course started under leafy trees and picnic benches on a small rise above the riverbank, the air hazy with humidity. Underneath us, the picnic grounds were bright green from spring and summer rains. The trail sloped down to the boat ramps, meeting a gravel road on the riverbank, the acrid smell of gasoline and tar filling the air. As it flattened the first auto bridge came into view. We passed underneath to the high-pitched hum and rhythmic bumps of cars on the grooved pavement far above. Suddenly, the full expanse of the river lay straight ahead, blue-gray and rippled, deep-green trees lining the opposite shore. The second bridge was a mile and a half beyond.

With my arms pumping, some of my breaths turned into gasps as I struggled to keep pace. Lazy clouds held in the oppressive heat, the grate of cicadas from nearby trees penetrating the dank air. At last we charged up a slope to some shade, turning around without pause to head back. Some of those guys could fly, showing all the lung power in the world. My runs were punctuated with the worry that I would deplete all the oxygen in my body. But while I was moving, doubts about my decision vanished.

All was lost, though, once I'd witnessed that initial football practice. In the back yard the next morning, as though drawn by magnetic force, I burst out crying as I watched the try-outs again. Back inside, I searched for something to read, anything to distract me, but my agitation was overpowering. Mom wondered why I was so upset but I choked on the words when I tried to explain. When Dad came home from campus for lunch, I leapt into his study and blurted it out. "Football practice began this week," I said hoarsely. "Everyone knows the plays but me. I can't wait until next year; I'd be so far behind I wouldn't last a day. Don't you see," I stammered, "I've wrecked my only chance. How could I have done this?"

Dad directed his gaze into the distance. I buried my face in my hands, fighting the urge to gouge out my eyes.

"I know it seems late," he finally responded. "But if you're sure you want to try, I could do this: I could call the head coach later to day before the afternoon. He's an honorable man, though tough, as you know. I can see what he says."

I felt myself sink deeper, repeating that it was too late. Considering his words carefully, Dad looked out the window and repeated his plan, stating that I'd probably have to meet with the coach immediately to have any chance. I relented but couldn't escape the self-hatred that had overtaken me.

Later that afternoon, Dad told me that he had spoken with Coach Mueller, who, if I were willing, would meet me that very evening. What did I have to lose? In the twilight Dad drove me to a street close to our old house on Wyandotte Road. He would pick me up in a half an hour, down the block. I managed to ring the doorbell and was ushered to a side porch. A moment later, the coach strode in, exuding his usual intensity. He looked me in the eye and briskly shook my hand. "Steve, tell me your thinking," he inquired.

I gave it my best shot, telling him of my errant decision while certain his eyes could bore holes through my skin. Finally, he sat straight up. "I believe that I understand your thinking, Steve.

You've missed some crucial sessions but there's still time. If you bring a physical exam form in tomorrow and let the cross-country coach know, I'll get equipment fitted for you and order you a playbook. You'll have to learn our systems thoroughly."

Had he just said yes? Stay of execution granted, I headed out in the dusk to find the car. Dad looked pleased as I nearly melted into the seat with relief. Saturday morning I was on the practice fields, part of the large, uniformed group. It took no time at all to get used to the intensity of two-a-day drills in the overpowering heat. I fought my way up and made the junior varsity squad. Our Saturday morning games were a pale afterthought to the excitement of the varsity contests under the lights the evening before, but I caught a few touchdown passes, rare for our Midwestern-style running team, and relished being part of a team. Without Dad, what would I have done?

The following summer, desert sands stretched endlessly, red-orange, tan, yellow, and pale brown. The peaks of Arizona's Monument Valley were primordial, sheer rock emerging from the desert floor. We pulled over and Dad handed me the steering wheel for the first time, at age 15. Soaring over the highway, the car rocketed forward with the slightest touch of my foot on the gas. I sensed that my life might soar, too, if I could ever transcend my yoke of order and duty.

Finally reaching Southern California after our cross-country drive, we spent a day at Uncle Paul's ravine-perched house near LA. With our cousins, Sally and I raced soap-box cars down the steep driveway. Before long a huge white Cadillac pulled up out front. Out climbed Uncle Bob, tall and confident. Pausing, he measured the slope with his eyes, slowly placed his artificial leg in front of his good leg, and walked magisterially down the path. He waved over at us, a jaunty smile on his lips, wearing his self-assurance like a crown. The amputation, it was clear, had not kept him down.

I felt like a stranger in the sun-washed, hip LA Basin. Yet Bob reached out, letting me know that it would take some time for me to get the hang of the pool cue in his den, while he hosted us there in his large, modern home overlooking the San Gabriel Valley. He helped me overcome the awkwardness I was feeling.

His four kids—additional cousins, roughly our age—seemed to look at Sally and me askance, which I attributed to our semi-hick status from the Midwest. What I didn't know was that almost precisely seven years before, when Dad was gone for my entire third-grade year, Bob had flown to Columbus to take him to psychiatric facilities in Southern California and, during the final months, invited him to stay in a spare bedroom of their family home while finishing his recovery. What did their family know about Dad, and our family, that I didn't?

A week later we were on the road back to Columbus. Mom wanted to see Lake Tahoe and its deep blue waters but Sally and I protested. My new girlfriend was waiting; I'd finally found someone I wanted to get close with. Even more, I needed to prepare to make the varsity football team as a junior. Sally, too, had commitments, including choir and cheerleading tryouts. After we begged, Mom and Dad relented and we stayed straight on the interstate to Salt Lake City and beyond.

Looking back, I feel ever guiltier over my selfishness. Mom desperately wanted to see that lake, to plumb its cobalt-blue depths. Something about deep waters drew her in, reminding her of long-ago train trips from Ohio to Cape Cod as a teenager, when she served as a camp counselor and taught sailing. She longed to escape land-locked Ohio and her duties there. Sally and I didn't know of the pain and terror she'd endured, always in silence, as she continued to wonder whether Dad and the family would survive the next assault of his mind.

If I wanted to meet my goals I couldn't let up. I've always had multiple plans, taking on many projects at a time. My plate is always full, the food spread thin to cover the china. A half-full plate might allow reflection back from the polished plate, a straight-on look that might be too revealing. With the plate filled, I can bypass any self-searching.

Early in my senior year, Sally and I pondered the future. She asked if I'd really leave home for college. I replied that if I got accepted, Harvard would be great.

"But won't you be scared, being so far from home?"

"Maybe at first," I countered, "but I'd like the challenge."

"I don't know if I could move that far away," Sally continued. "It might be too scary. And for Mom, wouldn't it be better if I were close by?" In her own way, Sally sensed the vortex lying beneath the family silence, completely identifying with Mom.

I didn't know which was stronger: excitement over the prospect of departing Columbus or guilt that I'd be letting my sister down, maybe everyone else too. Sally might need to sacrifice huge parts of herself to stay close. *Be brave—take the risk—move away!* I wanted to shout in her ears. But how could I bring her to a place of confidence when I was as confused as I was about my own life?

Each season left its mark. Fall afternoons in the receding light, relentless football practices, victories each week under the stadium lights. In the winter, patchy snow lay on the ground. Basketball season was harder, my skills having peaked back in junior high. The blossoms finally burst forth in April, as track workouts burned my lungs. If I got to bed after 10:30 p.m., I fought panic that I wouldn't get enough sleep.

On weekends, I saw my girlfriend, Barb—striking eyes, long brown hair—at her house, a long block down the tree-lined street joining our street at an angle just beyond the front yard. She was kind and funny, sometimes sarcastic, which I found unsettling but also a relief from the unrelenting seriousness that weighed me down most of the time. I usually felt uncomfortable around people who seemed casual: Didn't they know how important it was to stay focused? But sarcasm had a bite, revealing a difference between appearance and the deeper reality underneath. Barb and I went to movies, hung out with friends, and gradually got more physical. Were we falling in love? I wasn't sure, but the odds were good that we'd get married one day just like most of our classmates. I clung to the stability of knowing she was there.

Dad remained at home during my high school years, teaching graduate seminars and the huge intro to philosophy class, reading long into the evening, and pondering the futility of the Vietnam War as the sixties wound down, especially once Cronkite changed his own mind about the U.S. effort. Too many days he seemed blank and withdrawn, in a kind of retreat from the world. My activities locked up my time. I watched from a distance.

For many people with serious bipolar disorder, episodes increase in regularity and intensity across their adult years. In what's called the "kindling" theory, it takes a large amount of stress during late adolescence—for example, experiencing maltreatment, confronting a major loss, or perhaps overusing drugs that prime the central nervous system for disaster—to spark the initial episode. But after that, the episodes emerge more spontaneously and regularly in the way that a raging fire escalates after it's kindled. This was clearly Dad's pattern. After his initial, age-16 bout, it took eight years for his hospitalization at Byberry. But between his mid-twenties and forties, things got far worse, with severe episodes every year or two. Inexplicably, though, he reached some equilibrium by middle age.

Still, he sometimes exuded an intensity I couldn't place. Once the animated psychedelic film *Yellow Submarine* had been released, the Beatles' title song played relentlessly on the radio. On a whim, I asked Dad to listen to the lyrics on our phonograph ("We all live in a yellow submarine . . ."). Intrigued, he cleared out the family room and positioned himself precisely between the two speakers for maximum stereophonic effect, playing the song over and over. Afterward, his eyes were ablaze. "The meaning is dark," he said, a strange energy driving his words. "The yellow color of the submarine and the theme of the song betray a fundamental cowardice in the human condition." He gazed over to the wall. "This song conveys the weakness of our species." A profound insight? Or were Dad's meanings filled with a logic I couldn't see? As always, something lurked just out of reach.

During the fall of my senior year, I mailed in seven college applications. But my main concern was football. Somehow, I'd made the first team, and the new stadium was set to open right near our house. The whole team knew—how could we forget?—that the Golden Bears had won 20 consecutive games, state champions two straight years. Could we seniors do it? Between my courses and the never-ending practices, I hardly saw Dad.

The first Friday in September we took a three-hour bus ride for our opening game against a northern Ohio powerhouse. I pulled my "away" jersey, bright gold with a black 87, over my shoulder pads. But during warm-ups in the setting sun, I felt mucus, tons of mucus, in my stomach, and kept swallowing hard to keep it down. Something didn't feel right in my head. I left the lines of calisthenics and threw up by the side of the field. It was just a gob of yellowish bile, as though I'd cleared poison, like a migraine but without any aura or headache.

Under the lights, in a fury of hard runs and defense, we squeaked by, 7-6. The block I made from my left-end position—elbows out, hands into my chest, slamming that big defensive tackle into the ground—sprang our fullback's 40-yard run, our only touchdown. The next week we inaugurated our new stadium with a resounding win. Each subsequent week yielded a victory, some close, most lopsided. In the middle of the season, we were winning handily at home. I was in on offense and we were close to scoring. Our quarterback called a pass play, faking a handoff right. The defensive back took the bait; I cut left, wide open. But it was a bullet when a touch pass would have done; I lost it in the lights and it bounced off my chest. It didn't matter: We kicked a field goal and won, 59-0.

But my world caved in. I quickly showered and skulked home, the shame burning my skin like acid. Dad had been at the stadium, though I wasn't sure how he'd arrived. With a desperate look in his eyes, he walked toward me as I lay in my bed. "I'm proud of the way you and the team played," he said. But all I could do was watch his valiant attempts from afar as I sank farther.

The season's final week, at 9-0, we were one win from a third straight state championship. Light-headed from the flu and a fever, I forced myself into school and played every quarter, as I had all season. After another shutout victory, the celebration began in the locker room, coaches beaming, players whooping. Dehydrated and dizzy, I showered and walked home, falling asleep in a heap for 11 hours. I missed the party at the home of one of the star players, where beer and who knows what else was brought in. I'd never had a drink except for little-kid sips when I was tiny. I needed to stay pure, in control. I hated missing out but felt strangely relieved. What would I have done there?

By late April, as the lawns and trees turned a radiant green, letters appeared underneath the mail slot at home on our hallway's slate floor. Each time I ripped open the envelope and saw "accepted" underneath the university insignia, a surge of pride washed over me. I'd known all along that if I got into Harvard— the oldest and highest-ranked school—I'd attend. Just after I accepted, the Kent State shootings took place in May of 1970, 100 miles north of Columbus. But I felt untouchable, a glass layer between me and such a fate. With a draft number of 38,

I was next in line to Southeast Asia, but a college deferment had me heading to New England instead.

Which would be stronger: the surge to depart or the guilt I felt at leaving? I counted the days.

New England

I've often wondered what Dad felt as he began his college career at Stanford in the autumn of 1939. He must have made the move from Pasadena shortly after September 1, the day Hitler's troops overwhelmed Poland to initiate World War II. If he thought about it at all, he must have realized that his delusional mission to save the world from the Fascists three years earlier was a complete disaster. The Fascists continued to escalate their preparations to take over Europe; Dad had barely survived his hospitalization. Undoubtedly, he tried to block out that period of his life altogether, moving forward to take up the study of psychology and philosophy up in Northern California, keeping his half-year siege locked up somewhere as a distant memory.

As for my own start of college, ominous clouds occluded the Boston skyline as we exited the turnpike in our station wagon. In Cambridge, heading up Massachusetts Ave. toward Harvard Square in the steady rain, vans and trucks appeared through the windshield wipers, young people lifting boxes from tailgates and trunks, covering their heads with jackets or newspapers. Was I really one of them?

The next day was sparkling, early fall in its glory. "Will you be scared, Steve, living in a dorm like this?" Sally asked as we walked up the three flights to the suite in Massachusetts Hall. The sign on the side revealed its date of origin, 1720.

"I think it will be kind of cool," I replied, a bit too jauntily.

For our final dinner we found a restaurant in another part of town. It was festive, the air outside soft. But with the farewell looming, the scraped feeling inside my eyes and throat had thwarted my appetite. We finally headed back to campus. Glimmering in the moonlight, the silent Charles River was on our left. Just a few more minutes and my new life would begin.

The problem was that my legs seemed to be cast in cement. Who would I be once I was outside this sticky sense of duty and familiarity, this tangle of awkward silence? Which was stronger—the force pulling me toward a different life or the one holding me in the car, the gravity of a heavier planet?

Harvard Square had little traffic at 10:00 p.m. Dad made a sharp right turn into the Yard, the gate open all day for cars to drop off eager freshmen before orientation. We were the last ones there in the darkness. As he pulled to a stop, the car held a ghostly silence.

"Thanks for everything, everybody," I managed to say in a hoarse whisper; "I can't believe you drove me all the way out here just to see me off."

"We've had a good time here in Cambridge, haven't we?" said Mom.

"I'll miss you all," I replied.

"I'll miss *you*, Stevie," Sally said, as my heart tugged until it almost snapped. Images flooded my mind: the tiny girl who bit my arm, my constant companion on family trips, our made-up language when we were young, her ballet recitals, our cats. The calls to the house years ago when friends of the family would ask: "Is this Steve or Sally? I can't tell your voices apart!"

Dad looked proud but tired. It would be a long drive back

to Ohio the following day. "All best, son," he said, reaching back to shake my hand.

Just as I prepared to say farewell to Mom I saw her shoulders shaking up in the front seat. A moment later her whole body heaved. Chin down, arms limp at her sides, she had burst into silent convulsions. The tears streamed down her cheeks, her face wracked in despair. Everyone froze. Who had ever seen such emotion from her? Finally she sat up.

"I was overcome," she murmured, embarrassed. I awkwardly reached across the seat. "Stevie, we're so proud," she said, trying to smile.

"Good-bye, Mom; I love you." I gave her the best hug I could at my cramped angle. Too late, it dawned on me what kind of support I'd been for her the past 17 years.

"Good-bye, Steve, we all love you."

I somehow left the car, turning to wave as three hands appeared through the car's windows. The taillights slipped away as Dad entered the flow of traffic. *There's no way I could have stayed back*, I told myself. With rubbery legs I lurched forward and pulled on the heavy door of my building. Had it been recast in lead? But once on the stairs, with each successive step I felt lighter, almost buoyant. Reaching the fourth-floor landing, I placed the key in the lock.

I was thinking of pre-med, maybe psychiatry or neurology. Those books of Freud I'd started to read in high school, discussing all that goes on in the mind of which we're not even aware, had pulled me in. I played freshman football, trekking across the bridge each afternoon to the mentholated smell of balms and athletic tape. I went to weekend parties in Harvard Yard, hardly believing how much some of the guys could drink, the sweet scent of marijuana pouring out from dorm windows. I'd overcome enough inhibitions to try both.

A notice about freshman seminars had caught my eye, especially the one on social deviance, a year-long course on behavior outside social norms, blending psychology, sociology, and anthropology. To get accepted, applicants had to be interviewed. At the small office in Harvard Yard, Dr. Perschonok was intense but kind, with a sharp nose and wrinkled brow. Once an idea took hold, his pensiveness gave way to delighted enthusiasm. Through his thick Eastern European accent he began with a few general questions and then politely inquired as to what form of deviance most interested me.

I opened my mouth but no sound emerged. Flash-frozen, I was back in right field, immobile. In what seemed forever but lasted perhaps 15 seconds, the shame spread over me like a rash. If I'd had any experience at all in discussing the realities of mental illness, I would have spoken of my father's experiences and perhaps the puzzle of serious mental disorder more generally. But I drew a blank. Clearly, I wouldn't get into this seminar or any other. Breaking the agonizing silence, Perschonok gently suggested a topic or two to help me recover. Defeated, I skulked from the room. I felt like walking further west, perhaps to Ohio.

No surprise as I rushed to the notice board the next day: My name was not among the admitted group of ten students. Yet a small waiting list appeared at the bottom, with my name somehow included. Each time I went back to check, I'd moved up the list. Some of the original acceptees must have found other courses. By the end of the week I'd miraculously moved to the top group.

Excitement filled the air, with radical ideas in psychology and politics dominating discussions, the stimulation constant. But who was I? A Midwestern carryover into football and pre-medicine, or an increasingly long-haired student with a few ideas? There was a faint vibration ringing through my mind, the faint pedal point of a distant melody. I couldn't put my finger on it.

Before returning to Ohio for Christmas, I wondered what

gift to get for Dad. Intrigued by the seminar on social deviance, I thought of one of its readings, R. D. Laing's *The Divided Self: An Existential Study in Sanity and Madness,* his philosophical and psychological treatise on the nature of schizophrenia. I was enthralled by its premise, that mental illness was the result of social forces and communication styles. Sure that Dad would be intrigued by its ideas, I purchased the paperback.

On Christmas morning I wondered whether I still belonged in the rituals I'd experienced since boyhood. When Dad opened the wrapping paper of my gift in the family room, over by the tree, he looked as though he'd been slapped, averting his eyes and mumbling a hollow thanks. Something had struck a nerve, but what?

A few hours later, the household was getting ready for our holiday dinner. As I walked through the living room I heard Mom and Dad nearby in the study, their voices furtive. "Why do you think he got me this book?" Dad asked, shock in his voice.

"Well, he knows something," Mom replied.

"Yes, he must," Dad murmured. But if I did know something, I wasn't sure what. How much did I know before I knew?

Back in Cambridge in early January, the winter yielded a few magical days after snowstorms, the river frozen over, trees covered in white. Inevitably, though, everything turned to gray slush within a day. Two months later I walked through campus, spring threatening to emerge from the bleak skies. Pools of shallow, dirty water covered the ground, replacing the ice from a few weeks earlier. Bustling, I felt almost clammy in my sweater but the wind was frigid whenever I stopped at a corner. I looked toward the river just in time to see a sharp ray of sunlight pierce the cloud cover. Reflexively, I raised my hand to shield my eyes.

Arriving on my landing, I couldn't see the key I'd retrieved from my pocket. Shutting my eyes, I tried to will away the inevitable, but the lightning bolt of light was now in place. After additional full-on migraines in high school—always in the spring, always following the experience of glare—I knew all too well what was coming. Twenty minutes later, like clockwork, the pain began to pierce the side of my skull. The worst part was always the inevitability, the certainty that nothing could prevent what was to come. After a few immobile hours, I felt again that I'd swallowed the contents of a swamp. Rushing to the bathroom, I heaved and retched over the toilet. Finally, I descended into a numbed sleep.

In the morning I lifted myself up out of my bed. I was back to normal but not just normal. Colors were vivid, tastes sensuous, the air fresh with possibility. My whole being had a brisk vitality. Why couldn't my body and spirit be this vibrant every day? I was astounded at the utter difference between debilitating pain and the transcendence afterward. The extremes were baffling.

Back from spring break, and after my dad opened up about his mental illness, things seemed strangely familiar but at the same time everything was different. For a few days I wasn't sure of my whereabouts. Was I actually in Cambridge? Or still lingering in Columbus? Or perhaps inside Norwalk Hospital, listening to screams on the ward all night long?

Rushing to class the following week, I stopped in my tracks. At the upper edge of my vision I made out faint yellow-green buds emerging from the branches of the ancient trees filling the lawn, the late-arriving New England spring finally here. Peering into a pale canopy of hope, I clutched my secret covenant. Years in the making, the fortress of silence surrounding my entire life had been shattered by Dad's words. In its wake lay an underground river, strong and swift, the current propelling me on a wave of family, history, and perhaps even hope. I now had a mission: to understand Dad's experiences and the mysteries of serious mental illness. His secrets had been locked inside him for years, as though preserved in amber. Who else had ever heard him talk like that?

But as the weeks went by dread competed with hope, as I sensed the family legacy of mental illness closing in around me. All my planning and control, each of my small accomplishments: Maybe they were just a house of cards, ready to collapse in the next breeze. By the early 1970s my twin and adoption studies had debunked the myth that parenting practices cause schizophrenia. Instead, genes were the main culprit. Deadly strands of DNA must lurk inside each of my cells, counting down to the end of my sanity. But when would it happen?

In high school I'd read *Lost Horizon,* a novel Mom taught and loved. After his plane had crashed in the Himalayas in the 1930s, the main character, Conway, discovered the hidden enclave of Shangri-La, protected from the world and its growing conflicts. Orienting to the mystery of the lamasery, he began to feel at peace. The High Lama soon told him of the miraculous nature of the setting: People who stayed there attained the ability to live for hundreds of years, approaching immortality. Unlike anyone else who'd ever heard the news, Conway was intrigued, embracing this miraculous opportunity. Finally nearing death, the High Lama appointed Conway as his successor. Filled with a blend of honor and apprehension, Conway hesitated, unsure whether he could manage the responsibility.

I identified, realizing that I'd been appointed to solve Dad's lifelong problems. Our talk had released a small dose of poison from the plastic skins of those long-ago balloons. Once out in the open, might it convert into an inoculation small enough to build protection and immunity? Or was it lethal?

The hardest times came at night. From my narrow dorm bed I wondered how Dad survived those months in mental hospitals. Mental hospitals! The worst places in the world, I was certain, stark settings for those who'd reached the point of no return. Some of his fellow inmates, with their misshapen heads, were society's hidden freak show, banished to live forever out of everyone's sight. When might I join the damned, next in line to lose control over my mind?

Each second I lay awake compounded the last. Vultures circling their prey, thoughts of Dad's madness crowded my mind. Through the fractured logic of the wee hours I became convinced that if I remained sleepless until dawn, I'd reach a divide. The morning light would be a signal that I'd crossed into irrationality, the chaotic flow of my thoughts unchecked. The only weapon was to hold on, white-knuckled, and try to sleep. Fighting panic, I somehow drifted off. In the morning I was shocked when my mind was still intact. But how many more nights could this go on?

Daytime brought possibilities. My energetic roommate Bill worked as a Big Brother at Columbia Point, one of Boston's worst housing projects. While there, he'd learned that a mom with two young boys but no dad in sight needed help. I took the T to meet them. There was something about boys needing guidance that drew me in. Jerry was eight but his eyes already had a probing, adult look. He pushed limits but showed real wisdom, craftiness interleaved with insight. Bobby, six, floated above the ground when he walked, his thin limbs lighter than air, his long blond hair a tangle. Over the next three years, on Sunday afternoons I showed them where to put their fingers on the laces of a football. We might take the train downtown to the Museum of Science or aquarium, ending up at their mom's crowded housing-project apartment, once they'd moved to South Boston. I saved up and got Bruins or Celtics tickets high in the nosebleed seats, the cigarette haze half-masking the players below. In the spring I found bleacher seats at Fenway for the Sox. I owed something to the world for my gift of sanity, as long as I had it.

That spring Barb told me that she'd met someone else back

at college. For a day or two I was crushed but soon felt relief. Not that I could ever end a relationship myself. The thought of initiating a break-up felt like ejecting myself into the blackness of space, drifting without oxygen through eternity. Yet Barb had done the work for me.

I half-dreaded the parties and mixers I attended, never quite knowing what to say for small talk. But at one, across the river at Boston University, I met a tall freshman who seemed intriguing and felt an instant spark. We walked the wet streets, talking until late. Heading to her dorm to pick her up the following weekend, I felt almost sophisticated in my corduroy sport jacket and faded jeans. Later that evening she filled me in, furtively, about her former boyfriend, an older guy from the Navy. "You can't believe the feeling when a guy you're into slowly undresses you. Every nerve in your body is exposed."

Excited beyond belief, I wondered if I could rise to the challenge. But our quick love affair overwhelmed me. What might it mean to be that close to someone? Could I tell her what I'd learned from Dad? In the end I couldn't bring myself to call her back. Loneliness was better than exposure.

Vietnam, how the brain processes information, the origins of creativity: Each evening dorm conversations grew intense. The grass I smoked took the edge off my worries, as excitement filled the spring air. The social deviance seminar was reaching its conclusion, probing why societies form ingroups and outgroups and whether psychoactive medications are overmarketed agents of social control or needed treatments for biologically based forms of mental illness. Scrambling, I tried to ride the crest.

In late May, the athletic department announced a meeting for freshmen intending to try out for varsity football in the fall. The whole thing felt like past history but the memory of my near-miss in tenth grade was close at hand. I entered the classroom to see a crowd of eager guys awaiting instructions from the assistant coach. Yet there was something about the way my stomach was feeling, plus all that congestion inside my head, that blocked my focus. I listened for a few minutes but coursework beckoned. Realizing that this chapter of my life was over, I tiptoed to the door. Just as I put my hand on the knob, the coach spotted me, as his derisive words rang out: "Look, men, there's one who's not sure he can stand the heat." The sound of laughter filled my ears.

Back in my room I tried to study but couldn't concentrate. Exhausted but strangely wired, I went to bed on the early side but my head was too clogged to sleep. The pattern had started back in ninth-grade football when I was a defensive back, trying to tackle a running back downfield who had already made a big gain. Knocked down by a blocker and lying on the ground, I tried to grab the runner's leg but another kid's shoe got under my faceguard, his cleat almost crushing my nose. It wasn't broken but I'd had trouble breathing ever since.

My runaway thoughts took over: Just as the first pale morning light would appear behind my curtain following a sleepless night, I'd drop over a sharp edge, my mind spiraling out of control. The pattern was clear. Dad ended up at Norwalk after three nights without sleep, beginning his lifetime of mental illness. How could I just wait out a descent into madness? I had to do something.

I remembered my migraines. When the pain reached its peak, the only relief was to give in to the crippling nausea and crouch by the toilet until my insides nearly burst. Maybe now, if I could rid that crud from my stomach and clear the congestion from my head, sleep might come. What other option did I have?

As though in a trance, I hauled myself out of bed, hoping my roommates were asleep. I chugged some water from the faucet to make sure there was something inside to throw up, having digested dinner long ago. I looked down at the smooth white porcelain of the toilet and the dingy tiles of the bathroom floor. I bent down, my knee aching on the hard surface, leaned over the toilet, and stuck my fingers down my throat, way down, the way I sometimes had to during the final stages of a migraine when I couldn't get it all out despite the raging nausea. What choice did I have? I was convinced that my sanity depended on it.

The first gags and retches ended up in a futile cough. But I kept at it and the eruptions began to convulse my body, yellowish mucus and bile spewing forth into the glistening water. Gasping, I rinsed out my mouth, washed my hands, and stumbled back to bed, where, exhausted, I fell asleep. My eyes were tinged red in the morning. My body may have suffered but the purges had saved me. Hadn't they?

Without any release for the images Dad had provided me, I couldn't digest what he'd said about his lifelong schizophrenia. Through the crudest possible method, I expelled what I'd taken in.

In June I saw my year-end report of all As. Yet for my most important course—understanding myself—I had barely passed. Each day the contrast stared me in the face.

Ron had always been offbeat, even back in junior high when I first met him. He was strong, loud, and intense. His dad was an engineer and his mom a teacher. He called them by their first names, which everyone thought was weird. Ron didn't smell good, especially after exerting himself in woodshop class. Maybe no one had shown him how to use deodorant. But he was super-smart and super-athletic. By high school, the coaches had molded him into an incredible defensive end. Ready to run down any ball-carrier, his neck collar and arm pads giving him the look of a gladiator, he played a key role on our undefeated teams. Ron got into Harvard on sheer academic and athletic talent.

During freshman year I often headed over to his dorm in the

evening. The living room was always filled with roommates, weed, and great music. We talked intently of psychology and world issues. But every once in a while Ron did something strange, like the time his mom sent him a huge box of cookies in the mail from Columbus, a week's supply at least. We opened it with a couple of other guys, each of us eating one or two. The next night, I headed back for more. With a strange look on his face, he told me they were gone. "Come on, Ron, what do you mean?" I asked. Where was he stashing them?

"I finished them after everyone left last night," he continued.

"That's impossible! There were at least a hundred cookies in there."

"Oh ye of little faith," he responded sardonically, his grin twisted. "I ate them all!"

A couple of his roommates soon came in and confirmed the story. That's Ron, their shrugs said; they couldn't believe it either. If Ron had an impulse, there was no stopping it.

The summer after freshman year I was back in Columbus and so was Ron. He called one night and we decided to drive over to the OSU campus and see what was happening. His hair was really wild by then, not just long like everyone else's but all over the place. Picking him up, I could see that his eyes were huge, his gaze intense and erratic. As we crossed the Olentangy River on a warm June evening, throngs of people crowded the sidewalks. "Do you see them, Hinshaw?" Ron snarled, staring out the car window.

"See who?" I answered, trying to keep my eyes on the road.

"All of them, right there!" Ron called out. "They look like people, but they're not. They're robots!" At first amused, I was now hearing alarm bells. "You can't tell by looking at them," he was now shouting, "but they're mechanical, pretending to be human. They're machines, gears and wires inside. People are mechanical grasshoppers!"

Had Ron smoked a joint? Or was he voicing a metaphorical

belief about human alienation? I somehow knew that neither was the case. He calmed down a bit as we went into a bar. Back then in Ohio, at 18 you could get low-alcohol beer.

Worried about him as we headed home, I asked if he wanted to spend the night on our couch in the family room. Like a lost puppy, he accepted eagerly. I set him up before going upstairs, where for once I fell asleep within minutes.

The next day, after Ron had walked home alone at some point early in the morning, Mom had a haggard look. "Did you see the family room this morning, Steve? Wrappers everywhere, records out of sleeves, everything a total mess. Loud music until four a.m. Neither your father nor I could sleep a wink."

I was stunned, suddenly guilty that I'd invited him over. Their bedroom was right over the family room but I hadn't heard a thing. Mystified, I apologized. Later on, Dad came over to talk. He had dark circles under his eyes but tried to smile. "You were just trying to help your friend, weren't you," he said. "He's not in very good shape, is he?" Dad had a sixth sense for particular forms of distress.

Back in Cambridge in the fall, Ron didn't go out for any varsity sports, even though he would have been first-team in anything he tried. Without warning, he dropped all his classes. If I saw him around, he looked otherworldly. One day he suddenly left Cambridge, no one was sure for where. A former roommate said a few months later that Ron had ended up in a mental hospital somewhere, maybe New York. "He's got schizophrenia, that's what I heard," said the roommate with a bewildered expression.

No one saw Ron again. He'd vanished into the ether. But he stayed on my mind.

Desperately, I tried to work it out. Dad had been diagnosed with schizophrenia since the 1930s—the often lasting condition with hallucinations, fixed delusional beliefs, illogical thinking, and difficulty processing and expressing emotions. Ron had developed it, too, but with a huge difference. Once Ron began his collapse, he never got better. Neither had my cousin Marshall out in California, Uncle Paul's oldest son, who had been in and out of mental hospitals since his first term at UC Berkeley in 1968, without any sign of improvement. Yet Dad seemed so normal much of the time, at times super-rational even if a little detached. How could they all have the same condition? In class, I drew genograms, squares for male relatives and circles for females, shading in the shapes for cases of mental illness. With diligence, I might crack the family code.

Each time Dad and I headed back into his study during a visit home, my heart accelerated. He might start by asking about my interest in psychology, speaking excitedly about his own fascination with both psychoanalytic models and behaviorism during his years in college. He discussed philosophy and the ideas that had always thrilled him—the origins of knowledge, the progress of science, the sense of ethics people live by. Cautiously, in the third person, he raised the topic of schizophrenia once more. "When one has heard exultant voices and angelic choruses praising the Lord all night long, as I have, such a diagnosis is understandable," he said. I had a glimmer of doubt but said nothing. Dad's pattern seemed altogether different, leaving a major problem to be solved.

Although shattering, everything he told me made a strange sense. There must have been *something* this huge, this catastrophic to have produced the vast hangar of silence surrounding my life.

Back in high school we took a summer family trip up to northern Michigan, a break from my cross-country workouts before the football conversion, Sally's chorus practices, Dad's summer teaching, and Mom's course prepping. Boyne Mountain was a small peak, but compared to the glacier-carved plains of most of Michigan and Ohio, it seemed plenty tall. Eager to take the chair lift and hike the trails, I asked Sally to join me. But her expression instantly revealed her long-standing fear of heights. "I want to," she said plaintively, "but the chairs are so high off the ground! If I looked down, I might faint. Really, Steve, I probably would."

Thinking fast, I replied, "If I sit next to you and we concentrate on the view, we'll be up to the top in no time. It'll be more fun than you think." I let her know how proud she'd feel and what a great hike down we'd have. After she finally relented, we walked from the station to wait for the chairs to swing around the bend and approach us from behind. When the chair hit the back of our thighs, we sat back as the guy swung the metal bar over our heads. With a surge, we lifted off the ground, rising through the pine forest with a rush of air on our faces as the slope receded beneath our legs, 20, 40, then 60 feet below.

The view was stunning in the now-cooler air. But looking over, I saw that Sally was stricken. Her grip on the bar was so tight that the color had drained from her hands. "I've never been this scared in my life," she croaked. "Look how high we are!" The chair rocked back and forth in the wind.

"Don't look down," I ordered. "Hang on. We'll soon be up to the top."

"*Steve*," she cried, her voice breaking as she grabbed my arm with one hand. "I can't stand this another second. I'm going to jump." I felt her abruptly re-arrange her body, her hands groping to lift up the bar, the ground far beneath us. This was no idle threat. The panic in her voice was unmistakable.

"Sally, if you jump you'll break both your legs," I spoke loudly, trying to stay calm. "You could fall on your head." Indeed, she'd have certainly died. "Stay right here!"

Should I grab her? But the seat was starting to rock. I concentrated on talking firmly, without a trace of doubt. "Sally, listen to me. Close your eyes; you have to." I craned my neck to look toward her. This was my only shot. "Good, keep them closed.

Now do this—think of our cat at home." It was Thai-Thai, our Siamese. Sally's love of cats was incredible. "Think of petting your beautiful cat and how good it will feel when we're back at home to see him. Think only of the cat. We'll be off this lift in a couple of minutes."

Hesitant at first, she began to sit back, her eyes tightly shut. I told her about things she liked: her friends, the cat, anything to keep her mind occupied. *Hurry*, I silently ordered the chair lift. She kept her eyes shut tight as I talked.

After a few interminable minutes the ground came up fast beneath us. I lifted the bar over our heads and held her arm, telling her to open her eyes before pulling her off as the chair quickly swung around for its return trip. The lush countryside spread beneath us. Though pale, she had her feet on the ground. Never had I heard her so thankful. "I was ready to jump," she said.

"Believe me, I know," I replied. "You had me worried."

I couldn't get over the vice-like grip of her terror. I wasn't sure how I'd known what to say to her up there; it had just come to me.

Beginning my second year of college, my new plan was to drop pre-med courses and major in social relations, the interdisciplinary department blending sociology, social psychology, and anthropology, now merging with the small experimental psychology department dominated for years by B. F. Skinner. It might ultimately lead to a Ph.D. in clinical psychology if I could put in the work and get enough experience both clinically and in research. Maybe, just maybe I could learn enough science to understand mental illness and use any skills I had to help people—the way I had helped Sally.

I sought field work, and the medium-security prison south of Boston offered the opportunity to teach a psychology class. Passing through the metal detector each week, I felt the trickle of fear spread over my skin. My co-instructor, a senior, and

I brought up classic psychology experiments and showed films of these in a sterile, cinder-block room. Each inmate received a certificate at the end of the term, a small item, but one that might make a difference at a parole hearing. It was the least I could do, I thought, for those who'd turned abuse and deprivation into hurting others as well as themselves.

I headed back outside the gates each week but didn't gloat over my freedom. My own incarceration felt internal. How might I break out into a more authentic way of living, beyond my constant overscheduling, my lurking fear over what I'd learned but dared not share? More than I knew at the time, I identified with the inmates.

The fall semester was relentless, with endless reading lists and countless papers to write. Autumn faded fast, the trees devoid of leaves before October was over. In November spits of snow alternated with clear, freezing days. Every week or two, after hours of congestion and unease, I hauled myself out of bed for another torture session in the bathroom. By mid-year I'd lost ten pounds.

Every few weeks I walked over to the textbook section of the bookstore, a vast windowless annex. Row after row of new books gleamed, listed alphabetically by course. I always started in the "P" section housing the psychology books. But even the subareas of psychology—cognitive, developmental, biological, personality, clinical—loomed large. Down the aisle lay the other "Ps": paleontology, philosophy, physics. Opening a book at random, I scanned the dense opening paragraphs. I was entering other worlds, but how could I get immersed without becoming lost?

On some daring afternoons I went to other aisles: "A"— astronomy, anthropology, Asian studies; "B"—botany, biochemistry. In the dull glare of the fluorescent lights overhead, each book called out. But I feared that I might lose myself if I entered worlds of thought that were too different from my own.

Quickly retreating back to the "P"s and psychology, I took a deep breath. I had returned to the place I needed to keep my focus.

The battle lines were being drawn. Could I learn anything important if I were afraid to truly explore? Might I transform the knowledge of my family into anything useful? Every night, even the ones I didn't end up in the bathroom, the questions swirled.

The Iron Suit

8

During holiday visits to Columbus Dad and I sometimes saved our final talk until he drove me back to the airport, affording half an hour in the cocoon of the car. The streets and freeways faded in the intensity of the discussions. Ever more, I became initiated into the secret world of madness.

In one of our conversations when I was close to finishing college, it became clear that Dad wished to bring up additional information about the treatments he'd received. ECT was at the top of the list. Although stereotyped as barbaric in *One Flew Over the Cuckoo's Nest* and other aspects of popular culture, ECT can be an extremely effective intervention for severe forms of depression. Yet during much of the twentieth century it was used indiscriminately and even punitively for almost any form of irrationality. Back then it featured overly long pulses of current, which often caused major side effects such as memory loss. In the earliest days, before anesthetics were used, patients might break a limb from the seizure-induced thrashing. It's still not known exactly how ECT works. Placing an electric charge through a person's skull and thereby inducing a brief grand mal seizure alters a great many neurotransmitters and brain processes. But which of these explains its beneficial effects on serious mood disorders remains a mystery.

Dad told me of his terror regarding the procedure back in the fifties. One such session at Columbus State Hospital, when Sally and I were quite young, stayed on his mind. The technicians, he told me, would place a steel arc on top of his head and clamp cold, metallic electrodes to his temples. After waiting—always the waiting—a surge of current would commence at his psychiatrist's signal, sending his brain into a convulsion. His doctors had surmised that the medications he was taking weren't doing enough. Talk therapy, such as it was, only scratched the surface. At the time, his diagnosis was chronic schizophrenia, but little matter: ECT was used indiscriminately during that era.

On the morning Dad was recollecting, he was lying flat on a gurney, listening to the squeak of its wheels echoing through the corridor. Pushed by an attendant, he was heading to the special room, the place he dreaded above all others. With his arms and legs strapped, he saw the globe lights glaring down from the ceiling, passing above his face every few seconds as the slow journey unfolded.

Above all, he must show no fear. Keeping his pride intact, he said, was essential. Once inside the room he'd be injected with medication, enough to make it impossible to sit up. He'd be powerless once more.

Finally inside the door, he braced himself. He saw the nurses, scurrying to record his vital signs. The technician entered, the one who would trip the switch to allow the current to flow into the wires attached to the clamps. Would the crackle of electricity produce smoke from the side of his skull? His head, in fact, felt like scorched earth each time he awakened.

Out of nowhere a question entered his mind: Where were Alene, Steve, and Sally? Did they still exist? The house on

Wyandotte Road, the small kitchen where his son sat on his lap, the back yard framed by trees: They were all a faint memory, a film long since ended and the theater empty. Fighting panic, he wondered whether he'd ever see the brick and stone buildings of Ohio State again. Was he still a professor, or had that been someone else in a different lifetime? And what about Pasadena, his boyhood home with all his brothers?

How had he arrived in the hospital once again? He must have lost control in the classroom and at home. A vague recollection of flinging his golf clubs into the neighbor's yard appeared before his eyes, but the medicines had clouded his memory, making his life a permanent, dull present. By now he was inhaling the sticky scent of electrode paste and the metallic aroma of the ionized air from the previous ECT session with another patient. After his own procedure, he would try to figure out where he was, the headache overwhelming. Could he face it once more, this surge of power that made him feel like a charred husk?

There was one ritual from deep in his past: The Lord's Prayer, which had comforted him as a boy and provided relief during earlier times of despair. Lying flat, he began to move his lips, but the guttural whisper was barely audible.

> *Our father, who art in heaven, hallowed be thy name.*
> *Thy kingdom come, thy will be done*
> *On earth, as it is in heaven.*

Several young doctors, undoubtedly trainees, were observing the procedure from a corner of the room, writing notes on clipboards. Glancing tensely at the patient, they heard his monotone, their expressions revealing sharp concern.

> *Give us this day our daily bread, and forgive us our*
> *trespasses . . .*

"What's he doing?" one of them called out to the lead psychiatrist, Dr. Southwick, who presided over the session. "Why is Hinshaw muttering?"

. . . as we forgive those who trespass against us.

Dr. Southwick considered his patient on the padded table. Glowering at the trainee, he retorted with enough force that everyone could hear, including the patient. "What the hell do you think he's doing—he's praying! How else do you expect him to deal with his fear?"

> *Lead us not into temptation, but deliver us from evil.*
> *For thine is the kingdom, the power, and the glory, forever.*
> *Amen.*

A rubber guard now coated his mouth, its bulky mass nearly making him gag. Maybe his teeth wouldn't crack as he began to convulse. The final anesthetic was now administered and he began to drift off. Everyone held still for the signal. It was happening again, the white heat moments away from penetrating his skull. Not for the first time, everything went black.

Dr. Southwick nodded. The lights grew dim; the machine angrily hummed. The charged pulse held its beat for one full second, then another. His body gently writhed, and writhed again.

At least, Dad recalled from his study nearly twenty years later, no one was able to stop his prayer. He understood that Dr. Southwick had been his ally, standing up for him in front of the residents. As he ended his recollection his face revealed a combination of bitterness, fascination, and resignation I'd never before seen.

Staring alternately at the clock, each other, and the window that opened onto the Boston night, Mom and I sat on the orange-brown polyester hotel bedspreads and waited. Where could Dad be? The dinner reservation had expired hours ago.

Their weekend trip to New England had been marked by the informal tours I led around the Harvard campus and through Boston's comically crooked streets. It was a chance, too, for Dad to visit his longtime OSU philosophy colleague, Manny Lebowitz. Manny had left Columbus to teach at Brandeis a few years before but was now undergoing cancer treatment. Dad had departed for the hospital in the late afternoon, saying he'd grab a cab afterward to meet us at the hotel before dinner. Yet visiting hours had long since ended. Always punctual, Dad had never stood anyone up for appointments or social gatherings. Exasperated, Mom and I dared not speak our ultimate fear.

Suddenly we heard a key turning in the door and saw Dad enter the room, panting despite the cool evening air. Startled, he glanced over at us.

"Where were you?" I asked as calmly as I could. Treading cautiously, Mom mentioned something about the time and our dinner plans. Dad's gaze shot far beyond either of us, his look frantic.

"Where do you think?" he called out angrily. "Manny may not make it; the prognosis is grim. I decided to walk here afterward. What's the matter? What time is it, anyway?"

It slowly dawned on me: Manny, brilliant and kind, a fellow pipe smoker, was one of the few people Dad had ever spoken with about his past. Dad had been bereft when his colleague had moved to Boston, even though he had told me matter-of-factly that academics often get better offers at other universities. Right now, on full display right in front of us, Dad was revealing his grief and confusion along with more than a touch of agitation. When he left Manny at the hospital, nothing else mattered to him than the need to keep moving, to let the night's breeze and the pavement under his feet absorb the blow.

When I asked psychology professors about schizophrenia

versus manic-depression—the older name for bipolar disorder—I received dismissive looks. Why bother with formal diagnosis, they nearly scoffed; it's the underlying psychological conflict that's of the essence. Even as late as the seventies, clinical psychology was dominated by earlier, completely environmental notions of diagnosis and causation, which denied any biological roots of serious mental illness. Given the general ignorance on full display, it's safe to say that stigma permeated my very courses at Harvard.

Not that I mentioned my real reason for asking. I kept my interest general, academic. Courtesy stigma prevented me from raising the most important issue my family and I were facing: Dad's accurate diagnosis and the potential for responsive treatment.

Every spring I got a couple of migraines, real ones with the flashing lights, throbbing pain, and nausea I couldn't control. Eventually I went to the student health service. Any mention of the vomiting I forced on myself in order to sleep was too personal and too humiliating, so I left that part out. Self-stigma was part of my own curriculum.

The first doctor was decisive: I had a dust allergy and must clean my room regularly and change to hypoallergenic sheets. The second doctor, totally derisive, had obviously never been wrong about anything in his life. My migraines, he sniffed, had nothing to do with glare or genetics, even though Dad, all his brothers, my grandfather, Mom's mother, and Sally showed nearly the identical pattern. "You might leave the darkness of a theater and believe that the glare outside is a trigger," he declared, "or strive for biological causes. But the emotional content of the film is the true culprit."

Those expert doctors, so confident and sure of themselves! I railed at them, if only in my mind. Who among them had a clue—especially those who'd treated Dad, years before, by tying him to his bed at Norwalk, providing insulin coma therapy at Byberry, or dispensing antipsychotic medicines and shock treatments when Sally and I were young? The all-biological types were as bad as the all-psychological ones. Then and there, I made a vow. Whatever I ended up doing in this field, I would always remember that what we know in social sciences, psychology, and medicine is a tiny fragment of what needs to be learned. The only accurate stance is one of humility—and integration of diverse perspectives.

I feel the same way today. The human brain is made up of trillions of synapses receiving and firing signals every second; the miracle of human consciousness somehow emerges from those chemical actions. Those who bask in their supreme knowledge are deluding themselves, their patients, and the scientific community.

On a bright spring day near the end of my junior year I took the Red Line into downtown Boston and then the Green Line to the Museum of Fine Arts, one stop past Harvard Medical School. Pitch-black clouds loomed on the far western horizon, though the sky was bright and full of glare straight above. Once inside, I kept returning to a van Gogh painting, with spiraling blues of the sky and vibrant golds of the field, surrounding a building in the town where the artist had been recovering after his stay at the St. Remy asylum. The swirling, jagged paint strokes were electric, the colors and shapes mesmerizing. Staring, I tried to grasp the essence of the painting.

Near closing time peals of thunder boomed through the museum as the air pressure plummeted. Rushing out to the train with the crowds, barely ducking the squalls, I swayed in the steamy air of the crowded car. Almost back to Harvard Square, my heart sank: The initial zigzag of the aura now shimmered in front of my eyeballs. I futilely prayed that it was just some kind of afterimage but knew better. After I made my way back to the dorm, all I could do was lie down, helpless, until the crushing pain and waves of nausea took over. What was the trigger—the sudden drop of air pressure from the storm, accompanied by the sky's alternating glare and gloom? The emotions incurred by van Gogh's brushstrokes and madness? Or the genes permeating every cell in my body? The reasons crowded my mind as the throbbing intensified.

Things weren't as simple as I sometimes thought. They still aren't.

Back home during spring break of my junior year, I drove to see Sally at Ohio Wesleyan, a half hour north of Columbus. She'd decided not to go East for college; Ohio Wesleyan would be safer and not as far from home. She had a boyfriend and talked about her classes, excited but a bit overwhelmed to be on her own.

I took a risk and told her what I'd learned from Dad. As easily as we talked about most anything, the conversation became strained. It was hard for her to feel close to him or the whole situation. "He's never talked with me the way he does with you, Steve. Besides," she went on, "he's so distant from Mom, and she really needs support." I felt privileged but half guilty that he'd chosen me. I'd entered a selective club, one to which Sally and Mom hadn't been invited.

Sally went on to say that Grandmother lectured her when she was home, believing that she shouldn't have boyfriends and that she was acting entirely too modern. Her own migraines were getting worse. Following the aura, headache, and nausea, half her body sometimes went numb as she became semi-paralyzed for a few hours.

"I can't relate to the problems Dad's telling you about," she continued; "I don't feel part of it. He doesn't get who I am."

The gravitational pull to stay in Columbus had been strong but I'd followed my instinct. Yet from afar I kept an eye on everyone, the tug enormous. I wanted to rescue Sally, to push her toward freedom; but she didn't have the support from Dad she needed. I wanted to rescue Mom, who had spent her marriage keeping Dad's episodes from ruining the family—and walling off her own emotions from the complete irrationality of his illness. And I wanted to rescue Dad, getting him an accurate diagnosis, now that I was increasingly sure the doctors had been wrong his whole life. But how might I break through my own locked-down style?

"I've learned to love the Midwest, Steve," Dad said, back in his study. "We never had true seasons in Southern California. I couldn't get over the fall out here when I first arrived, the changing leaves. I love the winter and find the snow exhilarating. And the spring is gorgeous. Actually," he continued, "if you're happy with your life and work, you can be fine just about anywhere."

During our continuing talks, I envisioned him during his early days in Columbus, going to and from campus as the seasons changed, playing volleyball, badminton, or golf after work and on weekends. But now he viewed the seasons mainly through the windows of his study. Too often he seemed passive and listless, always needing a nap in the afternoon. So much of his life now seemed to take place solely in his mind. What had happened over the years since his promising start? Had the accumulated episodes taken an eventual toll, or was the cost linked more to the misguided, even barbaric hospitalizations and treatments he'd received?

His half-year delay in starting twelfth grade, I now understood, resulted from his involuntary stay on the back wards at Norwalk. His weak left hand and wrist—evident when he slammed the door on his hand as he hurried to pack the car for our long-ago California trip—also stemmed from his leap to near-oblivion. But I was seeing the pieces one at a time, long after the box had been overturned. When I thought about my first 17 years, my anger smoldered, especially over the silence, role-playing, and constant low-grade fear that accompanied me each day.

Yet a central question was now preoccupying me. Did Dad really have schizophrenia, or had he been misdiagnosed for the better part of 40 years? Didn't bipolar disorder serve as a better explanation? Another puzzle to solve, once again on my own.

I began to take summer positions on the East Coast, working with kids with learning disorders or serious developmental disabilities. Following my junior year I landed a counselor slot at a residential summer camp in New Hampshire for children with autism and other disorders. Camp Freedom stood on the shores of Ossipee Lake, the deep-blue water glistening between silver birches. The far point of the land afforded a head-on view to the north of Mt. Washington and the Presidential range, looming majestically in the distance. The best perspective was from a canoe while the oars dipped in the still waters. To the east lay the long, dual humps of a low mountain, symmetrically framing the horizon. The pay for counselors was miserable but the experience unmatched. I couldn't get over that my young Harvard professor, Bruce Baker, had founded the program to study and treat kids everyone else had given up on. Shaping language skills and reducing self-destructive behavior were grueling but the learning was nonstop. We might just change the world—or a part of it.

At the end of the intensive orientation, it rained for three days straight and the lake overflowed, delaying the opening. After canoeing to our raised platform tents to retrieve our damp backpacks and moldy clothes, a group of us drove down to Cape Cod until the camp dried out. Swimming in the moonlight in a lagoon not far from the ocean, I saw something I'd never witnessed, yellow-green traces in the water and sandy shores, in the form of phosphorescent microscopic animal life, a seeming reflection of the infinite stars above. On rare occasions the world could be magical.

Once camp opened, if I wasn't on night duty with the kids in the bunkhouse, I would sneak off and get high with a co-counselor or two. I was paired with John Whyte, a brilliant Swarthmore student totally into psychology, about to enter a dual M.D.-Ph.D. program. The first openly gay man I knew well, he talked with me about everything in his life. Instantly trusting him, I reciprocated, discussing my insights about Dad. I continued to scrutinize my every mood. Would my future mirror Dad's past? If my mind went too far, would I end up insane myself? Did Dad have schizophrenia or manic-depression? Having someone to communicate with lifted my burden, if only temporarily.

I arose one Saturday morning to the clangs of the wake-up bell to join John, coming from another tent, and Sheri, the third of our trio, who'd been on night duty with our kids, who exhibited a mélange of severe behavioral problems. I felt both light-headed yet heavy on my feet. I must have looked pretty bad, as John and Sheri ordered me to the infirmary. The former nurse, with tons of experience, was up for the weekend, watching as the new nurse placed a thermometer under my tongue. Taking it from my mouth, she studied the mercury reading, her eyes disbelieving. A second later she fainted straight away, fearful for my life. Mary, the old hand, deftly recovered the thermometer, which fortunately hadn't shattered, and read it out loud: 105.7.

Lowered into a tepid bath to bring down the fever, I saw visions of campers and the surrounding trees dancing and shimmering. It's as close to a hallucination as I've ever experienced. The hospital was 45 minutes away over two-lane roads, but no doctor was on call at the rural setting. Probably from the force of the fever, I began a migraine aura by that evening, followed by dry heaving, as I lacked enough fluid to actually throw up. The next morning, a nurse arrived early. "98.6," she said, peering at the thermometer. "How did you get back to normal?"

Back at camp, I needed a day or two to regain full strength.

John had become ill, too, along with several other staff. One theory was that the flood waters yielded breeding grounds for mosquitoes that caused a slow-onset viral pneumonia, though I had no other symptoms. John and I stayed in a drier, wooden structure to recuperate, where we smoked some really good weed. After we reached a peak buzz, he went to the dining hall to get us leftovers, the campers long asleep. We walked out to the shore, the sand still warm, hazy starlight above us.

"John," I said, "you're not going to believe what I just saw in front of my eyes."

"With that grade-A stuff we've been smoking, I wouldn't be surprised with anything you told me," he noted sarcastically.

"Well, I saw the image of a postage stamp, with the profile of Abraham Lincoln."

His response was dry. "That's not too exciting."

Yet I replied straight back: "Right before my eyes, though, the profile of Lincoln changed to the Easter Bunny."

"Now that's trippy," John retorted.

"But the Easter Bunny and Lincoln merged into a profile of my dad's face!"

John summed up. "When you're high, Steve, you would make a psychoanalyst very happy."

The next year I wrote a senior thesis on the community mental health movement, surveying how professionals implemented the latest treatments for youth with developmental disorders around the country. I served on a multidisciplinary team at a community mental health center that used undergrads as in-home therapists. I was assigned to a 14-year-old boy who had never spoken outside his family's house. He gradually opened up, revealing worlds of emotion and insight. The debates raged at case conferences: Did he have aphasia, extreme social anxiety, or a closed-off family system? The mental health field seemed divided rather than integrated.

At group supervision sessions, the topic one day was anger.

The leader, an astute African American psychologist, sagely commented on its uses as a signal for change. But I was sure that she was speaking in tongues: anger as a signal? For me, any sign of irritation erupted instantly into white heat. Once a feeling started, it couldn't be contained. No wonder I'd worked so hard at keeping my emotions in check.

By day ideas went off in my mind like little firecrackers, as Sylvia Plath put it in *The Bell Jar*. I might find a calling in psychology one day. But at night, ever more often, things ground to a halt as the sense of doom overtook me. I ended up back in the bathroom, the forced vomiting harder to enact each time.

I had a new girlfriend, Penelope, a Wellesley student. Intense but fun, with huge, sparkling eyes, she had the kind of warmth I craved. I even brought her back to Columbus for Christmas holiday. We were getting closer, but how close? I told her about Dad but kept my torturous evenings private as long as I could. How did I expect to receive emotional intimacy if I wasn't even open with myself?

One evening in the winter, in the library until late, I missed a phone call from Dad. My roommate Tim had taken it, reporting that Dad said he wasn't at home, but left no specific return number. "Your dad seemed really eager to talk with you," he noted. But when I called Columbus the next day, and the next, there was no answer.

My honors thesis drafted, I returned to Columbus for spring break, three Aprils after my fateful journey into Dad's study. Back in the same room, he told me that that he'd phoned, a couple of months before, from a partial hospitalization program at OSU. He'd lost control during the winter. Paranoid ideas had taken hold. His dosage of Mellaril was increased.

My mind reeled. Dad's episodes were still happening! How would he have sounded on the phone that night, if only I hadn't been buried in the library? Something needed to be done, and fast. But how? The information he'd been imparting to me had lifted me beyond my closed-off childhood but also bur-dened me like an iron suit, stifling any movement. My arms and body were wilting from the strain.

At a high school friend's house the next day, I heard his mom ask how I was doing. "Great," I told her, trying to believe it myself. "My senior thesis is done; the sky's the limit for me."

"Well, you don't look so great," she replied, eyeing me care-fully. "Actually, I've never seen you so tense."

Graduation was coming up in two months. It felt like a walk down the gangplank.

Dawn

9

The following September, a few weeks after most school programs had started, the Therapeutic Center opened, a brand-new program for a dozen kids who'd been either thrown out of the Boston Public Schools or never allowed to start because of their intractable learning and behavior problems. Massachusetts was the first state in the nation with an inclusive special education law, providing a model for the federal counterpart to start the following year, 1975. A few weeks out of my second summer at Camp Freedom, I'd somehow been hired by the Massachusetts Mental Health Center as the center's coordinator. I sported a seventies-style mustache and headband, but my intensity for this kind of work brimmed just beneath the surface.

Yet had twelve children and adolescents more different from one another ever arrived at the same building? Who was more bewildered: the kids themselves, their parents, or the staff who'd soon be teaching them?

Angela was seven, with black braids capped with pastel beads meticulously prepared each morning by her devoutly religious mother. Clapping her hands with her head bobbing, she strutted into the classroom, singing Stevie Wonder, Otis Redding, scat beats, and Motown. Her uncanny voice then shifted to gospel songs she'd heard in church on Sundays, which she echoed perfectly. She looked everywhere except in the eyes of the person across from her, smiling radiantly and closing her eyes as the sounds of her singing overtook her mind and body. But just try to get her to pay attention to something other than music and she flailed on the floor, lashing out as though tortured. She was encased in a glass vial, where the beats reverberated. Who might get inside her autistic shell?

Then there was James, 15, sturdy and freckled, rigid as a statue from the tension coursing through every muscle in his body. He gritted his teeth while his shoulders and arms twitched spasmodically, whether from inner agitation or the powerful antipsychotic medications he was taking, no one was sure. When a teacher gently tried to usher him into his classroom—"OK, James, it's time to start"—he screamed at the top of his lungs, his voice cracking with rage, slamming his fist into the closest object he could find: "Don't say OK! Don't say OK!" What did the word signal to him? It was a mystery, but people quickly learned that certain terms just couldn't be used with James. He'd destroyed a room or two of his clapboard Boston house.

Victor now arrived, eight years old and adorable, coming from a home of six siblings, all of whom had been neglected and abused by their drug-addled, cognitively delayed parents. He'd cuddle in your lap and shoot baskets at recess with an infectious laugh, but printed words on a page looked like hieroglyphics to him. The odds of his ever learning to read were long. Was it the beatings, the days with almost no food, or the genes he inherited? Or some toxic combination? When he lost control of his emotions, he sobbed a single plaintive cry: "Sorry, sorry, so sorry, sorry, sorry, so sorry." It was undoubtedly the only term that might have prompted his family to stop the hitting, at least temporarily. Where would Victor end up?

Ernesto was there, too, nine years old but spending most of the day in a fetal position. He'd never spoken and probably never would, but his intense brown eyes let you know that there was a lot going on inside, even though a lack of oxygen after birth had deprived him of any means of communicating in words. Every once in a while, especially at home, he would come alive with animation, pointing and gesturing, imploring his siblings to tickle and feed him as he giggled uncontrollably. But how would he adapt to school? He'd never been to one for more than a few days. Away from his adoring family, he seemed bewildered, reclining into his tuck, groans and chirps forming in his throat, his bird-like frame retreating from the world.

What about Ronald? Nearly 17, he sauntered into the classroom, took one look at his peer group, winced, and then reached for the knife in his pocket. A knowing look from his teacher, Phil, told him to hand it over so he grabbed a pick instead, tending to his hair. *What am I doing here with this group? How did I end up with these crazy kids?* His expression spoke volumes. Maybe it was better than juvenile hall, but he seemed incredulous. *Am I this messed up, too?*

There was another girl, Darlene, 13, from a housing project. She spoke with a gorgeous Southern drawl but struggled mightily with school subjects, working barely at a second-grade level. Her disruptive seizures were poorly controlled. Some of the program's medical consultants wondered whether her overstressed and under-resourced family made sure she took the pills regularly; her IQ was too low to remember herself. Still, over the years she'd had enough Dilantin that the tell-tale signs of deteriorating gums were in clear view every time she emitted her dazzling smile. She knew that her teeth were too big for her mouth but couldn't squelch her delight at being alive. Would she ever learn to fend for herself?

Over the first weeks, we established classroom routines, as our diligent young staff worked overtime each day. A reward system was implemented, linked to lessons that were geared to each individual's level. Signs of progress began to appear on the program's behavior charts. I supervised the teachers, made home visits, and conducted parent management sessions after school. The responsibility was enormous, but this kind of work was exactly what I'd been waiting to do all through college.

Darlene attended the adolescent class. One morning she arrived alongside her peers in a fog, dazed and slightly agitated. In class, she stood up, almost staggering, and wobbled. Phil, her head teacher, quickly took her arm and walked her to the hallway. A moment later, as if on cue, it started: She convulsed and collapsed in a heap, the contortions rocking her body, as a grand mal seizure overtook her. Shielding her from harm, we got her into the office, where she lay semi-conscious. But moments after she revived, her eyes rolled up toward her forehead and she convulsed again, the flopping movements possessing her.

Status epilepticus, Phil and I both knew—the pattern where one grand mal seizure closely follows another. If the chain doesn't stop, brain injury and even death can result. The paramedics rushed in within minutes of my call. Phil followed the emergency squad in his car, while the other teacher and I covered the rest of the kids until the school day ended.

Hurrying to her room in the vast Harvard Medical School complex that afternoon, I arrived to hear the doctors plead with her mother to ensure that the meds were taken every day. Darlene was hooked up to an IV drip of Valium, her huge smile back in place despite her obvious confusion. Clinical reports were starting to come in that this "tranquilizer," first introduced a decade before, could be addictive if prescribed indiscriminately for anxiety or sleep, even though it had been originally touted as a non-addictive alternative to barbiturates. Yet in front of my eyes it was saving her life, shutting down her uncontrolled seizures. Another miracle of modern medicine, but for Darlene and so many kids, far more basic miracles were needed: communication, knowledge, and understanding. If only there were enough staff, programs, science, and dedication to go around.

I wondered whether I possessed the qualities to make a difference. In fact, I was awaiting miracles not only for the kids at the Therapeutic Center but for myself. The way it was going, I might need one or two.

The previous June, stark white against the deep-green lawns, massive tents filled Harvard Yard, as golden sunshine infused the scene. More than three hundred graduation ceremonies into the sequence, I was somehow part of it, marching with the tiny group of *summa cum laude* graduates at the front of the procession. I got called to the stage to receive the Ames Award, for the graduating senior best blending social action and scholarship. Among the throngs were Mom, Dad, Sally, and Grandmother, who'd all driven out together. The best part was that I'd one-upped those New England prep school guys who thought they'd owned the place since freshman year. I secretly gloated: Midwestern public-school kid makes good!

Yet no academic honors could replace the massive holes filling my mind and body. Any plaudits I'd earned were quickly worn thin by my nights of torture. The thread of my life was unraveling. I was maintaining my weight, barely, but what would all the learning be worth if I couldn't help Dad? Who else was going to solve the massive problems he'd experienced since he was a teenager? I kept asking myself which group was worse: the psychoanalysts who thought they could cure him through figuring out his fantasies or the wave of biological psychiatrists who were sure that the right pills and jarring shocks would restore him to health? Where was the needed integration, or any admission that things were actually a lot more complex than these single-minded perspectives would indicate?

Amid the pines of Camp Freedom for a second time following my graduation, I hoped that one day I'd be able to conduct such programs, training young staff, advocating for society's powerless citizens, and performing research on child and family outcomes. But would I ever get to that point? Each day, following the morning classes and languid afternoons as the kids went swimming in the lake, I searched inside myself for signs of congestion and sleeplessness, bracing myself for the unspeakable ritual in the communal bathroom—everyone else, I prayed, long asleep. But who was I kidding? The self-induced gags and retches were getting more violent, and the thin wooden walls of the wooden outhouse in the woods masked no sound at all.

By day, I brimmed with energy and resolve. By night, I was increasingly unable to rein in my mind. Perched on a steep slope, my fingers tearing at grass and stones, I doubted I could stay above the darkness. Even more, the mountains and lakes of New Hampshire gave me more feelings of rapture than most relationships I'd been in. How would I ever form a deep connection?

Halfway through the program, Bruce Baker called me into the director's office. "How's your summer going, Steve?" he asked brightly. "Any job prospects yet for the fall?" Weary, I shook my head, concerned over any future I might have at all. He told me of a call he'd received from a psychologist in Boston who was looking for a Master's-level person to head a new school program. He told her straight away that there was a fresh B.A. with lots of experience right at his camp. Before I knew it, I was down in Boston for an interview. By mid-August, the job as coordinator of the Therapeutic Center was mine, and the intensive planning began.

Prior to the school's opening, I took a short trip to Ohio. Dad and I didn't plan our sessions together. Instead, the themes flowed from talk to talk. He was now discussing his times in mental facilities in Ohio. "Sometimes, teaching a class, my mind might begin to soar. My ideas would become highly irrational. I believed that I held the key to the secrets of philosophy. Soon, I was back on the ward." Each time, he said, was strangely familiar. I now understood: Dad *expected* the episodes, considered them inevitable.

He went on to speak about his brother Bob. "His migraines may have been the worst in the whole family. All the brothers had them, along with our father." Years earlier Bob had begun to prescribe himself pain medications—as an M.D. he was able to do so—at first oral barbiturates but later self-injections. Complications eventually set in, as a clot developed near the injection site. Finally, his leg had to be amputated.

What a difference from the cover story about Bob's sedentary life I'd heard in junior high school. At last I was peering behind the heavy covers that had blanketed most of my life. What more had happened that I never knew?

"As a result," Dad continued, "he's now showing signs of kidney failure. He'll begin dialysis soon. Because of the expense of going to the hospital, he'll do so at home." Dad's savior and my advocate, Bob was now reduced to this. In our family, even those who made it big might be headed for a fall.

But my chief concern was solving the puzzle of Dad's diagnosis. Time was getting short.

Penelope and I had split up. A couple of friends from Camp Freedom asked me to go on a three-day mountain expedition over Columbus Day weekend, a needed break from the rigors of getting the new school program off the ground. We would spend most of our time above the treeline in the Presidential range of northern New Hampshire. Yet what if I felt congested at night amid the highest peaks on the East Coast, with no place to purge myself? The signs on Mt. Washington revealed that the strongest winds on earth, 231 miles per hour, had occurred there. But the mountains beckoned.

Early snows had hammered the high country, the soft carpet of yellow and orange leaves at the trailhead giving way to freezing air as we continued our ascent. The crystalline blue sky glistened above us, while sweat accumulated in our inner layers despite the cold. We huddled in group cabins for campstove dinners, the stars overhead pinpricks of light from eons away. Tired but jubilant, I somehow made it to sleep. The next day, we hiked past Mt. Adams to Mt. Washington, snow drifts swirling in the howling winds. The clarity of the air was astonishing. Far below, in a 360-degree view, lay Canada, Vermont, Massachusetts, and, just visible at the horizon, the Atlantic.

At least I had a refuge against the frantic, dead-end places in my mind. Deep in nature I found a momentary truce. But like most truces, it wouldn't last.

Change was in the air. His junior faculty stint at Harvard over, Baker was off to UCLA. The board of directors found a new director for Camp Freedom. I was offered the position of program director, second in command, to coordinate the staff and oversee the treatment programs.

I met Celeste over Thanksgiving weekend, under frigid skies at a farm outside Boston. Long shadows from the trees and farmhouses covered the blinding snow. Petite, athletic, forthright, and fun, she was going to be a doctor of some sort. I desperately wanted to see her again. She must have felt a spark, too. In the winter she and I and a couple of others drove to Camp Freedom for the weekend, the camp empty except for the snow covering the ground under the birches. The denuded trees were tinted gray and silver against the hills and mountains. Cross-country skiing across the ice-encrusted lake provided a counterpoint to the canoe trips of the summer. The flames in the office fireplace kept us warm all night. Punch-drunk in love, I was giddy with connection.

"Tell me about your family, Steve," Celeste asked me one day.

"Well," I answered, "Dad's a philosopher and Mom teaches English at Ohio State. My sister's going into speech therapy." But I couldn't get out much more, with the stakes this high. What might she think about our family?

"Tell me more about you," I asked, "and come closer when you do."

My drive for connection was a blind hunger, but how real could it be if I wasn't all there myself? Keeping my evening rituals from her was getting to be impossible. The tightrope I traversed was as wide as a piece of string.

Back in Columbus over spring break, I talked with Dad once more before he headed off for a philosophy conference. Pacing through the house, I couldn't bear waiting another moment to see Celeste. I called the airlines and advanced my ticket, flying stand-by and making my flight by minutes. From Logan airport, I rushed over to her place.

"What are you doing back?" she said, surprised that I'd made the effort. Her eyes sparkled. We held each other. For a moment, the longing inside me felt as though it might overcome any void. "I need to see you all the time," I stammered, surprised by my conviction. "We need to make love right now." Slowly her eyes narrowed. Too late, I realized what was coming.

"Steve, this is too much," she said with a touch of defiance.

"But Celeste," I pleaded, "don't you feel the same way? I know you do."

"Not like that," she replied, her voice steely. "I need room."

I grabbed my bags and left for Cambridge, the wind knocked out of me as though I'd been blindsided on the football field. Burying troubles in the intensity of love, as if love were mainly about escaping pain, wasn't the answer.

In the lush days of June I was back again in New Hampshire, this time as the one in charge of the staff, conducting orientation week. To cap off preparations, my ultimate task was to complete the master schedule. Past program directors had pulled an all-nighter to construct it, integrating the pre-camp evaluations of each child to form a huge grid of kids grouped by skill levels, classrooms, and teachers. It couldn't be finalized until late in the week, when all the information was in place. But the deadline was urgent. Over the weekend the first cars would pull up, anxious parents huddling around their offspring before leaving them on their own for seven weeks.

Yet I'd never stayed up all night in my life. I'd always completed assignments far ahead of time, anything to prevent being up too late. But it was now or never, the whole program depending on this crucial night. With papers and reports scattered across the plank desk, I reworked the huge chart over and over, no small feat prior to personal computers.

The clock radio showed 4:30 a.m. Trying not to panic, I reminded myself that I'd pushed myself to the limit out of sheer need. I decided to take a quick look outside, then get a few hours of rest, despite my worry that I'd sleep through the bells and miss breakfast, ignoring the pungent smoke from the stone chimney in the massive stone dining hall.

The small cabin was located right on the shallow beach of Ossipee Lake. I opened the front door and peered out over the plate-glass-smooth water. Not ten feet in front of me, wisps of mist danced in columns all the way across the bluish-black liquid, two miles to the opposite shore. I stared as the sky gradually lightened overhead above the primeval scene. Turning east, my eyes were drawn to the color, a glorious blend of off-white, yellow, pale orange, and purple, as the dawn sky slowly gathered toward a deep red-orange directly over the summit of the low symmetrical mountain on the other side of the lake. The only sound was an occasional cry from some early-morning bird.

Pivoting to face the camp behind me on the shore, I saw the mass of huge pines towering above the sandy grounds below, as the first shards of daylight penetrated the shadows. Scanning back again to the lake, the sky ever lighter, I took in the entire scene once more, overwhelmed by the monumental nature of the world around me. Able to hold my gaze no longer, I walked up the three steps to the cabin, closed the door, and drifted off to sleep for a few precious hours.

My double life—energetic program director by day but defeated and tortured soul too many nights—was exhausting. Added to the mix were the deep problems emerging at camp. The new director was rigid in all the wrong ways, deciding on a disastrous course of action after failing to consult the needed players. Parents were upset, staff were tense, and the kids weren't learning as they should have been.

Mid-summer, the board convened a crisis meeting, faces grim as the members emerged from their car journeys from Boston and southern New Hampshire. The next day, Baker and the board president called me to a meeting. "Without revealing much detail, Steve, we can tell you that we need new leadership," they said grimly. "Would you be willing to become the acting director for the remaining weeks of the program?"

Shocked, I said yes. A hundred extra pounds had just been added to the barbells I was struggling to keep aloft. That evening, a brilliant doctoral student and longtime staff member of the camp pulled me aside with a gleam in his eye. "I just want you to know, Steve, that as long as everything thrives at the camp when you're at the helm, I'm right there behind you. So is everyone else." He looked into the distance. "But when things start to slide, it's just you, buddy. I'm out of here."

Trying to laugh at his sarcasm, I ignored the shiver coursing through me. I moved into the director's cabin, studied the financial books, and secretly prayed for no incidents before the last camper pulled out of the dusty parking lot in mid-August. At the final staff banquet, my sigh of relief was heard throughout New England.

As late summer turned into fall, rings appeared under my caved-in eyes. I was down ten more pounds since college. "Are you

OK?" staff at the Therapeutic Center asked as we began our second year. The nighttime rituals were increasing in frequency and intensity, though I kept those secret.

We'd hired a new teacher, Roberta. Two years older than I, she was mysterious, fascinating, political, and exotic. She'd lived in San Francisco, studied Gurdjieff, and planted community gardens. She relished teaching the toughest kids in the program. Wise and thoughtful, would she be passionate, too? After getting to know her, I walked by her apartment in North Cambridge in the early fall, bracing myself to ask her out. To my amazement, she agreed.

It was time to take a risk. "I should tell you something about my family, especially my dad. He's told me about his experiences in mental hospitals. He's had quite a life." I looked down. "I have this idea that he's been misdiagnosed for many years."

"Tell me more," she replied, not a hint of judgment in her voice. Tentatively at first, I even mentioned my nighttime torture sessions. As we continued talking, half ashamed of my straight-and-narrow life, I told her how I admired the risks she'd taken. But she came right back. "You've taken different risks, but risks just the same—the programs you've run, the responsibilities you've had." Deep in my bloodstream, pride welled up.

In late September, back in my apartment bedroom, another doomed night had begun. I'd realized since late afternoon that with my congestion, unsettled stomach, and raging mind, I wouldn't sleep unless I once again purged myself. Near despair, I was moments away from hauling myself out of bed. But for an extra moment I just lay there. Out of sheer weariness I decided to delay the inevitable.

Once more on the verge of lifting myself up, understanding the cost to myself of any more waiting, I held still for another few minutes. It was a terrible risk: My life with an intact mind was at stake. But to my amazement, I began to sink into the sheets, a strange lethargy overtaking me. I tried to rally, nearly panicking, but then started to drift, nearly drugged. The next thing I knew my alarm clock was sounding, eight hours later. Stunned, I shot up out of whatever dream I'd been having. Hurrying to get dressed, I wondered what had happened.

I met Roberta in Haymarket Square on Friday afternoon. We walked through the crowded rows of fresh fruit and vegetables, vendors barking out prices, thick pizza slices for sale, the constant expressway noise off to the right. The day had started bright but it was now gray, misty, and cool, typical New England. Close by was the North End, where John's father, William Foote Whyte, had written his classic, *Street Corner Society*, decades before. All the while I held on to a secret, a spark of warmth despite the gloom outside. *I don't have to torture myself any longer. All I have to do is lie there.*

Roberta was delighted. "Let your body do the work," she said, nourishing the tendril of hope inside me. Late that fall, I had surgery on my nasal passages. I received relaxation training and behavior therapy to condition away fears that I might not sleep. But it was all after the fact. Following that night in late September, I never made myself sick again.

I remain shocked over how bad things got during my prolonged crisis. I couldn't have kept up the forced vomiting much longer; the physical and emotional consequences would have been dire. Was the whole thing related to a fear of going mad? Or to a kind of superstitious conditioning, based on my migraine experiences? Or was I symbolically purging the information about our family's long-hidden curse? No matter: Stigma was the main culprit. I managed to dodge a bullet, one aimed straight for my heart.

A couple of weekends later Mom and Dad flew out. We drove to New Hampshire as the leaves reached their peak. It was the kind of autumn day I'd always dreamed about, every color imaginable framed against the royal-blue sky. They'd visited me at

Camp Freedom and knew how I felt about the lakes and mountains.

On our final day it clouded over, preparing for a real rain. Dad took a nap in the car while Mom and I hiked the small, dual-humped mountain across the lake from Camp Freedom. I'd seen it a thousand times silhouetted against the eastern sky but had never ascended it. Moderately steep, it was just right for a short jaunt. Mom was eager to join.

The trail and the fallen leaves on the ground emitted a damp, earthy scent. But halfway up, Mom suddenly became exhausted. I waited for her to get her wind. "Go on up to the summit," she said, hunched over. "I'll poke along, and you can catch me on the way back." I was shocked. Mom had never let up with anything she'd ever done.

I jogged the rest of the way and got an occluded view from the summit back over the lake to our camp, before hurrying down to find Mom, who was trudging forward, not far from where I'd left her. I stayed by her side as we slowly made our way back to the trailhead. A few weeks later, she said on the phone that she'd been diagnosed with bursitis, but that proved not to be the case. Within days a specialist correctly diagnosed rheumatoid arthritis. Over the next years, her medications changed from 16 aspirin tablets a day, plus low-dose steroids, to gold injections, penacillamine, and finally anti-cancer drugs, in a desperate attempt to stop her immune system's attack on its own connective tissue.

"The stress of caring for me all those years has undoubtedly played a role," Dad told me back in his study, his voice somber. "Her rheumatologist believes this to be the case as well." All I could do was agree.

Mom kept up with her activities, funneling her huge empathy to become a leader in the Arthritis Foundation, serving on the national board. But the consequences were unmistakable. Her entire nervous system and immune system had been on alert as long as she'd been married, handling impossible situations without communication or support. Although I can't prove it definitively, I'm convinced that stigma was the major cause of her system-wide, 40-year-long disorder, in which her body's defense system attacked her own connective tissue.

The next time I saw Dad, for once I set the agenda. "Listen," I implored. "There's no way you can have schizophrenia." I told him it must be bipolar disorder and that treatment with lithium would be far better for damping down or even eliminating the episodes. My own reading had convinced me of the need for a new diagnosis.

Dad had been vice-chair of the philosophy department for some years, partly, I surmised, to compensate for his decreasing rate of publications. He often seemed listless, which is how the depressions associated with bipolar illness often appear. Every night he took part of a Doriden tablet, a sleeping pill a generation beyond the barbiturates he'd received back at Byberry in the forties. Sleep problems are rampant for people with bipolar disorder—even between episodes—but the medication robbed him of natural sleep. He often drifted off during late-afternoon department meetings and took an hour-long nap every day to catch up. Even more, Doriden was potentially addictive. And what about the Dexedrine doctors had prescribed him during the late fifties and early sixties for low moods? He was lucky he hadn't become dependent on such pills. Adding in the ECT he received while hospitalized when Sally and I were young, just how much unneeded treatment had he actually received over the years? Like dry tinder, my rage kindled. Something had to change in the mental health field—and for Dad. Finally I remembered my ace in the hole. I made plans to see Uncle Bob in California.

The decision became final. I would become the official director of Camp Freedom for the following summer. Baker was back in town from the West Coast, meeting with me about the coming program. He didn't give long speeches, so when he launched into a talk about Camp Freedom's first summer, eight years before, I was on full alert. A fresh Ph.D. out of Yale, he'd wanted to help children with developmental disabilities and perform research at the same time. After finding a site and creating a board of directors, he founded the camp. One of the children during that first summer had the rare diagnosis of Prader-Willi Syndrome, a genetic condition marked by major cognitive problems and severe overeating, often leading to obesity. The boy was overweight, and with the family's permission, the camp instituted a program of caloric restriction and exercise to reduce his body mass. But the summer turned hot and, without the staff's knowledge, he became dehydrated. Found semi-conscious in his bunk, he died.

"Then and there," Baker said, his face impassive but with emotion infusing his words, "the camp could have closed forever." The debates over this tragedy had been his sternest test, but he persevered. All the while my insides were doing a nosedive. The Therapeutic Center was a few minutes away from some of the world's foremost medical centers but Camp Freedom was nearly an hour's drive over side roads to a community hospital, as I knew firsthand from my first summer's fever. At 23, was I ready to take on my biggest responsibility yet?

I told myself that evening that I would have to forgive myself if anything tragic occurred under my leadership. On another level, I had received this opportunity only because I'd resolved the crisis of my self-induced vomiting the previous fall. Without stopping such self-torture, I wouldn't have had this or any other chance to make a difference.

In March, I drove out of Cambridge in my first car, a used Fiat, destination California. I stopped shaving and a beard slowly emerged, even though it never quite fully covered my cheeks. After a week I finally traversed the LA freeways, in the land of Dad's youth. The air was sweet with the scent of blossoms but too often stagnant from the brown sludge lingering above the valleys. When the winds cleared things out, the grass on the hillsides was emerald, sparkling snow on the mountains ringing the city. How could a place be so enchanting and depressing at the same time?

My official reason for the trip was looking for new Camp Freedom staff among Baker's UCLA students, but my secret mission was to visit Bob. He lived in Brentwood, far from the sprawling house I'd visited years before. Now on home dialysis, he sounded weary but glad that I'd called. "Certainly, Steve; let's set up a time for you to come over."

Sea breezes softening the air, I drove through West Los Angeles. The town house was small and elegant, but there was no mistaking the medical equipment in the next room. Bob was gaunt, his goatee not quite masking the sallow skin of his face. His eyes widened as I walked in. He and I faced each other.

"Steve, your father says that you did quite well at Harvard, extremely well."

"Uh, yeah," I said, looking down, "I guess so."

"Yes, well, I think you're being modest. So, tell me about your current work and what brings you to LA." Explaining as best I could, I told him that I'd be applying for clinical psychology grad schools in the fall—and that UCLA's program was high on my list. All the while I was waiting for an opening to talk about Dad. What was there to lose?

"Bob, I've been talking with my dad a few times a year since I started college. The main thing is that I just don't believe he has schizophrenia. I mean, how could he get so much better the way he does in between his episodes and still have chronic schizophrenia?" I went on to say that I thought he should be on lithium. Hardly pausing for air, I emphasized that he simply had to have better treatment.

Lithium is a natural element, the lightest metal on earth. For reasons that are still obscure, the intuition of John Cade—the Australian psychiatrist who pioneered work in this area—has held up, as lithium regulates bipolar mood cycles. It alters neurotransmission in a number of ways, with its largest clinical effect the lengthening of the period of normal functioning between episodes. It's the original, and still unsurpassed, treatment for helping to prevent a lifetime of uncontrolled bouts of bipolarity.

Now that I'd blurted this out, Bob looked down for a few moments, pensive. Had I overstepped my bounds? When he looked back at me, pain showed on his face.

"Steve, with my health issues, perhaps I've lost touch with your dad more than I should." I thought of him at age 18, the first one out of the house, witnessing his younger brother sprawled on the pavement below the porch roof.

"But you mean to say that he still has a diagnosis of schizophrenia?" he went on. "He's remained on antipsychotic meds?" I nodded. "Let me get this straight," Bob continued, "he's never been tried on lithium?"

Bob went on to say that my analysis was undoubtedly right. Back in 1954, around the time Sally had been born and Dad was severely ill, he reiterated that he'd been able to secure his brother an early prescription for Thorazine, the first antipsychotic drug, which had just arrived from France. "If I'm not mistaken," he went on, "your father was the fourth patient in the U.S. to receive it."

At the time, he said, a diagnosis of schizophrenia seemed plausible, but the field's knowledge had vastly improved in recent years. He shook his head, whether in disbelief over Dad's level of care or chagrin over his own lack of involvement in recent times, I couldn't tell. He asked for the name of Dad's psychiatrist, recognizing the name of Dr. Southwick. "Let's call him," Bob said, to my amazement. "Actually, it's after working hours in Ohio, so I'll call first thing in the morning."

When I reached Bob the next afternoon, he told me that

Southwick disclosed he'd recently taken a continuing education course on manic-depressive illness. Prompted by Bob's call and this recent course, he'd finally realized his diagnostic error.

"That's a switch," I said quickly, and Bob agreed. Southwick was to contact Dad, take him off the Mellaril right away, and start him on lithium within two weeks.

I was incredulous—and seething. Was it really this simple to change a 40-year course of misdiagnosis? Yet why had it taken my 3,000-mile journey to point out what should have been obvious to an evidence-based clinician? What was the matter with the field of mental health? I felt vindicated, certainly, but my deeper emotion was anger.

I drove back East, making a stop in Columbus on the way to New England. I'd called ahead to let everyone know I was coming. Mom wasn't thrilled with my beard but didn't say much about it; she couldn't really hide how glad she was to see me. With all the commotion over the unexpected visit, it was hard to find solo time with Dad but we managed a few minutes. He told me that he appreciated my having spoken with his brother Bob out in LA. Forty years too late, he'd received a new diagnosis and a new treatment.

Had I done the right thing by advocating? At least I'd done *something*. For a precious moment, I felt relief.

The following summer at Camp Freedom was marked by a hurricane that slowly made its way up the Eastern Seaboard, with reports of imminent destruction emerging from the camp radios and single television set. The sheriff ordered us to evacuate to the local school gym, located on higher ground. For two days I was in crisis mode, overseeing the move of the campers and staff out to the school and back again. When the ordeal ended, the storm's winds lashing the camp's grounds but with no major damage incurred, I felt as though I'd been run over by a small truck. Even over steak and lobster for the staff celebratory dinner, with my appetite something of an urban legend, I longed for sleep.

At a van Gogh exhibition in Paris the following winter, the bilingual catalogue discussed his self-portraits, contrasting the early ones with those he painted toward the end of his life, after experiencing searing bouts of mental illness. I was on my first trip to Europe, now that I'd resigned from the Therapeutic Center and applied to graduate programs. The catalogue described the swirling backgrounds of the late portraits while lauding his control of the paintbrush despite the chaotic forces in his mind. "Art can go no higher," it concluded.

I stared back at the intrepid face of van Gogh and the torrent of brushstrokes behind his gaunt face. Torment and control, genius and madness, heredity and experience: These were the topics bound up with my family history—and the subjects I'd be focusing on for my entire career.

Admissions letters from graduate schools awaited my return in early April. Overwhelmed with the imminent decision, I figured that pick-up basketball might clear my head, so I headed to an outdoor court. The guy I was guarding was wearing hiking boots, heavy and intense, just like he was. After a missed shot, he forced his body over my back for a rebound. As we both went up for the ball, I felt the heel of his boot smack the back of my ankle just as my heel hit the ground. I toppled to the pavement.

When I tried to stand, it felt as though I'd stepped into an elevator shaft. Three days of excruciating pain and two misdiagnoses later, a specialist said that my Achilles tendon was torn, requiring a full-leg cast for three months and a partial cast for two more. I was destined to direct Camp Freedom for a final time on crutches. Three days late, I called UCLA to say I'd attend their Ph.D. program.

Roberta and I had to figure out whether our relationship

would continue. We were getting more serious. "I don't know about Southern California," she hesitated. "Not exactly a feminist haven." I countered that maybe she could move out the following spring, once her job was done and I'd settled in to my first year there. Her compassion had given me strength and girded me through my worst crisis. I looked forward to a future together.

The last summer of Camp Freedom was loaded with the usual daily triumphs and tragedies, but a new life awaited me on the far edge of the continent. My cast came off at the end of the summer and I started some rehab to strengthen my withered leg. On my way to LA, I stayed over in Columbus for a couple of days.

"How are you feeling about moving to Los Angeles?" Dad asked from behind the wooden desk of his home study. He was animated but fully in control. "I have colleagues in philosophy at UCLA."

"Well, New England was pretty great, but this should be a real challenge. And I'll be near where you grew up. Maybe you could visit?" Dad assented eagerly, noting that he always relished the chance to return to Pasadena.

The year before, Uncle Harold—Dad's oldest brother—had died from alcohol poisoning. Bob's status was tenuous as his dialysis continued. How exactly had I escaped all this?

I had, right?

I finally got to my most important question, about the lithium. Dad's new diagnosis and treatment had been in place for over a year. He replied that he had received frequent blood draws at the onset of treatment and that he was distressed by the fine-motor tremor he had developed, altering his elegant handwriting. Yet he summed up that he hadn't had this kind of assurance—of being protected from another episode—for as long as he could remember. His awkward hug removed several tons of weight from my body.

Half a week later I grabbed two huge suitcases from the luggage carousel at LAX. On the freeway to Westwood, the post-midnight sky was a strange orange-black, with millions of city lights off to the sides. I entered my small studio apartment two blocks from the UCLA campus, with flowering vines right outside the door, and fell asleep in a heap.

In that land of smudged skies, aromatic flowers, and searing sunlight intermixed with occasional winter storms, I was on the verge of discovery. I wondered where the current might land me.

The Thought
Experiment

10

We'll lead off today's seminar with a question," stated Kay Redfield Jamison from the head of the huge oval table. "It's a thought experiment." Forthright, supportive, authoritative, and energetic, Jamison was a dream mentor and supervisor during my year-long internship following four years of grad school. Such internships provide the capstone experience for clinical psychologists in training. There was no mistaking the quality of her mind, which permeated each pronouncement.

All 20 psychology interns and psychiatry residents stopped their conversations. During our intensive rotations through the Affective Disorders Clinic at the UCLA Medical Center, we performed intake assessments, conducted therapy sessions, and in some cases led groups. The clinic had become a top venue on the West Coast for patients with serious depression or difficult-to-treat forms of bipolar disorder. The weekly seminar provided the glue and theoretical background for its activities. As the clinic's director and seminar leader, Jamison usually began by discussing a provocative new finding or sharing a clinical case. Why had she switched things up today?

It would be another 15 years before she emerged with the disclosure of her lifelong bipolar disorder, through the publication of *An Unquiet Mind*. Even back in 1981, however, she was clearly attuned to the undercurrents of the field's increasing knowledge of genetics.

"Project yourselves into the future," Jamison went on. "Suppose you or your partner become pregnant—and there's a new screening test that can accurately detect the risk that the fetus will develop bipolar disorder." If Jamison didn't have my attention before, she did now. Even though the risk for manic-depression, she continued, would emanate not from a single gene but from several in combination, the science might one day develop to be able to detect risk with real precision.

"Assume that the screening test comes up positive. In other words, it's virtually certain that your child will develop manic-depression." She noted that if current screening tests were positive for Down syndrome or other forms of mental retardation, the family nearly always decided on an abortion.

Thoughts of Mom's sister flooded my mind. Although Ginny Ann hadn't been born with the chromosomal irregularity of Down syndrome or the profound intellectual disability she'd developed after her catastrophic fall down the basement steps, she'd emerged into life with some kind of developmental disorder. With prenatal detection, would she have ever been born?

Jamison had reached her conclusion. "Here's the question. Under this scenario, how many of you would elect to have an abortion for yourself or your partner? We'll take a vote. Raise your hand if you select the abortion, given such a test result."

For a second, the room went silent. A few trainees looked around sheepishly while others glanced down. Jamison repeated her query, calling again for the straw poll.

One thing was sure: My hand would remain glued to the table. My arm, in fact, began to ache from pressing down so hard on the wood surface. But as I looked up every hand in the room was held straight up, every hand except for mine and that of my best friend, Jay Wagener, a fellow intern and fellow Midwestern survivor of a gifted yet troubled family. Jay and I had connected early in the internship year, through co-leading a group for people with bipolar disorder in the Affective Disorders Clinic and, even more, through talking about the streaks of mania, substance use, and disruption in both our families. Friday-evening, post-internship-week treks to dive bars throughout West Los Angeles solidified our bond.

Incredulous, I wondered whether someone had sucked the air from the seminar room. But there was no doubting the consensus from the staff and trainees of a preeminent clinic for serious mood disorders. I quickly traveled back in time. If this kind of test had been available 60 years before, Dad would never have come into the world. Our family, lost in the ether.

And what about any kids of my own? For the past decade, ever since Dad's first disclosure, the idea had been too frightening. I was now starting to reconsider, but if such a test existed, how could any child of mine enter the world? The seminar readings were absolutely clear that the heritability of bipolar disorder is huge, even higher than the genetic vulnerability for schizophrenia, with the risk transmitted almost entirely through genes passed from parent to child.

From a distance I heard Jamison comment on the vote, yet I hardly followed the thread. As the hour concluded Jay and I stole a glance at each other across the table before heading our separate ways to packed schedules, our eyes wide and eyebrows raised. *Did that just happen?*

Over the next days I tried to salvage a moral to the story. All the seminar participants had been learning about the devastation often associated with serious mood disorders through some of the most difficult patients on the West Coast. The Affective Disorders Clinic was a magnet for crisis cases, people whose manias had led to involuntary hospitalization or whose depressions were resistant to traditional treatments. No wonder everyone had been so freaked out. But all the rationalization in the world couldn't remove the reality: The future leaders of the mental health field had just voted to eliminate my family members from existence.

I mentally reconvened the seminar and made a speech. *Don't you know my dad? The one who understood me when I'd given up hope, who persevered despite all odds? Finally diagnosed properly, he has embraced his new treatment. Yet you'd have prevented him from joining our planet—and remove our family's chromosomes from the gene pool?*

I'd been open with a few more people about my family, but in the aftermath of the thought experiment I said nothing to the seminar participants about the topic. Wouldn't I be known as a flawed member of a flawed family, unqualified or even ineligible to become a professional psychologist or scientist? Someday, I secretly pledged, I'd fill in the profession about Dad's life and our family's plight. But how would I ever get to that point?

The previous four years in grad school had been nonstop: Courses with huge reading lists, placements with clientele ranging from couples experiencing marital problems to teenage gang members, and case conferences that bordered on the interminable. But I didn't complain. The knowledge was red meat for my hunger to learn about brain science, personality theory, child development, community models, assessment and diagnosis, and blends of medication with psychological treatments for serious mental illness. After my three years as a school coordinator and camp director following college—with the lives of the kids on the line every day—my stint as a Ph.D. student actually seemed pretty luxurious.

My initial goal for grad school was to be able to continue to run schools and camps, but now armed with a doctorate. Yet when scheduled to present at a case conference or give a guest lecture, I was able to articulate complicated concepts; the words seemed to emerge from my mind unbidden. It dawned on me that I might know more than some of my professors about psychopathology. Over time, I developed the objective of integrating the biological side of the equation—genes, brain function, early risk—with the contextual side, including families, peer groups, and schools. A professorship might be just the ticket to create and spread knowledge.

All the while, small bursts of energy aided my efforts. I never reached irrationality, and my controlled existence stopped me from pulling any all-nighters. Still, my appetite for big projects, large ideas, and stitching together all sides of an issue just *had* to be fueled—and still is—by the DNA inside my cells producing surges of sub-manic intensity. When the bottom periodically drops out, especially if I sense I haven't lived up to my ultra-high expectations, my world suddenly turns pitch-dark. Inconsolable, I despair that all my efforts have been for naught. My mini swings are a pale echo of Dad's mega-episodes.

The late 1970s and early 1980s were a mind-bending time to be working toward a doctorate in clinical psychology. Genetic models had risen to prominence. The year before my internship, the third edition of the psychiatric bible known as the *Diagnostic and Statistical Manual of Mental Disorders (DSM-III)* was published. Greatly expanding on earlier editions, its goal was to make diagnoses precise, with clear symptom lists embedded in a web-like hierarchical organization. In short, it was a master scheme.

As a boy I loved maps, those two-dimensional guides to the world. During my high school football days the playbook I finally received was a revelation, as I devoured the intricate systems of plays, based on core formations and blocking schemes. As Camp Freedom's program director I created the maze-like organizing grid of our daily schedule, with the goal of promoting each child's targets for learning and behavior. Each time it was the grand plan—the 30,000-foot view—that drew me in.

But with maps there's only the bird's-eye view; no sight of the actual terrain. Playbooks don't capture the smack of helmet on helmet or the lung-burning panic of beginning the fourth quarter of a tough game. Master schedules can't convey the frustration of children who have trouble learning—or their families, desperately seeking any sign of progress.

Indeed, some of my most important learning during grad school took place on the ground. During my initial year at UCLA I'd started to work with kids who showed serious problems with impulse control. For a pilot test of self-management interventions at a local school, I worked with a group that included an extremely bright 12-year-old who'd been branded by his teachers and family as extremely impulsive, constantly acting without considering the consequences. Within the group he became involved in the exercises and role-plays, appearing to make real gains.

A few months following the group, I ran into him and his parents by chance on an LA street. His right hand was heavily bandaged. I subsequently learned that he had kept playing out in the garage with the pneumatic pump for the family's camper, despite clear knowledge he shouldn't take such a risk. He was so tempted by exploring and tinkering that he triggered an explosion of the compressed air, which blasted three fingers permanently from his dominant hand. Sobered, I understood that a scientific and clinical concept like impulsivity had grave clinical consequences.

I learned more in unexpected venues. One day I walked a couple of blocks to a travel agency in Westwood, not far from the UCLA campus, to book a holiday flight to Columbus. I was beginning to register that in Southern California, 75-degree temperatures in November were the norm. "OK," the guy behind the desk said, not a whole lot older than I. "Let's pull up your reservation. Last name?"

"Hinshaw," I replied, "with an 'i,' not an 'e.' And Stephen, with a 'ph,' not a 'v.'"

He paused. "Wait a minute," he said, looking me up and down. "Hinshaw? I knew a Hinshaw a few years back, east of LA, out toward the desert." Lost in memory, he gave a first name that didn't ring a bell. Because there aren't too many Hinshaws in the world, whoever he was discussing must have been a distant cousin.

"That dude was way out there," the travel agent continued, now getting worked up, his hands going in big arcs. "Man, talk about crazy. He was far gone, way out of touch. He heard and saw things that weren't there, strange ideas all the time. What a dude." Listening in silence, I had nothing to add.

"Wow," he concluded, shaking his head, "was he ever out there. What a wildcat! Anyway, let's get that ticket of yours going."

Feeling as though my family had been placed under a microscope, I collected the itinerary and envelope, wondering just how many insane Hinshaws there might be in the world. At least I'd escaped such a fate. Right?

I had actually introduced myself to Kay Redfield Jamison during my initial year in grad school. She'd made a presentation on mood disorders at a case conference I'd attended. My self-taught interest in bipolar disorder, paired with her brilliant talk, had me enthralled.

Not long after, I received an urgent call from Dad. He'd been in discussions with Bob, whose kidneys were further deteriorating. Bob's specialist had put out a call for any relatives who might serve as a donor match for a transplant. Dad wanted to help but was unclear whether the lithium he was taking—with its potential side effects on renal functioning—would make it too risky for Bob or himself.

Thinking fast, I cold-called Jamison, clearly a world expert on the entire topic. Certain that a secretary would screen incoming calls, I was shocked when she answered after two rings. I introduced myself, praying that I didn't sound too much like a lowly first-year grad student, and summarized the situation. She told me to come by the following week.

Through the warren of medical-center corridors, I managed to find her office. With rapt attention and incisive commentary, she provided the kind of authoritative feedback I'd been longing for. In the end, Dad and his doctor opted out of having Dad donate; the risk might be too high. No other matches could be found. Bob's fate seemed sealed.

The fall of my second year was eerily like my sophomore year at Harvard, as I was overwhelmed with coursework and clinical cases, with far too much to do in too little time. I worked frantically but my spirits ebbed. Roberta had moved to Southern California the previous spring, and we were working out how our relationship would continue. Most mornings I felt a gray cloud encircling my head and wondered whether I could muster the energy to make everything happen.

As October waned, evenings came on early, a cool haze emerging from the Pacific and lingering through the night. Unexpectedly, Bob's wife called to say that he was at Cedars-Sinai Hospital. After all the waiting, a donor match had suddenly materialized. It was now or never: He'd been rushed to the hospital for transplant surgery. Would it take?

On a misty evening a few days later, I drove into the unfamiliar turf of Beverly Hills and West Hollywood. Emerging from the huge hospital parking lot I found the elevator to Bob's floor. To my amazement he lay resplendent in his bed, smiling, jovial, thrilled to finally have a new lease on life. In the corridor his middle daughter Barbie—in between Sally and me in age and almost my twin in temperament—explained that this was the father she hadn't seen in years, laughing and full of energy. Sure, maybe he was jacked up on the high-dose steroids he'd been prescribed to fight rejection of the new kidney, but some of the joy was real. Uplifted, I experienced emotions I hadn't felt in months.

Two days later Dad called early in the morning, before my classes—a rarity. Instantly on alert, I expected bad news. "Son, it's a terrible tragedy," he said, his voice somber. "My brother Bob died in the hospital last night. The medications to fight the rejection took his life." He repeated the grim joke about saving the kidney but losing the patient.

Adding to the sense of unreality, the weather turned, as Santa Ana winds scorched the LA Basin. Howling gusts pierced the air, blowing the smog toward the beach. Temperatures soared, nearing 100. Any spark in the brush of the foothills ignited huge fires, smoke filling the air. When Dad arrived at LAX for the funeral a week later, hot ashes were dropping from the sky over the western portions of Los Angeles, imprinting small burn marks on cars and roofs.

His closest brother was suddenly gone at age 60. I kept thinking how far you could fall in our family. The pit was so deep that I couldn't begin to see the bottom of the void.

By the following spring my life began to feel brighter. I decided it was time to get to know Dad's family better. I spent time with Barbie, who'd become a photographer, a daring individual with an impish grin, newly emerging as a lesbian. After a talk with Dad's youngest brother Paul, now a soloist with the LA Master Chorale, I drove to Long Beach on a warm afternoon to visit his son Marshall.

Two years older than I, Marshall had been a standout student in high school, admitted to Berkeley for college. The only potential trigger for what happened was his use of marijuana around that time, but who didn't smoke a lot of weed back then, especially in California? Yet during the fall of Marshall's freshman year Paul received a call from the UC Berkeley hospital, stating that Marshall was a patient, having begun to hear voices and exhibit wild behavior. He didn't last a year at Cal, as his psychotic symptoms and diagnosis of paranoid schizophrenia persisted. Over the years he'd drifted up and down the state, sometimes in mental hospitals but often on the streets, including the decrepit windmills at the end of San Francisco's Golden Gate Park, where he decamped for a time.

He was now living near downtown Long Beach, in a board-and-care home, the formal name for California's for-profit flea-pits set up in response to the closing of most mental hospitals. The low-slung, decrepit building looked suspiciously like an abandoned Motel 6, with emaciated palm trees hovering over the lonely courtyard. Relentlessly smoking cigarettes, desperate men and women languished in their rooms or paced the grounds, heads down, many showing the disfiguring facial spasms of tardive dyskinesia, a movement disorder marked by grimaces, lip-smacking or -pursing, and excessive blinking. This syndrome sometimes follows the long-term use of antipsychotic medications. These medicines can often make a major difference by reducing hallucinations and delusions, but there's a risk of developing this side effect, which is itself stigmatizing because of its marked distortion of facial expressions and body movements.

At most board-and-care facilities, attending psychiatrists rarely showed up, and medication monitoring was poor at best. So much for California's enlightened policies of deinstitutionalization.

Marshall hated taking any medications, although when he stayed on his Haldol—a more potent cousin of Thorazine and Mellaril—his strange ideas and delusions seemed to clear somewhat. I walked him to my car and we drove to a fine beach on the other side of town. He had trimmed his usually unkempt hair and beard, but there was something in his eyes that didn't look quite right. We talked about life at his facility, his brothers and his sister, anything I could think of, but I was carrying the conversation. Every few minutes, his voice rose in pitch as he began a soft rant, a rapid mutter of half-sentences, his eyes rolling up in his head and his words spouting in an endless loop: "God the savior . . . Paul my father, not my father . . . Steve here, Steve not here . . . God the savior . . ." As he spoke, every muscle in his body was rigid.

This is chronic schizophrenia, I told myself.

I talked more with Paul whenever I could. He told me that over the years he would drive up to Berkeley and San Francisco, endlessly cruising Telegraph Avenue or Market Street in his car, hoping to catch a glimpse of his lost son. "The worst was when he came back down here after he couldn't remain in college," Paul continued, referring to the end of the sixties and beginning of the seventies. " 'This medication will cure him,' one psychiatrist told us. And the psychotherapists! One of them said to me, Steve, if you can believe it: 'Just give me a year with him, a few sessions a week, away from his family. I'll cure him of any schizophrenia.' "

As Paul lamented the audacity of the mental health professionals he and his family had encountered, I murmured sympathy but hid my rage. Why was it still all-biology or all-psychotherapy? Hadn't anything changed? Who were these modern-day versions of the know-it-alls who were so certain that Dad had schizophrenia—or who insisted on the gag rule of silence about what was staring our family in the face every day of our lives? I thought, right then and there, that the field of mental health needed a revolution.

I still do.

That summer, Mom, Dad, and Sally flew to LA for a visit. While I toiled on campus as a research assistant on their first full day in town, they drove to Pasadena to tour Dad's old neighborhood. Sally said that Dad was obsessed with seeing 935 North Oakland. He was still searching for clues, I surmised, *something* to explain his flight at age 16.

Over the weekend, Paul and his wife, Mary, hosted a family reunion. Among a crowd of cousins and other relatives I was surprised to see Marshall. At one point, looking for something to drink in the kitchen, I glanced out the window and witnessed Dad talking with Marshall in the back yard. Both of them were animated, gesturing hard, though I couldn't make out their words. Marshall looked particularly agitated. Dad was half-smiling but appeared to be in full lecture mode, gesticulating back.

The next day Dad explained. "Marshall claimed to be Jesus," he said. "Apparently, he has carried this delusion for some time. But I wouldn't stand for this. As a philosopher and person of belief, I questioned his arguments. 'Where's your proof for this blasphemy?' I asked him. 'Don't take it lightly to claim to be the Son of God!' "

A battle of the titans! Marshall's permanent state of psychosis and Dad's history of fluctuation between irrationality and ultra-reason provided the backdrop. I'd experienced Dad's compassion for those with disturbed behavior, but it was clear that his tolerance did not include ultimate questions about religion and faith. His acceptance had limits.

In early September a few relatives held a Miss America party, inspired by Barbie and her partner. The TV was the centerpiece, featuring Bert Parks and all 50 contestants. With our fake crowns and ongoing satire of the ludicrous competition, we laughed so hard that tears streamed down our faces. In serious moments, Barbie talked about her imminent move to Santa Fe, where she would be able to take her photography to another level. Having already packed, she and her partner were to depart the next afternoon for a two-day drive, using separate cars to fit everything in.

Tuesday morning I got a frantic call from Bob's widow, who was hardly able to speak. After departing, she reported, Barbie and her partner had spent the night in Phoenix. The next morning, they got up early to hit the road. But from her rear-view mirror, Barbie's partner saw a car careen across the median and hit Barbie's vehicle head-on—a drunk driver, killing her instantly. "She was twenty-six just like you, Steve. I can't believe it."

I sat in stunned silence. How was I left on this battlefield, increasingly strewn with bodies? I wasn't sure the black cloud would lift. The only thing left was to remain duty-bound, helping those remaining.

Late in my grad school years I heard from my Uncle Harvey, the other half-brother of Dad's, a virtuoso pianist and professor of music at Nebraska. He, his wife, and oldest son, Harvey Jr.—Chip—would be visiting Southern California soon. Roberta and I made plans to meet them for dinner.

A musical prodigy, Harvey exuded his usual nervous energy paired with gentleness. His wife, Marcy, was deeply interested in my graduate program and Roberta's community work. Sitting on the opposite side of the table at the pizza restaurant, Chip had a faraway gaze. With his sweet, almost innocent smile, he appeared to inhabit a slightly different world. He talked about his community residence, where he'd lived after his mental hospitalizations, and his girlfriend, another ex-patient. I wondered whether it was his condition or the medications he took that gave him such an ethereal feel.

He'd been diagnosed with schizoaffective disorder—a condition that features the mood swings of bipolar disorder but also the persisting irrationality of schizophrenia between episodes. Intriguingly, the people in our family with marked schizophrenia patterns, like Marshall and Chip, came from Dad's stepmother's side of the family, whereas mood disorder and substance abuse problems emerged from the side of Eva, Dad's biological mother.

It was the last time I saw Chip. He fatally shot himself a couple of years later, just past his thirtieth birthday. Once again, I felt the devastation of our family history. Numbed, I was becoming used to the pattern. How had I managed to hang on to my sanity: through my intensive work ethic and blocking off feelings? Or just the blind luck of the genetic draw? I couldn't figure it out then. Even now, I'm still not sure.

At an international symposium held by the Affective Disorders Clinic during my internship year, Jamison invited Professor Mogens Schou, the Danish psychiatrist who had risked his career on rigorously testing the effects of lithium on bipolar disorder. Schou had read with intense interest Cade's small studies from Australia—ignored or ridiculed by much of the psychiatric profession—and put them to the test.

At a small session in front of the trainees, he rolled up his sleeves to reveal his arms, grotesquely covered in purple splotches. "This psoriasis resulted from taking lithium for six months," he told us. "I insisted that my staff and I experience the medication first-hand. Of course we would never subject any patient to a medication that we hadn't tried ourselves." Pointing directly at the psychiatric residents, he asked whether they would ever prescribe a medication they hadn't first themselves taken. I hadn't expected this level of inspiration, disclosure, and challenge.

In another talk he described his team's clinical trials of lithium in the 1960s. Lithium is different from nearly all other psychoactive medications—number three on the periodic table, a natural element, mined from the earth. Its discovery as an agent that can dampen the risk for subsequent bipolar swings has saved countless lives from suicide. As one of the first Europeans to advocate for this medication, Schou had been ridiculed in major medical journals for promoting a pill that lacked rigorous testing. But to do so experimentally would mean that some patients would need to be randomly assigned to lithium and others to placebo.

"I was in conflict," he told us passionately. "The extraordinary suicide risk of manic-depression was well known. I could not have lived with myself if anyone on placebo deteriorated to the point of suicidality." The research plan he devised was ingenious. His team formed pairs of patients with bipolar disorder, matched on gender as well as severity of their episodes, with a coin toss deciding which member of the pair received lithium and which received placebo. A given pair would stay in the study only as long as needed—that is, at the first sign of worsening of either member, their trial stopped. The research team then broke the code, revealing whether the person who'd relapsed had been on the active medication or the fake pill. Crucially, they had pre-calculated precisely how many pairs would need to be in the "placebo relapse" versus "medication relapse" groups to detect a statistically meaningful benefit, so that they could test as few pairs as possible. At that point, the entire study could be stopped.

"As it was," he concluded, "nearly every single one of the paired subjects showed relapse on placebo. We now had experimental proof." The rest was history, as lithium quickly became the first viable preventive treatment against subsequent manias and depressions. By the early 1970s, following further trials, it was approved in the United States.

Role models like Schou gave me hope. Perhaps it was possible to be rigorous and ethical at the same time—to integrate rather than split.

Every Tuesday night, Jay and I co-led our therapy group for adults with bipolar disorder. With their lives of unbridled highs and crushing lows, the members were eager to learn and to support one another but sometimes devastated by their growing awareness. Beyond feelings of specialness, creativity, and sexual power during hypomanic periods, they now understood that they would crash and burn unless they accepted the reality of their condition. The group process supported their identification as people with a condition that mandated ongoing treatment. Why hadn't there been anything even remotely like this, I wondered, when Dad was young?

At a late-fall meeting one of the members, Deena, in her late twenties, came in with a distracted look in her eye that grew increasingly frantic as the evening progressed. In rushed sentences, she discussed her recurring vision that she would jump from her moving car onto the freeway once the group dispersed. The next moment she was talking about the smell of her own death. Her logic was deteriorating fast.

The group members traded eye contact: Everyone realized that something was desperately wrong. When asked, Deena admitted that she hadn't felt the need to take her meds in recent days, as the voices in her mind had told her to stop. Suddenly, without warning, she bolted from the room, sprinting through the door toward the staircase. Jay and two members quickly followed. We had to get her to the hospital before she tore off again, perhaps never to be found. I stayed with the rest of the members before disbanding early, once she'd been found in a nearby café.

Deena was in the midst of a mixed state, with a huge lack of inhibitory control and occasional olfactory hallucinations, not just hearing or seeing things that weren't there but actually smelling imaginary aromas. She was experiencing the worst combination of the frantic energy of mania plus the self-destruction of major depression.

Jay and I slowly walked her to the hospital, one on each side, making sure that the emergency intake staff knew the story. The life-and-death nature of our work stared us in the face during each group session.

During his visit several months later, Jay and I had invited Professor Schou to one of our Tuesday evening groups. The members had read his publications; he was a hero to them. In his mid-sixties, he exuded intelligence, caring, and a deep calm. Content to be an observer for the most part, he finally relented to some closing comments.

"One day," he said, quietly but with emphasis, "group sessions like this, rather than medication alone, will become the primary treatment for people with manic-depression. The group process will serve as a signaling system, as signs of a new episode or an escalation can be detected and tracked by one's peers." Medicine, he explained, might then be reinstated, or the dosage raised, in consultation with the patient's doctor.

His candor floored me. Bipolar disorder was by that time discussed almost exclusively in genetic and biological terms, but here was the world's expert extolling the essential nature of social interactions and social support. I reminded myself to keep an open mind and think broadly rather than narrowly.

In late January, Dad flew out from Columbus for the last part of the week-long international conference. It was a classic El Niño winter, with deluges of rain soaking the Southern California Basin. On a day of partial clearing Dad explored the beach community around my apartment in Venice, which housed many unconventional types. The roller skating craze had come and gone, and the locale had become a mix of grungy and ultra-hip. A few years before, Marshall had roamed the walkways of Venice with his flowing hair and beard, proclaiming himself as Jesus. When I'd moved out to the beach after my first year at UCLA and people learned my name, I heard gasps as they realized that Jesus of Venice Beach was my own cousin.

As the sparkling blue-gray of the Pacific yielded heavy breakers, Dad had the day to himself. During my tight schedule at the medical center I imagined him near the ocean, taking in the scene. Dodging the fitful traffic, I hurried back to the apartment in the late afternoon. He brightened as I entered, recalling how much he loved his boyhood home of Southern California.

"I walked for hours today," he said. "The ocean was magnificent. What a scene on the boardwalk." I replied that Venice is indeed a trip.

"I found an intriguing restaurant for lunch," he continued. "Sitting next to me, I can tell you, were some pretty interesting characters." My antennae were lifting.

"I could relate to them right away. Hearing their discussion at the nearby table, I knew instantly that some of them had spent time in mental hospitals."

Intrigued, I paused, asking him how he could tell.

"Steve," he explained, looking straight at me, "when you've been in mental hospitals as much as I have, you can spot the psychotics like yourself right away."

I stared right back at him. Beyond the picture window, a flood plain filled the huge empty lot behind the apartment, half a mile from the beach. Seeking an answer, I gazed into the hardened earth, filled with pools of water. Had I heard him correctly: the *psychotics* like yourself?

A reply was forming in my mind. *Dad, you're attending a major conference on bipolar illness and hearing talks on genes and medication advances. You've read the scientific reports I've sent you since I started grad school. Don't you realize you're a person with bipolar disorder—a highly genetic condition producing irrational highs and blank lows—rather than a madman, a "psychotic"?*

But the words never emerged. Who was I to tell him how to think about himself? All the readings I'd sent him, all the explanations he'd heard about bipolar disorder in recent years had only scratched the surface. Nothing had put a dent in his fundamental self-image: his perception that he was one of *them*, not *us*. Brutally hospitalized at 16, he had formed an identity based on a sense of deep moral flaw. Stigma had been his constant companion.

As the sky darkened outside the realization crashed over me. Given up for dead in a mental hospital and tied to his bed as a teenager, sensing utter irrationality all around, Dad came to understand that his supposedly magnificent ideas were utter nonsense. Later hospitalizations, at Byberry and Columbus State, had further degraded him. Nothing he might learn in middle age had any chance of altering what he knew deep inside—that he was fundamentally different, insane, and not fully human.

Bitterness washed through my system. Diagnoses and treatments late in the game have no hope of altering deeply ingrained identities. We'd better listen to what the people we're supposedly treating are telling us.

Grad school was winding down, but the real curriculum was just beginning.

A Deeper Layer

11

Increasingly aware of his slowing body and mind, Dad decided to take partial retirement at the same time I was finishing grad school. Under this plan he would teach one or at most two quarters per year, which graciously allowed the philosophy department to recruit a younger and more vibrant faculty member. Sally, Mom, and I kept a secret: I would fly in from California to surprise him at his official retirement dinner on campus.

On the Ohio State Oval I witnessed a golden twilight as the warm May evening waned. I hurried to the faculty club and reached Dad on the front steps, where he was talking with colleagues. I tapped him on the shoulder. "What are you doing here!" he cried, beaming.

Filling the evening were speeches and the reading of laudatory telegrams and letters from philosophers around the world. Dad gave generous remarks about his 35 years at OSU, with the promise of more to come. Yet just prior to the festivities the current department chair pulled me aside, whispering that it was a blessing Dad had decided on early retirement. Other faculty members had been lobbying for him to step down; he was beginning to be a liability. "He admires you, Steve, enormously. Maybe you can help him deal with his new status. Good luck." Weighed down with burden, I faced the evening.

Mom was working through her crippling arthritis every day, preparing for surgeries to replace, with implants, major bones in both of her hands and both of her feet. Eventually both of her knees were replaced, too. Her energy and activity level never abated, but the pain was relentless. And as Dad's partial retirement loomed, Dad seemed to be drifting. Watching my parents in their separate orbits, how could I provide any gravity, any stability? The shadow of stigma had shielded our family from the light of open communication for its entire existence.

I stayed on for a few days after the ceremony, the skies rank with humidity. When I talked with Dad in his study he seemed blank and devoid of energy. Was this the product of his now-official retirement or instead the form of depression that often follows mania?

During the internship Jamison had each Affective Disorders Clinic trainee sit in on a clinical interview she performed, an old-school method but one that can be utterly compelling. The patient she interviewed in my presence had experienced a lifetime of bipolar disorder, with wildly productive and sometimes destructive manic states but now in a severely depressed phase. I'd been expecting cries of despair, but instead, this distinguished-looking man didn't move a muscle for the entire 50 minutes. His face was as blank as granite while he described, with chilling distance, his lifetime of huge dreams, inventions, ruined business ventures, and failed marriages. All emotion had leached from his body. *This* is bipolar depression, I told myself, with newfound respect for the utter severity of mental illness. It helped me understand Dad's blank, rigid periods of low mood.

Crossing the line once again between son, medical consultant, and advisor, I begged Dad to contact his doctor, pushing for the addition of an antidepressant medication to his lithium dose. It was increasingly known that lithium was better for squelching manias than lifting depressions. I couldn't stand to see Dad fading in front of my eyes. But as I implored he just stared. Powerlessness clung to me like the fetid air all around.

Once I was back in California, Dad finally relented and contacted his psychiatrist, who wrote a prescription for a new antidepressant, which lacked a proven track record. Soon after, I received a panic-stricken call. "I can't see well," Dad said. "Driving is now a hazard. My ophthalmologist suspects macular degeneration, and the new medication may be partly to blame." Indeed, it emerged that some of the newer antidepressants of that era could produce exactly this side effect. Specific medications for the depressions that linger following manias weren't uncovered until the twenty-first century. The most established of these is lamotrigine (Lamictal), which lifts bipolar depression in many individuals.

Ominous signs had been appearing. During a visit to Southern California with Mom when I was in grad school, Dad seemed lethargic and even confused. His hand tremor was worse than usual. Because one of lithium's effects is to suppress kidney functioning, lithium levels may climb because the chemical is not cleared adequately, especially for older patients. The following morning Mom told me that things were getting worse, as he couldn't even manage to put a key in a lock and had vomited during the night. I hurriedly called UCLA hospital, where he was admitted. With grim resignation, I realized that his confusional state, lethargy, and nausea were all signs of a lithium overdose.

There are few, if any, magic bullets in mental health. I was going it alone in advocating for Dad, but my solo act was teetering. Like battery acid, bitterness and self-blame seared my skin. Often the silent third party during our conversations, Dad's bipolar disorder had reared its head once more.

* * *

I received a post-doctoral fellowship at the Langley Porter Institute of UC San Francisco. When I arrived, the psychiatry department chair was the eminent psychoanalyst Robert Wallerstein. As I was finishing two years later, he yielded to the equally eminent biological psychiatrist Sam Barondes, who studied basic cellular processes. Their approaches were diametrically opposed. Everywhere I looked, the splits in the mental health field seemed unbridgeable.

Roberta had already moved up to Berkeley, to begin her social welfare Master's degree. We rented a house together and finally decided to get married. Who else would have ever supported me? But I was continuing the patterns I'd developed as a boy, too often lacking the spontaneity to go beneath the surface of my routines and control. I had opened up with Jay and a few other friends, I played touch football and basketball as much as I could, and I continued to search for the grand scheme that might solve the riddle of mental illness. But within the most important areas of my life I felt closed off rather than expansive. Far from soaring, I was slowly sinking.

Even so, my academic record continued to grow. My dissertation research, now getting published, revealed that for children displaying major problems with attention and impulse control, the combination of biological treatments (medication) and psychosocial interventions (behavioral and cognitive therapies) made the biggest difference, especially for their social interactions. I applied for a few faculty jobs, turning down several offers because, by now, Roberta was pregnant. Instead I accepted a visiting lecturer position at Berkeley. In the fall I walked excitedly to campus to teach courses and pursue my research, a newcomer with a temporary job amid giants of the field. I knew that it wasn't wise to stay in such a non-tenured position, so the following spring I accepted an assistant professorship back at UCLA. There, at least, I was a known quantity, and we could stay in California. With seven-week-old Jeffrey in the car seat, we drove down Interstate 5 at the tail end of 1986, back to the arid Southern California landscape.

The previous spring, Dad had joined Mom in Palm Springs, where they rented an apartment for several months. As the March days lengthened and the early sunrise suffused their upstairs bedroom with searing light at 5:30 a.m., Dad's mood soared. While visiting them I heard him talk nonstop, unable to rein himself in. Back in Columbus Dr. Southwick had been worried about the side effects of Dad's now-tiny lithium dose and had pulled him off altogether the year before. All spring I hoped beyond hope that Dad's symptoms would stop at the milder phase of hypomania. It was touch and go. Sometimes people with bipolar disorder witness a fading of their cycles later in life, but in other cases, things only intensify. As of yet there's no certain prediction.

Back in Columbus a month later, Dad eagerly attended a talk at Ohio State by R. D. Laing, whose book *The Divided Self* had been the Christmas present I gave him several months before our first major talk. Laing was influential in both psychiatric and existential philosophical circles; Dad had continued to follow his work. After the lecture, he introduced himself and invited "Ronnie" to the house. Somehow, Laing accepted. They drove back and after a brief hello to Mom, Dad pulled out gin, bourbon, and two glasses from the cabinet. Closing the sliding door to the study, he engaged Laing in drink and talk until quite late, before Laing caught a cab back to his hotel.

By that point, Laing had been open in print about his own psychotic experiences, and Dad undoubtedly divulged some of his journeys. I would give a large sum for a tape recording of their discussion.

Dad remained elevated for several months but escaped a major escalation into full-blown mania and hospitalization.

Absent lithium and any real therapeutic support, he managed—through pure luck—to stay sane.

By this time my talks with Dad were changing form. As we sat in his study he began to pull letters and handwritten journal entries from manila folders in his packed file drawers, spreading them across his desk. Some were handwritten notes on yellow legal pads; others were exquisitely typed, double-spaced documents. How long had he been keeping these writings? Who had ever seen them?

In many of them he focused on his boyhood. One entry described how, after his father remarried, his stepmother secured Virgil Sr.'s permission to be the one to look after Junior's discipline. The other boys were getting older, and she saw in him a boy young enough and pliable enough to engage in firm control. Dad reminded me that she'd been a missionary to Latin America, in charge of a religious school. He told me that she praised him in front of houseguests for his academic skills and religious faith but held him to a high standard.

It might start with a small infraction, like failing to put down the toilet seat or talking impudently. She would confront him and order him to her room to await stern punishment. Dad had saved a letter she'd written to her sister in 1925:

> One day this week I was out in front, buying vegetables from the vegetable man, when I saw the children coming home from school down the street. I heard Junior's voice ring out roughly, "Shut up! Don't blow your nose so loud. I'll knock you in the bean!" I came in thinking that was pretty rough and strong coming from one five year old, so as soon as he came in, I asked him, "Junior, were you saying all those things to the little boy down the street that you play with?" He looked a little blank, and then shook his head and said, "No, I didn't say it to <u>him</u>." Then I asked, "Who did you say it to?

They were pretty rough sounding words to anybody." He then said, "I didn't say it to anybody."

And then he began to cry . . . and amid his sobs he said, "I said it to the <u>wind</u>."

Would that not get to you? The <u>wind</u>! Anyway, even to the wind they were not nice words to be yelling on the street.

In the margins of the letter, Dad had added a handwritten note:

When I had finished crying, I was asked to go to the bathroom and bare my buttocks in the corner for spanking. "Never say shut up to anyone or anything," said my stepmother.

A hard switching followed.

Many of Dad's typewritten journal entries focused on the spankings, which grew more intense as he got older. He began one with a recollection of first grade:

Accustomed to stern discipline at home, I found the open classroom atmosphere at the progressive school a welcome change. I soon took advantage of this freedom by acting . . . as I would never dare to act at home in front of my stepmother. In short, I soon became a smart alec. One day as I persisted in talking and laughing with my seatmates (in French class, which was taught in a more structured than open manner), our teacher became exasperated and said: "I don't like your attitude." Whereupon, quick as a wink, I stood up, climbed onto and stood on my desktop, and replied to her: "Well, how do you like my altitude?"

The students laughed and, carried away by my spontaneous outburst, I was unconscious of my rudeness or at least of its possible long-run consequences. Little did I know . . .

He was sent to the principal's office, where a call was made to the family home to report the misdeed. His stepmother answered.

When I got home the whole situation suddenly changed . . . No one else was at home; so she seized that moment for purgative punishment. This spanking was surely the longest I had ever received. "We'll do this once a week until you have learned your lesson," she softly but sternly said. "Plan to be spanked, just like today, for the next three weeks. You may pick the day of the week and the time of the day."

And so it was to be: I <u>asked</u> her for a spanking three more times.

From a continuation of the typed essay, I read the following:

Minor offenses were at first simply verbally corrected after a hard slap or two on each cheek. If such offenses were repeated, I would be asked to go to the bathroom and wait. Out would come the bar of soap and a wet wash cloth while my mother proceeded to vigorously wash out my mouth with soap. The actual washing was not so bad, but her righteous indignation and her size (about five feet four inches tall, but over two hundred pounds in weight) made even such punishment frightening . . . When I was a little older she gave up the soap for castor oil . . . Greater offenses always merited spankings, always bare, at first in the bathroom downstairs and later in my bedroom upstairs . . . The spankings were always hard and always hurt (about 15 to 20 spanks at first), yet even as a five year old I never cried during or after such discipline [as] a matter of pride, defiance, and masochism . . .

Dad wrote in one of his journal entries that although the term was not used at the time and although Nettella's intention was to shape his moral behavior, he came to believe that he was a victim of what today is called child abuse.

I quickly recalibrated. It wasn't just the loss of his mother when he was three; it wasn't just the make-up of his DNA. Something in those punishments had molded his view of himself and the world. What he particularly recalled was that, after a transgression, his stepmother would make him go upstairs and *wait* for the inevitable punishment.

Sometimes the wait in bed was short, sometimes long (an hour or more), but it usually seemed long. Her eyes and face were always very stern at such times, but her manner was that of a high school principal about to punish some tenth-grade girl for breaking rules . . . She spoke calmly but with moral fervor, knowing that no infraction of rules she had laid down was to go unpunished . . . At length, she would always ask: "Do you think you ought to be punished?" I would meekly assent . . . I would then climb on the bed on my knees (in the punishment position) . . . In righteously indignant gestures [she] proceeded with the inevitable—the rhythmic, hard spanking. I can still vividly hear and feel the spank! spank! spank! of this and the many other spankings that were to follow . . .

. . . I believe that it was the first time I was razor strapped that she suggested it would be better if I were tied when strapped so as to avoid injury from my involuntary movements while being whipped . . . As her father, an upright, German-American Methodist, had strapped her, now she must strap me. I am convinced she loved me deeply, and that she thought strapping was necessary to shape me into a good man.

As she initiated the punishments, recalling her missionary days in Latin America, she invoked Spanish to initiate the ritual.

"Presentame, por favor, tus naglas desnudas para zurrarte" or "Please present to me your nude buttocks so I may spank (or whip) you."
"Immediatamente, Madre," I would reply.

Early on, his older brother Bob was occasionally punished alongside him. Dad wrote about their difference in attitude.

When I was young she expressed some astonishment when, on being spanked in turn with my next-older brother, I never cried or cried out even though he did. Later on, she commended me for not crying out when she strapped me harder than she had her senior girls. Astonished though she might have been at my early stoicism, she frequently praised me for it, chiefly because, I have come to think, my silence insured even greater privacy since the on-going ritual . . . was less likely to be overheard.

Right after a particularly hard spanking or strapping, Dad told me, she would rub olive oil into his wounds, providing some relief. The feeling turned into sensual pleasure as he attained puberty, when he began to associate sexual release with his being bound and punished—and then soothed—by his stepmother.

Important research reveals that for bipolar disorder, despite its extraordinarily high heritability, maltreatment can also be a major part of the equation. Individuals with the propensity for manic-depression who also experience trauma tend to have earlier onsets and more frequent, difficult-to-treat episodes. Such experiences predict a worse course of their illness. Simple answers and miracle cures are not in the cards. Integration rather than division is essential.

* * *

As a new parent, I couldn't get over seeing Jeffrey's almost infinite number of changes of expression in the course of an hour, much less a day. UCLA had an infant-care center right in the psychology department, a floor down from my office, so I could feed him while I was at work. But Roberta, now in a new Master's program in public health, longed to return to Northern California. I was ambivalent. UCLA had resources galore, and I was well regarded there. Yet several faculty, despite their best intentions, treated me as a continuing apprentice. Nothing seemed easy.

Research was emerging in the late 1980s that the specific genes responsible for schizophrenia and for bipolar disorder were on the verge of being discovered. The excitement was palpable, but it would take several decades for the sobering truth to emerge that no single gene is responsible for any form of mental illness. Complex gene combinations, in interaction with the environment, yield vulnerability. Emerging knowledge of the ways in which genes are activated epigenetically—through chemical and other environmental signals—has shattered the "nature versus nurture" perspectives so strongly promoted throughout the history of psychiatry and psychology. In the ultimate argument against such a simplistic dichotomy, it may well be the case that the genetic vulnerability for certain forms of psychiatric illness is, in fact, an acute sensitivity to the effects of maltreatment, life stress, or other forms of contextual influence. With such facts in mind, either-or arguments no longer make sense. In short, to understand the origins of mental disorder and to overcome stigma, we have to think broadly and with a multidisciplinary perspective.

Once I'd begun grad school at UCLA in the late 1970s, Mom began to make winter trips to Palm Springs, to help with her severe, systemic rheumatoid arthritis. The warmth will do you good, her rheumatologist had said. Dad could join her in a few weeks once he finished his winter-quarter teaching. Mom loved the desert, its indigo sunsets and Native American art. Whenever possible I made the two-hour drive from LA to see her on weekends. During afternoon drives outside the city limits she opened up. The vast sands beneath the towering peaks all around provided the right context.

During my assistant professor years at UCLA, she told me one afternoon that she had an especially difficult topic to bring up. Speaking about the early years of her and my dad's marriage, she grew tentative. "There was an early sign," she said, "of what was to come." She paused. "This is hard to discuss, Steve."

For the first year of their marriage, they lived in a rented house on the other side of the Olentangy River, not far from campus. She loved that house, she said, which symbolized the promise of their life together. They were looking forward to starting a family one day. Eyes on the highway, the vast sands on all sides, I listened intently.

"But, Steve, your father had what might be called, well, a kinky side. One night, near bedtime, Virg came over to me with a plea. He asked me to tie him up, before we were going to make love."

At first she didn't know what to make of his request, but the look in his eye told her that he was completely serious. " 'Just like my stepmother used to do to me,' he said, 'when I was growing up and she punished me.' " Hardly believing what Mom was saying, I froze.

Mom continued. " 'Tie you up?' I said back to him. Steve, I didn't know what to think. I couldn't imagine what I'd got myself into, a Midwestern girl like me. Most of my friends had married their high school sweethearts. Here I was with this magnetic philosopher from California, with a past I knew nothing about."

For a moment, the only sound was the hum of the tires on the flat gray pavement.

"I quickly planned my response. I knew that I needed to be clear with him. I told him distinctly: 'Virgil, I'm not your step-mother, I'm not your keeper, and I'm not your mistress. I'm your wife. I won't tie you up.' "

I silently calculated. His stepmother had tied him to his bed to deliver her punishments. So had the orderlies at Norwalk, to prevent his wandering at night. Fellow inmates at Byberry had secured him to a pommel horse before beating him.

The picture was coming into focus. Was there any other way for Dad?

For decades Mom had carried a crippling load—of Dad's madness, of society's imposed stigma and silence regarding anything related to mental illness, of needing to stay hypervigilant to ensure our survival as a family. The effort had pushed her immune system into high alert, prompting her debilitating arthritis. But her spirit had never broken.

She was finishing her story. "Then and there, Steve, I knew that things in our marriage would never be as I'd planned."

The stillness inside the car was absolute.

Progressive Decline

12

On a damp night in the early spring of 2009 I gave a reading in Berkeley about my recently published book, *The Triple Bind*. In front of the sizable crowd I discussed the book's central premise, that cultural pressures have made teenage girls ever more vulnerable to depression, binge eating, and self-harm, especially those with genetic vulnerabilities or experiences of maltreatment. As girls increasingly experience the message of needing to be both nurturing and kind and academically and athletically competitive—while doing so effortlessly and with a "hot" look—helplessness and internalization frequently result.

Once the question-and-answer period began, an elderly gentleman sitting near the back was among the first to raise his hand. He stood up shakily. The crowd strained to hear his articulate yet faltering voice. "I want the audience to know," he said, "that I am experiencing déjà vu. Many years ago I was a student of Professor Hinshaw's father, the esteemed Virgil Hinshaw, at the Ohio State University." An audible murmur sounded.

Trying to mask my shock, I replied to his question and several others. Afterward, he slowly walked to the podium and introduced himself as Joel Fort—a prominent Bay Area psychologist with strong interests in legal and ethical issues as well as substance abuse. He had fought for progressive policies all his life and had even testified in the Patty Hearst case during the seventies, countering the defense claim of "brainwashing" after her abduction. The topic he most wanted to discuss, however, was Dad. We ended up seeing each other a number of times before he passed away in 2015. During those years Joel surpassed 80 years of age and showed progressive signs of physical decline. Yet he was still enthusiastically engaged in remembrance.

In 1946, I learned, he had been admitted to OSU as a precocious 16-year-old, in an early version of today's honors programs. He was drawn to the fields of philosophy and psychology. Particularly captivating, he said, was a magnetic new professor in the philosophy department, Virgil Hinshaw, Jr., from whom he took an introductory course. He'd met with Hinshaw in the professor's office, and the young faculty member and his colleagues had invited him and other students to talks in the community. New worlds were opening up. Joel deeply appreciated the mentorship, particularly because he lacked a real peer group on campus.

The next year he signed up for an advanced course, an erudite tour of the philosophy of science. The dense syllabus, mimeographed a bright purple, rang out with major questions: In what ways do scientific theories form? Can ethics be based on a foundation of logic? How can progress in human thought be measured? Sitting at a restaurant in Berkeley, his hand shaking from a palsy he was developing, Joel told me that each lecture was more enticing than the last. The philosophy department was transforming, he said, inspired by their most recent hire to pursue twentieth-century logical positivism as well as the classics.

Toward the end of the fall '47 quarter, chairs creaked as the students hurried into the small amphitheater. Joel, the enthused sophomore, marveled at his good fortune. Whispers and bustling ceased as Professor Hinshaw entered the classroom, black hair swept back over his forehead, his gaze intense. What new vistas might be revealed today?

But from the first words at the podium, Joel knew that something was terribly wrong. Hinshaw gazed above their foreheads, a far-off look in his eye. Haughty and self-assured, he spoke without notes, his voice strangely commanding.

"Today we consider our origins," he proclaimed. "Behold the primordial era, filled with dinosaurs, cavemen, and primitive love. The secret of humanity lies therein!"

The students stared at their notebooks, but the syllabus yielded no connection between the scheduled topic and these rash pronouncements. Hardly pausing, their professor wove a tale of the beginnings of modern humans, focusing on the emergence of empathy from the caves, with man and woman in eternal rapture.

"Battling the elements," he was now shouting, "overcoming predators, finding its way, humanity prevailed. Cooperation emerged from stark, brute competition! Primitive lust transformed into sensual, deep love! The human species rose to new heights!"

Was this some kind of joke? Joel had initially wondered. But the conviction in his professor's voice made it clear that whatever was happening was no laughing matter.

Hinshaw was finishing his impromptu lecture. "The Lord has overseen the evolution of our species. The newly formed human spirit will never be broken!"

As he recounted the story, Joel's face filled with a blend of compassion and horror. It had dawned on him during the lecture that Hinshaw's inspiration had come from the 1940 film *One Million B.C.*, starring Victor Mature, Carole Landis, and Lon Chaney, Jr. A fable depicting the plight of early humans, the movie was woefully inexact, mixing cavemen and cavewomen with dinosaurs. Even so, it had been nominated for two Oscars. Completely lacking in accuracy and utterly melodramatic, it was just the kind of film that Dad would have lambasted when in his right mind.

Indeed, how did the thread of the course relate to this Hollywood epic? The linkages, it was clear, existed solely in the professor's fantasies. Despondent, Joel realized that his beloved mentor had become floridly psychotic right in front of the class.

Following the mystifying tirade, the students filed silently from their seats, eyes averted. Thinking fast, Joel formed a strategy. Back in his room, he pulled out the campus telephone directory. Lifting the black receiver from its cradle, he dialed the chair of the psychology department, Professor Julian Rotter, a noted personality and clinical psychologist. To Joel's surprise, the secretary put him right through, and he recounted what had just occurred in the classroom. Rotter was compassionate and forthright, giving assurance that he would take necessary steps. Indeed, rumors had surfaced regarding the new professor's instability once he'd finished grad school at Princeton, though no one could ever say precisely what had happened. When illnesses are stigmatized, mystery and innuendo take precedence over any truth.

A visiting professor was brought in to cover the final class meetings, but what would become of Professor Hinshaw? It was the suddenness that stayed with him, Joel lamented, the utter surprise of witnessing such complete irrationality from a mind he'd revered. Joel's first experience of serious mental disorder had floored him.

The following year Joel departed for the University of Chicago to complete his undergraduate years before pursuing graduate studies in psychology. Yet his lasting remembrance of Ohio State was how his professor's usual intellect and demeanor had vanished overnight.

Within days of the incident, I've surmised, Dad was committed to his first stay at Columbus State Hospital, the massive mental facility on the west side of the city. This was his third involuntary commitment, following Norwalk as a teen—where he received no intervention whatsoever—and Byberry as a newly minted Ph.D., with its insulin coma therapy and reported beatings. This time, his wild thoughts and fantastic pronouncements were masked by sedative medications and his initial experience with ECT. Why, he wondered, must I once again replace my clothes with the drab uniforms of inmates, with no belts allowed over the baggy pants, to prevent self-hanging? Each day's routine was interrupted by shouts of despair and rage in some corner of the wards. Who would get sent to solitary lock-up today?

Somehow, the episode abated within a few weeks and he was released. Back on campus for winter quarter, he never spoke of his detour into madness. He'd learned to pick up the pieces and forge ahead. If anyone were to know, they'd understand only that he'd become one of the forgotten—less than human, little more than a beast.

Although he wouldn't have phrased it as such, by that time Dad was clearly experiencing *anticipated stigma:* the fear of what might happen if the world were to know about his flaw, his mark. This expectation is a particular concern for groups with hidden or potentially concealable stigmas, like mental illness. If everyone can readily see your "difference," such as skin color or being bound to a wheelchair, there's no secret to keep. But if the issue is hidden, the choice of whether or not to reveal always lurks. What friends will you lose? What jobs won't you get? Will you ever attain an intimate relationship? Not only does anticipated stigma prevent disclosure but it stops people from taking on important life challenges. When trauma and maltreatment enter the mix, stigma and shame typically escalate, as victims tend to blame themselves—and keep such experiences secret.

Like so many others of his era, Dad did everything in his

power to hide what had transpired during those periods in his life when his mind had spun out of control. He expected the worst if people were to know—for good reason, given the abject stigma of the times. How different his life might have been had he been able to safely tell his future wife, his colleagues, and his friends about his lifelong struggles. How much freer he might have felt with the support of peers who had lost their way, just as he had.

Later that year he was introduced to a striking graduate student in history, Alene Pryor. Intensely attracted to each other after their blind date, they saw more and more of each other and later became engaged. His chapter on Einstein's social and moral philosophy was causing a stir, as were the sole-authored publications he'd written while a graduate student at Princeton. Once again, his trajectory was ascendant.

If only he could cling to the rational side of existence; if only he could maintain absolute silence about the chaos. No one might ever know.

My own name was climbing the academic ladder. I was conducting federally supported summer programs for kids with behavior disorders, writing empirical articles and theoretical papers on the development of children's mental health problems, and giving talks at national and international conferences. I was the favored son back at UCLA, which had opened a child study center the year I returned, a terrific base for the work I was doing. Yet I realized that I'd always be viewed by my colleagues as the up-and-coming youngster, a glorified gofer, rather than a true adult, an independent scholar.

Still, I wondered whether I could make it happen anywhere else. During my second year back in Southern California, Berkeley finally listed an assistant professor position. I couldn't imagine uprooting so soon and let it pass. By some miracle the slot remained unfilled, and the following fall I received plaintive phone calls from Berkeley faculty asking for my application. Moments before the deadline, I raced to send my materials via Federal Express. My having waited until the last minute betrayed my ambivalence.

Beneath the strategic debates over where best to thrive as a professor and father, behind the back-and-forth with Roberta about a potential return to the Bay Area, the real reason for my conflict went deeper. When he was reaching his thirties—the same age that I was now—Dad had already begun a slow, inexorable decline, fueled by his devastating episodes and brutal hospitalizations, including his journey back to 1,000,000 B.C. just as his career was launching. During the early years of his marriage, after he'd achieved tenure, he spent considerable time in hospitals following wildly erratic episodes, gradually losing his professional edge. Although many philosophers, mathematicians, and physicists perform their seminal work while in their twenties, Dad's misdiagnosed and maltreated mental illness had clearly sped his demise.

So how could I be eclipsing Dad? *He* was the one who'd set out to pursue life's fundamental questions; *he* was the one who'd rescued me when I'd been lost. Surpassing him felt like a betrayal. With the benefit of hindsight, I understand that I was experiencing survivor guilt, which emerges when someone makes it through a disaster while others succumb. Consequences include self-blame, guilt, and a view of one's own life as insignificant. Maybe I hadn't survived a plane crash, but it felt as though I were combing through wreckage of a different sort, and it was troubling to me that I'd dared to transcend the family legacy.

By winter, I'd made the finalist group at Berkeley and interviewed during torrential February rains, in the days when such storms actually happened. I spent the last morning of my three days of presentations and meetings beside the hospital bed of the former head of the clinical psychology program, Shelly Korchin. He was the psychologist who'd interviewed the

Mercury astronauts years before, founded the modern clinical psychology program at Berkeley, and took a liking to me during his waning years when I did my visiting professor stint. He'd become acutely ill with a relapse of his long-standing cancer but insisted on being a part of the search committee. He cast his vote for me just in time, surviving my visit and the crucial meetings just weeks before passing away. Though it took half a year to receive the formal offer, I was clearing out my UCLA office the following fall.

Following the anguish related to the decision, a strange thing happened when I arrived on the Berkeley campus. From my first morning I felt propelled by a jet stream. I knew instantly that this was my chance to make an independent mark. I'd almost stayed back in Columbus after high school out of unspoken guilt; I'd almost decided to play out my academic career at UCLA, where things felt like a sure bet. Each time something pushed me to forge ahead. Sometimes you just have to trust your gut.

Berkeley's psychology building is named for Edward Tolman, the eminent scientist whose classic work of the 1930s and 1940s revealed that even rodents running a maze use mental maps to guide their behavior. In essence, he was the founder of modern cognitive psychology. Yet Tolman quit Berkeley during the 1950s rather than sign the newly formed loyalty oath for California employees, a legacy of McCarthyism. After his protest registered far and wide, he returned to Berkeley in triumph a few years later, where he ended his career. Upon arriving, I felt that I was breathing rarefied air.

Still, many of my days were lonely. I was the only assistant professor in the department, and for much of the week I was a single parent because Roberta had entered UCLA's doctoral program in public health, commuting each week back to Southern California to work toward her degree.

But with the hills looming right above the campus and the Bay in sight, the quality of the air was striking. Starting in late

January and stretching until June, the Northern California spring yields new blossoms every few weeks in a continual reawakening. I created an undergraduate course on developmental psychopathology, covering the continuing interplay between biology and context to shape disorder and resilience. Things continued to heat up career-wise. I was awarded a major grant, as one of six investigators for a cross-site study involving a clinical trial of medication, behavioral treatment, and their combination to alter the trajectory of academic and behavioral problems of children with serious attention deficits and impulsivity. I sailed through tenure review, which I'd delayed with the move, and received full professorship a couple of years later. I had launched.

To find order amid chaos, scientists seek patterns. To organize the vast amounts of raw material in front of them, they create schemes and hierarchies. They classify.

It worked for the periodic table of elements, where ordered rows provide insights about the atomic mechanisms underlying matter. It worked, with adjustments to incorporate modern genetics, for Linneaus's classification of the plant and animal kingdoms into subdivisions, all the way down to species. It worked, too, for the eons, eras, periods, epochs, and ages of geological time, which organize the age of the earth according to strata and striations of rock (think, for example, of the Cretaceous and Jurassic). Medical classifications, involving symptoms, signs, syndromes, and diseases, have helped to save countless lives.

Shouldn't it be the same for people's impairing problems of behavior and emotion, which are now termed mental disorders? If only we could organize and classify this huge array of distress, we might leave the Dark Ages of uncertainty, mystery, and fear. No more guesswork; no more stigma. Used throughout much of the world, the *International Classification of Diseases* includes a section on mental disorders. In the United States, the *DSM* is the psychiatric bible. Its third edition dominated my learning during my internship.

Emerging into the world of scientific psychology, I was convinced that answers were close at hand. Mental illness should be part of a rational science. Through the placement of a person's unusual and troubling symptoms into a psychiatric classification scheme, progress should mount. The task would not be simple, of course, given the myriad ways in which humans interact with the world, the vast complexity of the brain, and the troubling lack of any "neural signature" for specific conditions. Still, diagnosis could remove personal and family blame by locating the problem in an ordered system. Treatment strategies would follow suit, each linked to a diagnosis within the classification. Mental illness might finally be solved!

But like many others in the field, I was slowly coming to a different realization. Such an architectural guide glosses over the realities of people's emotions, conflicts, coping strategies, and lives. Even more, different people with the identical diagnosis, like serious depression or bipolar disorder, may actually be quite different: Their similar symptoms can betray different vulnerabilities, risks, and developmental pathways. Multiple roads may lead to Rome, but these disparate patterns are masked by traditional diagnosis.

Even more, environments shape behavior at the same time that individuals select and interpret their particular contexts, meaning that *reciprocal* processes are frequently at work. Over time, repeated reciprocal patterns yield *transactions,* when reciprocal patterns spiral and consolidate. Finally, *transformations* emerge when even a small change in transactions brings forth a new configuration—as when a difficult life event pushes a vulnerable individual into serious dysfunction. Putting a diagnostic box around such complicated processes can obscure the living, breathing person in question.

Unlike inanimate objects, people respond to the ways they're classified. Receiving a diagnosis of mental disorder might lead to liberation, relief from shame and doubt, and the motivation to seek treatment, but it might also promote demoralization and dehumanization if the person's essence is lost—and if mental illness continues to be viewed as shameful. Coming to this understanding shattered my certainties. To make sense of it all, I knew that I'd have to grasp the complexity of transaction and to comprehend people's experiences, behind the diagnoses per se. To comprehend transformations, I needed to transform.

Dad was graduate secretary for Princeton's class of 1945, the year he completed his dissertation. On visits home I would see him dutifully typing up the remembrances classmates had sent him for the alumni newsletter. Every June, he traveled to Princeton for the graduation ceremony. Sometimes Mom accompanied him so they could make a weekend of it.

On one trip during the late 1980s they spent the night in Philadelphia before their return to Columbus. The next morning, Dad told me in his study a few months later, he became obsessed with finding Philadelphia State Hospital—Byberry—where he'd spent five long months in the spring and summer of 1945. Dad said that he'd searched maps and finally figured out how to get there, even though suburbanization had rendered the surrounding environs nearly unrecognizable. When they finally reached the site, Dad scratched his head: The only buildings around were abandoned ruins, with apartments, office structures, and malls nearby. It dawned on him that the monolithic structure was in the process of being razed.

Had the events there really happened? Were his recollections of the terror, beatings, and insulin coma treatments real? Or had he imagined the whole thing? He needed proof, but the proof was vanishing before his eyes.

* * *

With the raw material of Dad's writings now available to me, I felt like an astronomer with a more powerful telescope. One afternoon I scrutinized an undated yellow legal pad from his mass of files. The frenetic writing was a jarring shift from his usually elegant strokes. He described those months at Norwalk County Hospital when he was turning 17, following his abortive attempt at flight to save the world from Fascism.

- At one with the world—'in, but not of, this world'
- Celestial music of the spheres, all night long, since I slept so little
- In the Hallway of Hell, with micro-and macrocephalics . . .
- Tried to relive my own infancy and childhood, or the infancy of Vergil, the Roman Poet, especially as to the learning of language. Likewise, to probe the origin of all language, from the baby Vergil's/Virgil's first words. Are many of the Latin words echoic in origin, and related to the breathing patterns of a baby? Was I, in some respects, the Vergil of the Aeneid? Is there metempsychosis? Reincarnation?

No mention of refusing to eat the food—which he'd imagined to be poisoned—at the facility, leaving him at a skeletal weight and near death, yet plenty of evidence as to his grandiose thoughts.

Other pads revealed crowded passages, where his notes in the margins were dizzyingly connected by a series of wild arrows in some sort of jumbled code. Although recalling earlier times of mind expansion, he must have been plenty elevated at the time he wrote these lines, as well:

In madness and high enthusiasm, bizarre behavior is explained by the presence in the world of a mysterious power, which may enter the person and make him/her its instrument. In the Old Testament, power called <u>ruah</u> or <u>breath</u>. Thus Sampson's strength, the insanity of Saul . . . An age was anticipated when God would "pour out his spirit on all flesh" . . . Cf. applications to feels, grimaces, gestures, etc., that "recall," however subtly, some previous gesture in a similar situation: A hand to wipe away a tear now when there is no tear . . . an apparently warm buttocks when now thinking of or contemplating doing something for which such an act, when done as a youth or child, was thoroughly punished.

Why had it taken me so long? Dad completely anticipated his hospitalizations, which were as inevitable to him as the strappings his stepmother had meted out decades before. Mental illness and hospitalization were a deserved series of tortures, punishments he'd brought on through his lack of faith and his failings of character.

In one essay Dad referred to Goffman. For some of the sociologist's key books—like *Stigma* and *Asylums*—he had spent months living in a mental hospital in order to understand the experience. He coined the term "total institution" to describe the dehumanization inherent in giving over one's complete identity to a prison, hospital, or death camp. In his typewritten journal, Dad likened the act of forgoing his own clothes and anticipating judgment at Norwalk, Byberry, or Columbus State to awaiting, with his pants down, his early punishments, when he had to choose their mode, timing, and severity. In Dad's mind, the processes were one and the same.

When Jeffrey and I were back in Columbus over a holiday in the early nineties, Mom took us to the community residential facility where her older sister, Virginia—Aunt Ginny Ann—was housed. The rooms were beautiful and light, the antithesis of a traditional state institution. Now in her seventies, Ginny Ann had bobbed white hair. We noticed the staff's devotion to her, even though she hadn't walked or talked since she was a girl and even though it was clear from her vacant expression that she never would again. Still, her behavioral goals for independent functioning were posted each week for all staff to see. Years later, Jeffrey told me how frightened he was of the facility, with the wheelchairs and grunts and vague smells of antiseptic from the bathrooms. Silent tragedy had become the legacy of not only Dad's side of the family but Mom's. Still, the setting gave me renewed hope that the movement toward humanization might continue.

With their love of the desert, Mom and Dad decided to purchase a town house in Palm Springs, a few blocks from the apartment they'd rented each winter. The pool, framed by flowering trees and palms, provided an oasis, with Mt. San Jacinto straight behind, towering over 10,000 feet straight up from the sea-level desert. During my visits Dad and I found time to talk whenever we could. As always, the conversations revealed an alternate reality, more vibrant than most any other I'd experienced.

As he sat by the pool one morning before anyone else had ventured outside, I saw his poignant expression. His eyes tilted upward, a sign that he was seeking some kind of higher meaning. "Throughout my life I've longed for some way of understanding my difficult experiences," he said. "I've sought explanation for what was happening to me."

He took a breath. "There are times that I'd wished I had cancer."

Temporarily stunned, I listened in silence. "Cancer?" I finally repeated. Was Dad losing his rationality before my eyes?

"Cancer is a real illness," he calmly proceeded. "But each of my experiences was related to a *mental* illness. Think of the very term: an illness of the mind." He noted what it meant to a philosopher to have such a disease: Perhaps everything he'd experienced was fabricated, just a figment of his imagination.

"How I've longed to have a real illness," he summed up.

I knew better than to protest by proclaiming the reality of mental illness or reminding him of the current science regarding the role of genes in relation to bipolar disorder. The implication was clear. If people with mental disorders are convinced that the core problem lies in their own flawed character—and that their symptoms are somehow imagined—little wonder that engagement in treatment is low and self-stigma high. When brutal "care" occurs during one's formative years, as it had for Dad at Norwalk, any later book learning won't stand a chance of erasing one's core identity.

Dad had smoked since he was a teen, having started in earnest during his first episode of manic grandiosity on the streets of Pasadena. As befitting a philosopher, he gravitated toward pipes but still kept up with cigarettes. At the end of the 1980s, a few months before his seventieth birthday, he went cold turkey, in full knowledge of the health risks he'd been incurring. There was little fanfare but he was proud nonetheless. Yet within several months he began to experience problems with his voice. He couldn't maintain its volume; his words sounded raspy. When we spoke on the phone, I kept asking him to speak up. His doctor thought initially that he had a throat infection but medicines did no good. It was the first sign. Indeed, it's now understood that the nicotine in cigarette smoke may mask the onset of movement disorders like Parkinson's.

When he and Mom flew out to Northern California for our first Thanksgiving back in Berkeley in the fall of 1990, I watched him attempt to stand up or change direction. He would suddenly freeze, temporarily immobile. Although deeply proud that I was at Berkeley, he looked frail, having shed many pounds despite no change in diet.

The next spring he received an invitation to speak at the prestigious Gordon Research Conferences, which take place each year in New England. He prepared a paper entitled "The

Dialectics of Control," expansively blending Aristotle, Plato, Hume, Marx and Engels, and R. D. Laing. Mom traveled with him and attended his session. She told me afterward that when he tried to deliver his paper, he couldn't quite turn the pages of his notes, losing his sequence. Sadly, she noted the vast difference from his captivating lectures so many years before when his career was launching.

Nowadays when we greeted each other, Dad gave me a stiff hug, far different from his lifelong handshake. He traveled to the Bay Area that fall for his fiftieth class reunion at Stanford, for the Class of '41, but his facial muscles seemed encased in plaster. Classmates and friends commented on his changed demeanor and reduced strength.

The next summer I traveled with Jeffrey, five and a half, to visit his grandparents in Columbus. Dad and I took him to a playground one afternoon at the height of the stultifying humidity, watching his exuberant play on the swings and beams. Dad got an eager expression on his face; I could tell that he wanted to walk out onto the huge wooden climbing structure to join his grandson. Yet the instant I tried to help him up the small stairs to the platform, he became dead weight in my hands. He retreated with baby steps.

"What's happening, Dad?" I asked softly.

"It's the 'fraids,'" he replied, once he'd backed down. "When I was a little boy and something frightened me, I called it getting the 'fraids.'" Being afraid was now compounded by a growing inability to move. Firmly implanted on the sand, we watched Jeffrey careen through the structure.

Once more I took on the role of advocate. Dad was seeing a senior neurologist at OSU, so I typed out a cogent life history of his episodes, treatments, and hospitalizations to send back to Columbus. No surprise: The evaluation revealed the onset of a Parkinson's-like illness, replete with slowing, motor freezing, shuffling, balance problems, and weight loss, plus a tremor that looked different from his earlier lithium-induced one. More troublesome was the potential for Lewy-body dementia down the road, a complex variant of Parkinson's that involves not just motor areas of the brain but regions and pathways underlying cognition. Dad was initially prescribed L-DOPA, just as Ezra had been all those years ago. Yet no miracle cure was at hand, and his decline slowly continued.

The following year I noticed a sign at Berkeley for a conference to be held in a couple of months' time, encompassing the history of science. Cal and Stanford historians and philosophers would present on epistemology, theory of knowledge, and the progress of scientific thought. Maybe, I hoped, Dad could fly up from Palm Springs in April, stay over at our house, and attend. But could he fly alone? Mom and I decided that, if she could get him as close as possible to the departure gate and notify the flight attendants, he might be able to manage the trip. On the phone, Dad seemed eager.

On arrival day I drove Jeffrey to Oakland airport to meet Grandpa. In those pre-9/11 days we could stand right next to the gate and greet him as soon as he slowly stepped off the jetway. His face was gaunt, and the walk toward baggage claim seemed like a funeral march. At the escalator leading down, he inched his way to the edge of the moving stairs and started to lift his foot but stopped short, as though stricken. The people waiting behind us were clearly annoyed. I begged indulgence and the three of us slowly turned around and headed to the elevator. "I just didn't know how to coordinate my foot with the moving step," Dad said on the short ride down. "I'm sorry."

The next morning in the packed lecture hall, I couldn't get over how many speakers and attendees knew Dad, as they came over to greet him during breaks. It was impossible to miss their expressions as they saw his changed state. The talks were impressive: How did the first experimental science emerge in the seventeenth and eighteenth centuries? What issues remain in understanding how knowledge advances? Are Kuhn's ideas of scientific paradigms valid? Dad drifted off periodically but made an effort to follow when he was awake.

At the end of the afternoon we slowly walked to the other side of campus for the reception. Dad was thrilled but slightly confused. On the patio of the faculty club, drinking gin and tonics with him in the incomparable spring twilight, I understood that he had attended his last academic conference.

Nighttime in Palm Springs a year later, the sky was black velvet. Illuminated from within, the swimming pool was utterly still. Dad had deteriorated further. He could barely keep his balance when he stood up. Reading philosophy was now a thing of the past. Still intact, however, was his ability to contemplate and discuss the past.

It had been a good day. Grandpa relished the time with Jeffrey, whose happy but volatile temperament reminded him of himself as a boy. "How I wish I could go barefoot again," he said wistfully. In spare moments, he recalled his boyhood adventures: taking the streetcar to downtown Los Angeles, serving as squad captain for his junior-high sports teams, arguing with his brothers about economic strategies during the Depression.

After 9:00, with Jeffrey fast asleep following dinner on the patio, father and son headed outside, as I eyed carefully the stone path and stairs. The stars pressed down from above. We paused to look toward the massive mountains to the west.

"I've been contemplating," Dad finally said, holding on to the back of a chair for balance. I strained to make out his faint words. "What a marvelous life I've had. Imagine the people I've met, the students I've taught, the ideas I've shared. Some experiences were terrifying, especially the times in mental hospitals. But every experience was revealing."

I marveled at his stance. Many of his experiences were of the sort that I'd tortured myself for years to fend off.

His voice gathered steam. "In fact, I wouldn't trade any experience I've ever had. Not a one!" I was silent. "What a rich life I've had!"

When considering his plight I mainly felt agitation, regret, and anger, especially over the ignorant yet overly self-assured profession that supposedly treated him. How might I ever gain even a fraction of Dad's philosophical attitude, his sense of wonder?

We pondered the soft blue-green of the pool for a few more moments before it was time to return. I guided him by the arm in the dark as we inched our way to the front door of the townhouse.

The End
and the Beginning

13

With my expanded sense of mission, which included ever-stronger motivation to understand stigma, I hunkered down in my home study on a gray winter morning in 2003. My core reading that day was a book by the noted medical historian Gerald Grob, entitled *The Mad Among Us: A History of the Care of America's Mentally Ill.* Provocative and authoritative, the book highlights attitudes and practices toward mental illness from the colonial period through the modern era. Periods of reform and despair, Grob argues, are cyclic rather than linear, with the social action of one era too often leading to the repression of the next. The book's material is compelling, motivating a search for the kinds of change in mental health that might really last.

Reading intently, I felt my eyes begin to tire by late morning. For a break I turned to the sections of illustrations and photographs in the book's middle. Ordered chronologically, they were fascinating in their own right. One was an early lithograph of McLean Hospital outside of Boston, which included the formal title of "lunatic asylum." Others depicted attempted reforms, as the state hospitals became ever larger and more inhumane during the late nineteenth and twentieth centuries. As I thumbed through the last section of more recent photos, a caption caught my eye, stating that the picture above was of a men's dorm room at Philadelphia State Hospital, known as Byberry, in the 1940s.

Wait! Dad had been at Byberry right at that time. Suddenly I was on full alert, all weariness erased.

Authoritative sources reveal that Byberry was severely overcrowded and widely regarded as the worst mental hospital in the United States. It had been the subject of a *Life* magazine exposé entitled "Bedlam 1946" and was the partial inspiration for the book and film *The Snake Pit,* which raised the consciousness of the nation in the late 1940s about the plight of people placed in such warehouses. My eyes leapt to the photo above: a stark blackand-white image of a large room filled wall to wall with beds—utterly sterile, totally dehumanizing. The photo on the facing page portrayed wide-eyed, despairing women wandering aimlessly in one of Byberry's ghastly rooms. The crowding was so severe that there was no place to sit.

Over the following years I viewed newly created websites documenting the history of the Byberry monolith, which at its peak held 7,000 inmates, far above capacity. Photos taken by conscientious objectors who'd been placed at Byberry during the latter years of World War II—the same time Dad had been an inmate—were smuggled out, graphically portraying naked, gaunt men in stark, empty dayrooms. Raw sewage permeated hallways. Testimony from the 1940s documented beatings and deaths, at the hands of both staff and fellow patients. Officially suppressed, these accounts are now part of the institution's legacy of horror. Byberry had been the home of the ultimate in stigmatization.

That winter morning, the images from another infamous *Life* magazine issue jumped into my mind, the ones taken during the liberation of the camps in the spring of 1945. In those iconic photos, emaciated inmates lean blankly toward the camera from stacked double- and triple-bunk beds, eyes bulging, with starvation hours or days away. The settings were all too similar: the same rooms full of urine and excrement, the same bone-filled faces beyond despair, the same stripping of any semblance of dignity. The same utter hopelessness, outside the watch of mainstream society. The hair at the back of my neck stood straight up.

In his 1948 book, *The Shame of the States,* which unveiled the despicable realities inside U.S. mental institutions, Albert Deutsch described the conditions he observed:

> As I passed through some of Byberry's wards I was reminded of the pictures of the Nazi concentration camps. I entered a building swarming with naked humans herded like cattle and treated with less concern, pervaded by a fetid odor so heavy, so nauseating, that the stench seemed to have almost a physical existence of its own.

I'd long wondered whether Dad's accounts of Byberry had been exaggerated. Had he truly been beaten by fellow inmates as staff blocked access to the physical therapy room? Was the setting as depraved and inhumane as he'd intimated to me and recorded in his journals? Perhaps his psychotic thinking had been doing the talking. But the photographs, captions, and text before my eyes were no delusions. After all, Hitler's objectives were to rid the earth not only of Jews but also of gypsies, gay men and lesbian women, "mental defectives"—those with intellectual disabilities—and people with serious mental illness. As a student of history, Dad knew. As a patient, he bore witness.

In the car with his brother Randall, translating the road signs into German, had Dad actually been overseas escaping from a camp? Of course not. But he'd been preoccupied with the Nazis since he was a teen. His obsession, fueled by his grandiose mania and underlying despair, led to his near-demise at age 16. At

Norwalk, having lost 60 pounds after refusing to eat because of a Nazi plot only he understood, he resembled a camp survivor himself, given up for dead by the administrators. At Byberry, he wore filthy, institutional clothes, and crowded his body into the narrow bunk each night for a few hours of relief from the daily torment.

Without bidding, the ending of *Lost Horizon* raced into my mind. Conway had fled Shangri-La with a small group but realized that he had lost his chance at immortality. He was desperate to return but the question lingered: Had the entire scene at the lamasery been real, or was it just a figment of his overstressed imagination? While there he'd fallen in love with Lo-Tsen, a beautiful young harpsichordist. She'd departed Shangri-La with his group and soon accompanied him to a doctor, because Conway had become ill. Characters in the book who wished to confirm Conway's fantastic story about Shangri-La, and the near-immortality it conferred, later found this Chinese doctor, who revealed, in broken English, that the woman was not young and beautiful but old—the most old of anyone he'd ever seen.

These words served as the confirmation: Once she'd left Shangri-La, Lo-Tsen had quickly reverted to her true age, well beyond that of any other humans. The High Lama had told the truth: Shangri-La was real.

The revelations of that February morning served as my own confirmation. Dad hadn't lied. Underneath his psychotic thoughts and beliefs lay the reality of what was transpiring at Byberry. The stigma of mental illness was far from a small, tangential issue. Instead, it was life or death.

My project to understand this concept, I now realized, would go far deeper than I'd ever imagined.

Ten years earlier, with the multicenter treatment grant now awarded, I found myself at another interminable meeting in

Washington, DC, with a large group of psychologists and psychiatrists from the six selected research centers around the country. Our goal was to plan and design a definitive treatment trial. A core requirement was that each team must travel to the National Institute of Mental Health (NIMH) every month for planning sessions. These interdisciplinary meetings served as a defining moment of my early career.

But could those meetings ever drag on.

One of the NIMH scientists supervising the investigation was a brilliant developmental psychologist, John Richters. John was a bit different: He wandered the perimeter of the tables for much of the meeting time, making bird calls and warbles during any lull in the proceedings. Sitting still did not play to his strengths, as his subsequent diagnosis of adult ADHD made clear. Yet when there was a conceptual point to be made about research design or measurement strategies, his laser focus and incisive comments cut to the bone.

In spare moments outside the meeting room he told me about his background and upbringing, dominated by harsh, abusive discipline. "Think of *The Great Santini*," he told me, describing his military father. John stole cars at an early age and later spent time at juvenile detention facilities. His life went almost permanently off track, but well after the age when most young adults had graduated from college—without even a ninth-grade education behind him—he finally embarked upon higher education. He earned top honors and went on to become a distinguished grad student. Ever since, he'd won awards for his incisive analyses of developmental issues in child mental health. Feisty, demanding, obstreperous, and wickedly funny, John was a trip.

The meetings sometimes went on well into the night, as arguments raged about recruitment strategies for families, the correct assessment tools, the value of medication versus psychological treatments, ensuring that interventions are delivered with an eye to high quality and fidelity, and tailoring treatments to each child while maintaining the integrity of a randomized, experimental trial. The stakes were high, as the investigation was—and still is—the largest treatment study for children with mental health problems in the history of NIMH.

When things got deadly in the meeting room, John and I would sneak out to the hotel corridors. Every time we spoke the ideas ignited like a brush fire, sparks jumping from branch to branch. One afternoon he asked me about my background. Bleary-eyed, still on Pacific time, and wondering whether we should perhaps return to the meeting room in case a crucial vote might be coming up, I took the plunge. I brought up Dad, Pasadena, Russell and Einstein, hospitalizations, schizophrenia versus bipolar disorder, and the talks that had begun during my first spring break from college. I went quickly but left nothing out.

As I continued talking John's eyes got big. Soon he was nodding, gesturing, and leaning in toward me with each phrase. At one point he stepped back, lifted his hands up high, and then reached forward to grab me by the shoulders.

"Steve, do you know what you're telling me?" he half-yelled, his voice super-charged. "Don't you understand the importance of your dad's story?" He was six inches from my face. "Write about it and talk about it!"

I nodded back. This was my first public commitment, even if my public was at that point just one extremely animated individual.

Flying home on yet another transcontinental flight, I began to gather my thoughts. In spare moments the first outlines emerged. Over the following years I began to speak publicly about Dad, as well as our family and myself, having finally overcome the hesitancy, secrecy, and shame that had been the core curriculum of my childhood. In 2002 I published a monograph emphasizing the clinical reality of bipolar disorder through the example of Dad's life.

Analyzing our family's history impressed upon me, more than ever, the horrendous concept of stigma. Although I hadn't admitted it before, but the very term is noxious. When speaking it aloud, you can't help but notice its sounds—the occlusive "t" and "g" consonants—that spit out from your throat and then lodge there. Its meanings are equally severe, as the individuals in the degraded group are branded as outcasts: shameful, offensive, and less than fully human. Underneath the toxic cloud of stigma lie negation, repression, and banishment. For many stigmatized people, the accompanying isolation is tantamount to solitary confinement. There may be no sensation worse than being excluded from the mainstream, lacking any community or social support.

By the late 1940s, with the demise of Fascism, many social scientists believed that only a subgroup of people—those who'd been subject to punitive parenting practices—became stigmatizers or bigots. In fact, a major book on this topic, *The Authoritarian Personality*, was written by Berkeley psychologists and sociologists of the era. Over the intervening years, however, the core premise has changed radically. Prejudice and stigma are now viewed as the products of everyday social cognition.

In other words, any interaction with a group yields a flood of social information, so that one must quickly categorize fellow humans—as young versus old, sharp versus dull, tall versus short—to reduce the torrent of data and make sense of the social world. The key categorization, however, is deciding who lies within one's ingroup (kin and close contacts) versus the outgroup of potentially threatening strangers. Initial stereotypes of "difference" often become infused with negativity, morphing into prejudice and discrimination, when fundamental rights are denied to outgroup members.

Thus, stigma is not limited to a small group of prejudiced individuals but instead is nearly universal, especially against sub-groups branded as threatening and irrational, like people with mental illness. Indeed, stigma against people with mental disorders appears in every culture and society ever studied. Overcoming stigma, I now understood, would be an enormous undertaking, encompassing a fundamental change in attitude and empathy across the human race.

In 1994, I obtained a sabbatical from Berkeley. No chance for travel to exotic corners of the world, as Jeffrey was in second grade and I needed the time to devote to my research. But the time off from teaching allowed me to focus on my projects and make occasional trips to Columbus. Indeed, by now, Dad had sunk deeper into the Parkinsonian condition that robbed his physical abilities and limited his cognitive functions.

I flew home in early September. As always, Ohio seemed worlds away from California. Our back yard was beautiful, the late summer's warmth permeating the soft-blue sky, full of cirrus clouds. Geese forming huge chevron formations pointed south. Dad and I sat at the picnic table under the shade of the now-mature trees, a far cry from the frail sticks that welcomed us when we'd moved in over three decades before, only to have him disappear for nearly an entire year.

He started off by stating quietly that it was September 6, the precise date when, 58 years earlier, he had jumped from the porch roof back in Pasadena. I was taken aback, for once having lost track of my internal calendar. Nearly a quarter century after our first talk, his words of recollection transported me once again into his and our family's history.

I flew back in early January. Dazzling white, iced-over snow covered the ground, with temperatures far below zero. Mom and I took Dad out for lunch in German Village, a restored part of Columbus with red-brick stores, cobblestone streets, and homes from a century earlier now brought back to life. While Mom found a parking space, I helped Dad out of the car and guided him up the short flight of steps to the restaurant. Paralyzed momentarily, he stopped halfway, his body as frozen as the arctic air. As he looked over at me, resignation and despair showed through his stiff face. We backed down.

"I never dreamed that it would come to this," he said softly, incredulous. "Look at me, stuck like that. Who'd have ever thought I'd end up like this?" He wasn't so much feeling sorry for himself as expressing disbelief.

The following afternoon I initiated a talk in his study. I'd been mentally preparing for some time. This might be my only chance. I closed the sliding door behind us. The golden-toned wood and the deep-hued book covers contrasted sharply with the bare branches beyond the windows, covered with ice.

How many times had we sat here since my freshman year of college? When I was home during spring break, the pink and white blossoms in the yard dazzled during their fleeting existence. For summer talks, the leaves and lawn were a majestic green. We hardly met up in the autumn: I couldn't often get away when fall term was in session. On Christmas holidays, the outside world was drained of color while our connection strengthened inside the warm room.

My agenda was clear: I needed Dad's permission to take his story to another level. My conversation with John Richters the year before had solidified my resolve. But corralling Dad's attention was no easy task.

"I've got something to ask," I said from the small sofa, at the opposite end of the room from his desk, with all its distractions. Yet to my amazement, he was trying to stand up. With agonizing slowness he lurched over to his file cabinet, his fingers fumbling while he tried to open the drawer. After an age he peered inside the jumble of course syllabi and other materials. Hands tremulous, he sifted through the folders and grabbed the one he wanted. He walked stiffly back in my direction and held it out toward me.

As I opened it I realized right away that this was his summation. In his typed pages, written in the third person about himself, he referred once again to Goffman, who had contended that institutionalization involved a complete loss of identity:

> One is penitent, an "invalidated" human being. What formerly took a morning out of his day, now takes up to 5 months of his life. What formerly was momentary humiliation (of the protracted strapping that inevitably ensued), now takes months. What formerly was the first stage of the punishment ritual in which guilt was established . . . is now called a psychiatric examination or "degradation ceremonial," . . . wherein he is bereft of his civil liberties and, in effect, imprisoned in a total institution known as a mental hospital.

Regarding the arc of his life, I now fully understood, Dad viewed punishment and stigma as the central themes.

Yet I couldn't allow myself to become distracted. I thanked him but repeated that we needed to talk. After he'd eased his body back into a sitting position, I looked straight at him. "I've been thinking a lot about our talks over the years," I explained. "I would like you to consider something."

But was he really focusing on my words? His half-paralyzed facial muscles revealed nothing. I went on to say that I'd like to write about his life, using what we'd been discussing and the journal entries he'd shown me as a guide. I told him that I believed his life had lessons for many others.

"So, Dad," I asked as incisively as I could, "may I write about you and your life?"

He looked up. At first immobile, he slowly began to nod assent.

But had he really heard? I repeated the question. This time his answer was definitive. "By all means, son," he replied, faintly but directly, back to the formal diction he used for emphasis. For everything on the topic I've written ever since, Dad is my co-author.

It was the last talk we ever had in his study.

Somehow Mom got Dad to Palm Springs in March. I was to arrive the following week, but one evening early in their stay, believing that a night light in their bedroom was aflame, he threw a cup of water in its direction, shorting it out and creating a mass of smoke and sparks. Things were dire. Mom cut the trip short.

Neurological assessments back in Columbus revealed progression of the illness, diagnosed as Parkinson's with accompanying Lewy-body dementia. Parkinson's starts with depleted dopamine in the specific brain pathway linked to voluntary motor movements, but over time, abnormal protein deposits inside key neurons can spread to higher regions of the brain, producing dementia. By late May, Dad could barely make it out of bed to use the bathroom. There was no way that he could stay home. Not wanting to panic him with an ambulance, Mom arranged for an old friend and her brother, Buddy, to come to the house, lift him down the steps, and drive him to the hospital.

In June I was at a conference in New York City, departing as soon as my talk was finished to get to Columbus. Driving me straight to the hospital, Mom and Sally told me that Dad's mind was going pretty fast. I approached his bed to see his weakened body and drawn face. Still, he was alert. After noticing that I'd entered the room, he showed a radiant smile. "What are you doing here?" he called out as loud as he could. "I'm so delighted to see you!" I awkwardly hugged him as he lay in his bed. He seemed disbelieving of his good fortune that I had suddenly appeared.

It was soon time for another blood pressure reading. The

nurse shooed all of us out for a few minutes. When we re-entered after the short delay, Dad once again showed a startle of recognition when I caught his eye. "What a surprise! It's incredible to see you!"

He clearly had no recollection that I had been in the room ten minutes before. Every sign was ominous.

I tracked down any attending psychiatrists and neurologists I could find. Unmistakable signs of delirium, dementia, and general brain deterioration were grim reminders of his current situation. The following day Mom and I drove to several nursing homes, as the Ohio day turned from brilliant blue to milky white. He couldn't be retained at the hospital much longer. Maybe, just maybe, if we could find a good facility, he might emerge from the current crisis and regain some of his functioning.

Back in California to conduct my summer research programs—I was running two that year—I called Mom daily, as Dad had been discharged to one of the nearby facilities we'd checked out. Two weeks later, she reported bad news. Following an infection Dad had developed a fever. The antibiotics weren't succeeding in bringing it down. Still, I should remain put. But a few days later when she called, the gravity in her voice was unmistakable. Dad's systems were failing. I must get back immediately.

It was too late to get East that night so I booked a flight for the following day, a Saturday. With no non-stops to Columbus I had to change planes in Denver. I phoned Sally during the layover. She was home, in between visits to the nursing facility, and told me that Dad was resting comfortably. "You'll be able to see him tomorrow, Steve. I know it's frustrating to wait for the second plane, but don't worry."

On the startlingly warm night of July 22, I finally arrived at 10:30 after an additional two time zones of delay. Thinking I'd grab a cab home, I was surprised to see Mom and Sally near the baggage claim area, straining their necks to find me. But their faces told the story.

"Daddy died an hour and a half ago," Sally said. "I was back at the facility sitting with him. Mom had gone home to take a shower. As I was holding his hand I felt his breaths getting shorter and shorter. A few minutes later he took his last one."

Mom looked exhausted, feeling guilty that she'd left for a break but realizing the inevitability of what had transpired. We drove straight to the nursing home over the back roads of Columbus. Through the open window I viewed the brick factory buildings, now closed up forever, amid cricket chirps and light traffic.

Ahead of Mom and Sally, I rushed to his room down the linoleum corridors of the care facility. Feeling unreal, I opened the door and approached Dad's bed. I gazed at his rigid body and peaceful face. He was diminished, literally ravaged over the past several years. Still, his hair, nearly jet black until he was 70, was even now only half gray five years later.

Couldn't we talk just one more time?

The next day was a blur. At the funeral home to plan the burial and memorial, I looked again at Dad's body in the open casket as the loneliness hit me like a tidal wave. At the cemetery a morning later, the day was already sultry by 10:00, sweat dripping down the temples of everyone assembled—the small group of family and colleagues sitting under the trees. Numbly, I watched the casket mechanically lowered into the earth.

I flew back West for my programs but returned the following weekend for the service of memory at the church where Dad had sung in the choir for so many years. Hundreds were present: friends, university colleagues, family. It opened with a tender oboe solo and chamber music from a small group of Columbus Symphony players. The choir sang before Randall spoke warmly of his younger brother, recalling childhood memories, graduate

school at Princeton, and continued contact at recent family re-
unions. Too emotional to sing at the service, Paul spoke about
the warm caretaking he received as a boy from his older half-
brother as well as the sports they played together.

Then it was my turn. Looking out from the pulpit, with Mom
and Sally directly below, I began by describing Dad's life—his
early years, the loss of his mother when he was three, the family's
move to Pasadena, his academic successes, his flight to save the
world from Fascism, his hospitalizations, and his love of OSU. I
recounted the two stories of the number 100: my kindergarten
question about the populations of Russia and China and my
fourth-grade sleeplessness and despair, solved by Dad's telling
me I'd live to be 100 years of age via the miracles of modern
medicine. I spoke of his lifelong probing of the underpinnings
of the indescribable mysteries of everyday existence. I told the
assembled group that despite his misdiagnosed mental illness,
he was a warm and caring father.

Finally, I said that even though Dad had become essentially
a spirit in his final years, his spirit was still alive in me. I repeated
a short quotation from Bertrand Russell, which Dad had placed
at the end of his own self-description for *Who's Who*. Nearly
eighty years of age when he wrote it, Russell was describing love
and compassion:

> If you feel this, you have a motive for existence, a guide in ac-
> tion, a reason for courage, and an imperative necessity for
> intellectual honesty.

Throughout, I felt the familiar mixture of emotions: sadness
over the unrealized potential of Dad's life, anger over the ignorance of the mental health profession, and gratitude over having
been his son.

On my way to the airport the following morning, I asked
Mom to detour to the cemetery. We got out and walked to the

gravesite, where Dad's name and dates had been freshly chiseled in the headstone.

In loving memory, Virgil G. Hinshaw, Jr., 1919–1995

An hour later I hugged Mom at the airport, walked onto the plane, and flew back to complete the summer programs for a hundred-plus kids who needed help, in the hope that our findings might reveal the underlying nature of their mental-health-related conditions. Dad's words a quarter century before—and throughout the intervening years—had opened the doors and provided the spark.

The Rest of My Life

14

Every few weeks I visit my cousin Marshall at his apartment in downtown Berkeley. It's more of a cell than an apartment, about 8 by 10 feet, the walls stained a permanent yellow-black from nicotine. A twin mattress covered with age-old sheets on a metal frame, a tiny refrigerator, an antique television, a newer computer monitor that only sometimes transmits images, and a single chair comprise the room's only furnishings. The window is permanently closed, leaving the air inside the room so hazy with cigarette smoke that it's hard to make him out, much less breathe. The communal bathroom lies a few yards down the perennially empty hall.

He resides within a single-resident-occupancy building, two blocks from the Berkeley campus. Instead of an institution, where he would have undoubtedly spent the rest of his life had he been born half a century earlier, the residence is a warren of isolated rooms. Except for the gregarious and warm apartment manager Cathy, who sometimes returns on weekends to share home-cooked food with the residents, and a few fellow souls who know Marshall, it's as forlorn a place as I've ever been.

Now in his mid-sixties, Marshall has four teeth left. His shoulder-length gray hair and his scraggly beard are seldom washed. Just as when I talked with him four decades ago during my grad school days, his initial, enthusiastic words yield to raspy-voiced diatribes that become impossible to follow, especially above the din of the high-volume television. When I told him not long ago that I was heading to Chicago for a conference, he told me that I would be traveling to Chicago, Mississippi, not Chicago, Illinois, before launching into a spinning discourse on hidden geographic passageways. A planned visit to our house for an outdoor meal becomes, in his mind, a trip through a time portal to a different dimension. His internal systems of logic are inscrutable yet repeatedly honed.

For 48 consecutive years, Marshall has dealt with schizophrenia, which in his case is an unrelenting pattern of visions and voices, reasoning only he can follow, and an otherworldly style of interacting with the social world. Only a minority of individuals with schizophrenia show the utterly chronic pattern that he displays. If he were placed in an MRI scanner, the images would certainly reveal massive spaces where brain tissue is supposed to be. The newer-generation antipsychotic medications he takes help a bit: When he stays on them, his lucid periods of speech last a bit longer and I can feel his presence more acutely.

All those years ago when I was in school, I had three contrast points with Dad in the attempt to understand severe mental illness: Marshall; my other cousin Chip, whose schizoaffective illness led him to take his life not long after turning 30; and my high school and college teammate and friend Ron, whose unrelenting psychosis precipitated his disappearance from Harvard and the rest of the known world. Yet today, when I bring the groceries Marshall likes—fresh milk, white bread, ballpark franks, peanut butter and jelly, processed meats, sliced cheese, and as much instant coffee as I can carry—he grins from ear to ear. He pumps my hand, gives me a hug, and remembers to escort me through the hallways as I depart. As he says, it's the host's duty to do so. Each time, I'm floored by his overwhelming wish for contact.

Which should we choose: the overcrowded state institutions of the past, with their dehumanization and potential for abuse? Or the isolated rooms of a transient hotel, where people like Marshall sit all day—or, in his case, walk a mile down to the public mental health clinic twice a week to receive medications and a few dollars from disability payments? Should our choice be *then*, with the snake pits that took so long to dismantle? Or *now*, the threadbare, desolate rooms where isolation is the chief presence? Marshall is so bereft of human contact as to break the coldest of hearts. Anyone who contends that progress in the community "treatment" of serious mental disorder is enlightened must not have seen what I've seen.

My family legacy of mental illness accompanies me everywhere I go. My constant companion, it reminds me of what I escaped and what I still face.

Following Dad's death in 1995, Roberta and I devolved toward a permanent split. What held me back was the fear that I might not be with Jeffrey each day. After all, Dad had stayed with us and supported me when I was young except for those times he'd been placed in a mental hospital. What was my excuse? That my marital relationship wasn't what it had been? I found a new house three quarters of a mile away and the divorce was finalized by the end of the decade. I continued to see Jeff daily.

Now an adult, he is thriving, negating the concerns gripping me during my twenties—that having children would only perpetuate the dark side of the family history. It's essential to remember that, despite the high genetic liability of bipolar disorder and other forms of serious mental illness, the vast majority of offspring do not go on to develop the same conditions. Amid all the work involved, parenting is an act of faith.

During the 1990s, I continued conducting summer research programs for kids in trouble, particularly a series of camps for girls with significant problems with attention and impulse control. For one of these we hired an art teacher from San Francisco, Kelly Campbell. Her vibrancy, depth, and devotion to kids were evident from the start. Half a year later, she contacted me regarding a new job of hers, needing a referral for a student, and we began conversing. From our earliest moments, we were honest and open, supplementing the spark we both felt. We were married at Berkeley's Faculty Club in 2001, six years to the day after Dad's death. Two years later, Evan Robert Hinshaw emerged into the world.

We're different in temperament: Kelly is artistic, vibrant, even-keeled, and meditative, whereas I'm analytic, competitive, sometimes irascible, and incredibly goal-directed. Still, our connection has only deepened over the years. Early on, she helped me through a crisis I thought I'd never resolve. I'd begun drafting descriptions of Dad's life, but Mom was clear that going public would be the ultimate in shame for her. Yet how could I claim to be changing the climate around stigma if I kept our family's core messages buried? Listening impartially, Kelly stated that of course Mom was ashamed of the past but insisted that if Alene came to understand what the project meant to me, she'd eventually come around.

To my surprise, over the next years, as I began to give talks about our family and drafted the monograph on bipolar disorder using Dad's life as an example, several of Mom's oldest friends—all the way back from grade school in Bexley—read what I'd written. The secret was now out in the open, and they praised her for the courage she'd displayed throughout her married life. In the end, Mom fundamentally changed her attitude, asking for extra copies of the monograph and wondering why it hadn't been reviewed more widely. She was actually pushing for the family story to be widely heard.

For decades, I'd been reluctant to reveal our family's past, and my own. Yet by doing so, I not only freed myself but, against my initial judgment, propelled Mom to find a more open existence in her final phase of life. No one had ever bothered to listen to her years before: The medical profession had shut her out, and social mores kept our family's struggles enshrouded in silence. At long last, she had a voice. When shame and stigma are shed, hope can truly emerge.

A year after Evan's birth I flew to Las Vegas to give an all-day workshop on childhood behavior disorders. Sickened by the opulence of the suite in which I'd been put up, as well as the 100-degree heat held off by the overly chilled air conditioning high above the desert floor, I felt miserable. With travel I often feel unmoored, lacking the tether that keeps me bound to familiar routines. I also felt that I hadn't disclosed enough in my monograph, failing to tell what it was really like to grow up in our silent home.

After the workshop, which I somehow delivered on autopilot, my cousin Jim came to the hotel for a drink. He was the oldest son of Uncle Harold, Dad's oldest brother—the one with lifelong alcoholism. Jim lived outside of Vegas and was a fascinating guy, having provided the initial engineering for the glittering lights that made modern-day Vegas look as it does at night.

"I read what you wrote, Steve," he said as we downed an initial Sidecar. "I imagine that you've been getting some flak." Not quite sure what he was getting at, I listened hard. "Don't let anyone ever tell you that you were too harsh about my dad's and your dad's stepmother. I believe every word about what she did to your dad." He went on to state that his father's drinking problems led to a life that had been far different from the academic careers of the other original brothers, Randall, Bob, and Virgil Jr. In fact, Nettella was outraged with how Harold had turned out. She shunned him and, later, his wife and kids.

"She wouldn't even let my mom bring us to the house on North Oakland Avenue. We weren't good enough; our family was immoral." He knew, he told me, what it was like to be an outcast. "Keep telling the truth," he concluded. "People should know what really happened." His words pumped my motivation to keep pursuing the family narrative.

Clearly, scientists must be dispassionate and objective when testing hypotheses and theories, so their expectations and bias don't taint any gain in knowledge. Yet in the *discovery* phase of the scientific enterprise—before all the hypothesis testing and statistical analyses take place—inspiration, insight, and passion can guide where the research should head, and indeed, inform the right questions to ask. Particularly in medicine and mental health, narrative accounts can make a real difference.

At the same time, such narratives must be both real and accurate. Anyone can create a tale with a beginning, middle, and end, but is it reflective of the underlying truth? Crucially, I'd learned that Dad's experiences at Norwalk, Byberry, and Columbus State were not simply figments of his overworked imagination. His hospitalizations were as brutal as he'd depicted. Taking the battle to the next level will require legitimate stories *and* the best of the scientific method.

In 2004 I was asked by our dean to take on the role of department chair, becoming the first member of the clinical area of psychology to hold this title since psychology had split off from philosophy in the early 1920s. My main goal was to cross the major divide in the field: the biological, neuroscience, and cognitive areas of psychology versus the developmental, social, cultural, and clinical wings, bridging the fissures that had plagued not just our department but much of psychology half a century earlier. Through my understanding of Dad's early experiences, along with the primitive treatments he'd encountered, I'd learned the hard way what happens when fragmentation rather than integration carries the day.

I spent any spare hours working to understand stigma. To deepen my knowledge of what it really entails I began probing evolutionary perspectives. The underlying premise here is that natural selection has favored high levels of social contact in humans, as cooperation is essential for the survival of our physically unimposing species. On the other hand, complete trust in others might be disastrous, allowing opportunities for disease, exploitation, and subjugation. In other words, humans must traverse a narrow path between social contacts and caution regarding interactions. As a result, signals of social threat have become hard-wired into our minds and brains through natural selection, in the form of specific exclusionary "modules" or programs that place brakes on our interpersonal lives.

Across history and across cultures three universal signs of social threat exist. First, signals of parasites or disease, such as disheveled appearance, "sick" behaviors, or excessive grooming, trigger disgust and avoidance. Second, evidence of someone's poor cooperation—in the form of unpredictability, extremely low social status, or behavior that threatens to cheat others—elicits anger as well as banishment of the offender. Third, marked physical or cultural difference, including different skin color, custom, or religious belief, any of which might portend takeover by a rival coalition, can motivate hatred, exploitation, and even extermination.

The shunning of individuals displaying these signs is sufficiently universal to invoke the idea of deep, naturally selected roots of social exclusion. Indeed, evidence for such patterns permeates human history. Even more, members of other species shun their "peers" who reveal sick or overly deviant behavioral displays.

Lacking any background in evolution, the sociologist Goffman showed incredible prescience in his 1963 book on stigma.

He posited that "abominations of the body," "blemishes of character," and "tribal" differences were the universal triggers for stigmatization. His intuitions map almost perfectly onto the contagion, social threat, and coalitional modules of the evolutionary approach.

As for mental illness, the first two tendencies—wariness of contagion or contamination and exclusion of people with unpredictable behavior—are especially salient. Individuals with chronic mental illness may seem disease ridden, and irrational behavior may give rise to the view that the person is an untrustworthy social partner. On the other hand, "tribal" rejection linked to appearance and cultural difference would appear to be linked far more specifically with racism or ethnic hatred.

Evolutionary models can be reductionistic, even fatalistic: Think of Social Darwinism or the eugenics movement of the early twentieth century. These models are also difficult to prove experimentally. Still, the implications are chilling, as stigma-related responses to individuals with mental illness might well be automatic and unconscious. Even so, although deeply ingrained forms of stigma may be hard to overcome, they are not inevitable, because humans can recognize and harness such responses, especially if the fundamental humanity of those individuals experiencing mental turmoil is emphasized. Fostering humanization may be the single most important weapon in the fight against stigma.

Some years back I began seeing a therapist, partly to get beyond my periodic plunges. I talked about my history of holding things in—and my wariness of feelings. Saying good-bye to someone has always felt as though I'd lose contact forever. Even a hint of sadness might trigger a slide toward despair. Sensing a less-than-perfect effort in myself would spark an explosion of self-hatred. But when feelings are actually communicated, as I gradually learned, they might not be lethal. Over time, I began to get back on the planet of reality rather than the fantasy asteroid where superhuman efforts and the suppression of feelings seemed the only way to survive.

When I moved to Berkeley 25 years ago, I saw a different therapist for a time, one who used formal assessments to help guide treatment. Early on, he asked me to complete a widely used personality scale, the Minnesota Multiphasic Personality Inventory (MMPI). Despite my self-torture in college and beyond, my mini-swings of mood, the rage that lingers just beneath the surface, and the self-doubt that co-exists in tandem with my confidence, the overall scores from my profile were squarely in the normal range. Yet there was one index with a subtle elevation, the MMPI Paranoia scale. I was sure there'd been a mistake, as I'm usually trusting to a fault—the antithesis of paranoia. But a smaller subscale exists within Paranoia, called Poignancy. It was here that my score was particularly high.

People who provide the answers I did have an intense and emotion-laden approach to the world, believing that hidden meanings underlie each endeavor and interaction. They often feel misunderstood and, in fact, quite alone. It's true: I infuse everything in my life with emotion and a search for essential meaning. Despite the regimented approach to life I developed as a boy, I've been on the lookout for underlying currents for as long as I can remember, a hidden passageway to enlightenment during my often solo efforts to figure things out. Unbidden, memories flood my mind each day, placing me squarely back in the key transitions and battles of my earlier years. I may not show it outwardly, but my background noise consists of a deep intensity, a pale image of Dad's far sharper swings but laden with sharp emotion all the same.

Still, over the years I've learned to relish life's small but crucial pleasures: that song or symphony on the car radio so wondrous I keep driving just to hear it all the way through; the sound of a three-point shot hitting nothing but net as it swooshes through the hoop; the sight of Kelly, beautifully bringing out the best in everyone around her. Somehow, I've moved beyond the lockdown.

In 2010 I was contacted by a man named Philippe Fontilea, living in Southern California. He was convinced, he said, that he'd found a way to conquer the stigma of mental illness and wanted experts to help his effort. Phil's background was intriguing. He'd been a Broadway dancer, investor, rock climber, and more recently a rock-climbing instructor. He'd come to the realization that fighting stigma would need to begin early. The way to go about it, he believed, was to form high school clubs—without need for mental health professionals—in which kids could express their natural empathy and activism by discussing ways to counter discrimination and prejudice. Without rigid, adult-directed scripts, the students would devise ways to cross barriers, discuss "difference," and draw upon their interests and motivations.

The idea was utterly simple and utterly profound. He called the program Let's Erase the Stigma, LETS for short. Phil put together a summit of several hundred LA-area high schoolers, who gathered raucously amid rap music and break dancing in the spring of 2011 to learn about the LETS model. Once back at their schools, they established clubs the following fall. So long as a teacher agreed to serve as the club's advisor, weekly meetings were held. Guidebooks for the club activities evolved. A student recorded the club's activities each week, to help understand the active ingredients.

Our research team at Berkeley provided an evaluation, discovering that after a semester of club participation, members showed some gains in their knowledge of mental health. Revealing greater improvement, though, were their attitudes and their desire for greater contact, as well as their intentions to reduce stigma on a daily basis.

Other stigma reduction programs embrace the goal of teaching factual information about mental illness in high school health classes. Through this kind of intervention, student knowledge definitely improves. But at the same time attitudes tend to get worse and the desire for social distance may actually *increase*. In other words, simply knowing the facts about mental illness tends to reinforce all the wrong ideas and deeply held stereotypes. What's needed instead are contact, empathy, and action, in order to gain understanding of the human side of mental illness. When young people have the opportunity to become active in the service of reducing barriers among people, unleashing their desire to connect, there's real hope.

In April of 2012 I received an unexpected phone call from Glenn Close, by then an ardent activist on behalf of stigma reduction as a result of her family's intensive experiences with mental disorder. She asked me to serve on her scientific board of advisors. During our conversation, I invited her to LA to address the second LETS summit, starting the formation of connections. When Phil relocated overseas in 2014, Glenn's anti-stigma organization, Bring Change 2 Mind (BC2M), took on the oversight of LETS clubs. Our research group is now in the midst of a random-assignment trial of the impact of the clubs in multiple high schools. The hope is that LETS BC2M will thrive.

In future decades, might it no longer be shameful to admit a history of mental disorder or seek intervention that could reduce symptoms and impairments? The stakes have never been higher.

Not long after Kelly and I were married, Sally was hit by a car while taking a long, fast, summer bike ride back in Columbus. She plunged face-first through a closed window, almost succumbing to blood loss during the frantic rush to the hospital in the emergency squad. It was touch and go. After several surgeries she recovered.

She now works at OSU Medical Center and other hospitals in patient education and physician training. Completely dedicated and committed, she knows more about medicine than most everyone with whom she works, having become a linchpin in the growing movement to improve the knowledge base and clinical skills of health professionals. Mom's caretaker for many years while the debilitating rheumatoid arthritis progressed, Sally has stayed engaged in progressive political causes far more than I ever have, and she continues to ensure that her life has purpose and meaning.

To a fault, Sally and I are alike in our styles: impatient, routine-based, and intense. She's less forgiving of herself than I am of myself, and I wish her more flexibility and self-acceptance. We remain ultra-close, continuing to speak—metaphorically, at least—the same private language we shared all those years ago.

A few springs ago she and I planned that I would detour through Columbus on the way back from a trip to Washington, DC, to surprise Mom on her eighty-fourth birthday. I arrived on the small commuter jet from Dulles on a warm night in late May, booked a rental car, and drove the freeways back home. Mom couldn't believe her eyes.

The next evening Sally and I took her out to dinner, and Mom beamed throughout the entire birthday meal. With a tender look in her eye she exclaimed: "What a life you've had, Steve: your accomplishments, the places you've been, your family. You're the best son a mother could ever have." Two days later we drove out past Grandmother's old house in Bexley, reminiscing about our family's times inside its walls.

But on my birthday in December of 2014, Sally called to say that Mom had awakened in horrible pain, with fiery currents radiating down her back. Within three days she was in the hospital. Two evenings later I flew all night to Columbus, where Sally and I spent Sunday morning holding Mom's hands as she slowly stopped breathing in the intensive care unit. She was a few months short of her ninetieth birthday.

A neurologist colleague and friend in Berkeley, Bob Knight, had given me a heads-up before my flight: Mom had undoubtedly experienced an odontoid flare, he said, in which the chronic rheumatoid process triggers a sudden inflammation of the odontoid bone, located within the very top cervical vertebrae, pressuring the spinal cord. The two symptoms related to such a flare are fire-like pain shooting down the spine and death within a week, because the brain-stem-related circuits that regulate breathing shut down.

Perhaps her sudden demise was a blessing, given the huge pain and disability she'd have undoubtedly faced from the continuing arthritis if she'd aged into her nineties. Yet I miss her terribly. One source of solace is that, as with Dad, we'd held the needed discussions when she was alive. Not much was left on the table.

I've been to Columbus as much as possible ever since, to work out the details of Mom's estate and connect more deeply with Sally about our family's plight. Over the dark Imperial stouts that Sally cherishes, some of my learning has been painful. While I basked in the glow of Dad's wisdom and generosity when he was well—and received his long-held secrets about episodes of madness—she experienced a father who never showed the true pride in her he should have. Once, back in the 1970s, when she was home and took a message for Dad from an old colleague, the caller paused and said that he didn't know Virgil had a daughter. No wonder Sally had identified so strongly with Mom, who always supported her. I'd been favored for no real reason other than being male.

I only wish that, had the shame and internalized stigma about both mental illness and abuse been less cemented inside Dad, he could have better accepted himself and let both Mom and Sally in on his vulnerabilities. It must be hard for Sally to hear the kind of tribute to Dad I'm writing, when she never had the same spark of interest from him. Still, she knows how much I've always loved her, and her life is all about the empowerment of others, particularly patients with a range of physical and mental disorders. So many years after the shroud of silence enveloped us when we were young, we're both working to remove it, each in our own way.

How much more open *am* I? With our boys—Jeff, making it in the world of research and finance; Kelly's talented and musical son, John, learning the trade of gem-cutting overseas; Evan, entering his teenage years—can we hold to a different standard than what I'd experienced? Change is difficult: I'd still rather believe that, through some kind of magic, tough issues will simply resolve themselves without discussion. Silence begets silence; shame begets shame. Still, if Mom—who lived her entire life inside the deep shadow of stigma—could finally experience a sea change in her ability to open up, why can't I?

When Jeff was a pre-teen I took a risk one day and talked with him about his grandpa, who'd died the year before. After discussing philosophy and what philosophers do, I told him to imagine a time when he'd been really excited—and then to imagine being ten times more excited than that. The same for feeling sad: What would it feel like to be ten times sadder? What Grandpa experienced, I said, were moods that were really strong. It would be several more years before I learned of the work of Beardslee, including his family therapy model that encourages parents to speak to their children in understandable language about the realities surrounding the family. But I sensed I had to say *something*.

Fast in everything he does and with the benefit—and curse—of intensive social media, 13-year-old Evan is quick to judge as he, like everyone else his age, solidifies crucial attitudes about a variety of social groups. Open dialogue will be essential for him and every other teen. Might he come of age in a world filled with more openness and acceptance than now? It's today's youth who will make the key difference from here on out.

Not long after we began our relationship and she'd heard my family's story, Kelly told me that it must have been overwhelming to shoulder the burden of learning about Dad's past once I'd started college. I quickly replied that there was no other way: I simply *had* to learn the truth. A few years ago, my therapist raised a similar point, commenting that my discussions with Dad were one-sided, as he never asked for my reaction or checked in about how I might understand his disclosures. I countered that hearing of Dad's experiences in no way compared to the devastation he'd gone through. My price was small indeed.

With time, however, I've begun to accept the wisdom of their contentions. Without any outlet for the knowledge I was gaining and without any way to express the gnawing doubts I held about my own sanity, I experienced a war inside my mind about Dad's words and images during college and beyond, especially at night. I'm still shocked over my ability to have tortured myself for years on end. I walked the precipice for far too long. Finally—at the eleventh hour—I learned to trust in my ability to let go and let myself truly rest when the day's work was finished.

Still, when I think of Dad, what I remember most are those talks we had, the times in his quiet study—or even in the car with perhaps half an hour before we'd reach the airport—when the outside world disappeared. His words infused me with unexpected scenes of life inside hospitals, with knowledge of the California family I gradually came to know, and with his quest to understand the roots of the ultimate philosophical questions and his own plight. They forged my goal of engaging with mental health and battling stigma.

Only late in the game, during Dad's final years and then after his passing, did I finally understand another purpose of his. Without ever asking me directly, he was, I'm now sure, encouraging me to convey his story to the world. During our last talk in his study on that arctic January afternoon, he made the final handoff of his crucial message—linking his hospitalizations to his childhood punishments—while I secured his permission to let the world know about his life.

Over the past years, in fact, I've become his scribe, ghost-writer, and interpreter. It took a while to gain momentum but I've kept at it. My life has never been richer or more fulfilling. In what I consider to be the key challenge of my life, I hope to integrate science and personal narrative more than ever.

In the end, I hope that Dad might be pleased with what I've tried to say. I hope that telling his story, conveying our family's plight, and disclosing my own journey might yet help to turn the tide.

Epilogue

The winter sky quickly darkened as the overnight jet ascended toward London. In January 2009, the day before the inauguration of Barack Obama, I was on my way to give a keynote talk at the fourth International Stigma Conference on Mental Illness, held at the Royal College of Physicians, King's College. When the invitation had arrived six months earlier, I stared. Was such a conference even possible, with people from around the world converging to discuss shame and stigma? Given our family's history, it seemed unthinkable.

Before my talk, which was to be an account of my personal and family journey, I toured the exhibition on London's Royal Bethlehem, later contracted to Bedlam, the first permanent mental hospital in Western Europe, with an 800-year history. During the Enlightenment, wealthy citizens paid admission to watch the raving patients there, as though touring a zoo. Accounts reveal unspeakable horrors that were daily occurrences. Though I knew the history, the diorama floored me.

Beyond the troubling exhibit, the lecture hall was modern, its amphitheater-style seats packed with five hundred attendees.

After a number of presentations, I heard my name announced and strode to the podium as the lights muted. How still it seemed throughout the auditorium. How diverse the audience members looked, representing over 50 nations. With large images of my family projected behind me on the huge screen, I took a breath and began.

As I finished 40 minutes later, the room went silent. A second ticked by, then two. Maybe such a distinguished group hadn't wanted to hear such a message. Unsure of what to do, I made a move to step down when the explosion began, applause like a burst of gunfire, ascending in a crackling wave, palms pounding into palms. The ovation didn't recede for some time. Maybe things really *were* changing.

Even so, the mental health crisis remains firmly in place. Three times more Americans die from suicide (42,000 in 2014, the last year with solid statistics) than from homicide. But who would know of this fact from the news, which routinely features gun violence perpetrated against others but almost never discusses the inner pain related to depression and suicidal thoughts? Around the world, suicide is the third leading cause of death for people aged 15 to 44—and the *leading* cause of mortality for adolescent girls. Taken together, mental illnesses account for more disability than physical illnesses. For people in their forties, mental disorders predict a greater level of disability *than all physical illnesses combined.*

Mental disorders don't afflict *them*—a deviant group of flawed, irrational individuals—but *us*: our parents, sons and daughters, colleagues and associates, even ourselves. A quarter of the population will experience a significant mental disorder in a given year. Countless veterans and trauma victims suffer from post-traumatic stress disorder (PTSD). Rates of child-onset conditions like autism and ADHD are skyrocketing. Eating disorders contribute to major health risks. Substance abuse devastates lives, especially via the current epidemic of opioid-

and heroin-related fatalities. Together with thought disorders, anxiety disorders, and a range of developmental conditions, mental illnesses drain hundreds of billions of dollars annually from the U.S. economy and over a *trillion* dollars around the globe, linked to unemployment, related physical conditions, and sheer despair. Personal and family suffering far outstrips the financial burden.

Chillingly, serious mental illness reduces life expectancy by 10 to 25 years, through risky behaviors, poor exercise and health habits, proneness to chronic physical diseases, low access to health care, and self-destruction. Yet it takes over a *decade* for most people experiencing symptoms to seek help, linked to the shame and denial surrounding the entire topic. What if it took people ten years or more to understand and treat symptoms of heart disease or cancer? The headlines would never stop.

The paradox—and tragedy—is that evidence-based treatments for mental disorders really work. Cures aren't yet at hand, but interventions for mental illness are as effective, on average, as treatments for physical disorders. Yet utilization remains low. "Parity" for mental health is not living up to expectations, and the treatments most people receive are nowhere near the kinds of state-of-the-art, evidence-based interventions needed. Recovery is a definite possibility but far too often does not get realized.

In many ways, mental illness is the final frontier for human rights.

Haven't attitudes toward mental disorder fundamentally changed? Consider the flood of stories, blogs, and magazine articles linked to the topic, many quite moving. Disclosing inner turmoil and consulting a "shrink" might be seen as a badge of honor on the coasts. Yet, as noted earlier, rates of stigma and social distance toward mental illness have hardly budged in the past sixty years, and perceived links between mental illness and violence are far *more* common. Even worse, in half of our nation's states, admitting to a mental illness, or even a history of such, can result in loss of a driver's license, inability to serve on a jury or run for office, and automatic relinquishment of child custody. My history of depressed mood disqualifies me from driving or jury service? My eating disorder, if that's what my forced vomiting was, means I can't run for office or be a parent? It's a good thing such laws weren't in place in 1860: Lincoln could never have run for president, with his history of debilitating depressions.

The view that disturbed behavior emanates from evil spirits may be long past in much of the world, but moral perspectives still predominate. Popular culture depicts people with mental illness as either demons or brilliant misfits—like John Nash of *A Beautiful Mind,* the mathematician with schizophrenia who won the Nobel Prize. It's still acceptable to use abhorrent language to describe mental illness: *psycho, nut-job, wacked, lunatic.* National politicians, including our new president, imitate and mock people with physical and mental disabilities as if it's perfectly OK to do so. Where are the everyday stories of struggle and triumph, loss and recovery, and family connection that must be heard? Where's the empathy and identification, rather than fear-mongering, so urgently required?

To fight stigma, a key strategy over the past 20 years has been to convey that mental illness is a brain disorder linked to aberrant genes. As with alcoholism, the disease model should reduce guilt and blame. Indeed, psychological theory tells us that if negative behavior is thought to emerge from a cause that can't be controlled, like an illness—particularly one linked to genetic vulnerability—the individual will be absolved and stigma will plummet.

Experimental studies show that when people believe mental illness to be a genetically triggered brain disease, they *do* hold the individual in question less blameworthy. At the same time, though, they believe that the individual is essentially hopeless—

after all, immutable DNA is to blame—and unworthy of social contact. In other words, the biological/illness perspective often backfires, promoting pessimism and *increased* social distance.

On the one hand, we certainly don't want to revert to the idea that mental illness is a character flaw or simply the product of bad parenting. Most forms of mental illness are in fact moderately heritable, meaning that genes are clearly involved in underlying risk. But all-biology views are not the full story. Experience and context mold genetic vulnerabilities, and individuals and families must still make choices to seek and stay with treatment. It's not *either-or,* it's *both-and.*

Remember the evolutionary model of stigma, where signs of disturbed behavior are believed to trigger, nearly automatically, fear of contagion and avoidance of threat? The third evolutionary module—keeping one's distance from those thought to be members of a different "tribe"—was instead linked to racism but not mental illness.

Yet attributing deviant behavior exclusively to biological and genetic factors might inadvertently promote just this form of stigmatization. In other words, if unpredictable, threatening, and irrational behavior patterns are believed to result from flaws in the person's very DNA, that person may be thought of as genetically deficient, part of a deviant tribe, perhaps even subhuman. Unexpectedly, then, the biomedical perspective may unleash a form of stigma associated with utter hatred. If history serves, resentment, subjugation, and even extermination will follow.

Reducing stigma—that other form of madness, far worse in its consequences than mental illness itself—will take coordinated strategies: enforcement of antidiscrimination policies, access to high-quality care, a far different set of media messages, personal contact that fosters more empathy, and the replacement of silence with dialogue. Above all, humanization is the goal. Getting young people engaged in the fight for human rights is central to the entire effort. Each year that we maintain our current attitudes and practices is another year of lost productivity, wasted human potential, and unspeakable tragedy.

It will require an unprecedented team effort to make a difference. The knowledge is there and the pieces are in place. Do we have what it takes to mount the fight?

Acknowledgments

I would never have completed this book without the vision, faith, and skill of Don Fehr and Karen Wolny. Working with them has been one of the great gifts of my career. Don, my agent from Trident Media Group, immediately "got it" when we first communicated about a memoir that would also address larger messages about stigma. He put me through the paces—multiple revisions of a lengthy proposal—to present this book's essential message in the best possible light, doing so with vision and verve. In a word, Don is a force.

Karen, my editor at St. Martin's, has perennially showed patience, support, and expert guidance in challenging me to dig deeper, to provide an integrated voice, and to keep "on message" throughout the book's chapters. She never dictated precisely what to write. Rather, as a remarkably sensitive elicitor, she compelled me to take this work to a different level, always revealing considerable insight and compassion. Her blend of ultra-competence and warmth is nothing short of remarkable.

To have gathered the support of these experts means that I've been amply blessed.

My ongoing team in the Bay Area includes my colleagues and friends Allison Harvey, Bennett Leventhal, Mary Main, and Rudy Mendoza-Denton. Their unflagging support and spot-on critiques have been essential. Bennett pointed me in the direction of the incredible quote from James Baldwin, an excerpt from which serves as the book's title. Scott Lines provided a different kind of inspiration in helping me to understand so much about my past and present.

In the early stages, Betsy Rapoport masterfully showed me how to approach this kind of writing. I also received encouragement and critiques from the generous input of Katherine Ellison, Nan Weiner, and Lee Gutkind—the "godfather" of creative nonfiction. Linda Isbell played an essential role in linking me with Don Fehr and championing my efforts regarding this book. Among my enthusiastic additional supporters have been Shaikh Ahmad, Kyla Buckingham, Daphne de Marneffe, Howard Goldman, Sheri Johnson, Laura Mason, Nicole Murman, Lisa Post, and Robert Villanueva. Eric Youngstrom provided sage guidance regarding the concept of "Cade's disease" in the context of bipolar disorder. My sister and I will always be grateful to my friend and colleague Bob Knight, who instantly understood the consequences of Mom's odontoid flare during the last week of her life.

The support, love, and sharp editorial skills of my wife, Kelly Campbell—now Dr. Campbell—made the entire effort possible. Kel, I can't thank you enough.

Our three boys, Jeff Hinshaw, John Neukomm, and Evan Hinshaw, have shown me, full-on, the intergenerational pull that keeps our species going forward. Their close bond to one another is wonderful to behold.

Finally, my sister, Sally Hinshaw, didn't have the same kind of relationship with our father that I did. But as the book's dedication reveals, our closeness as siblings and her courage are always at the front of my heart.

Index of Medical Terms